HANDBOOK

OF

THE OLD-NORTHERN

RUNIC MONUMENTS

OF

SCANDINAVIA AND ENGLAND.

HANDBOOK

OF

THE OLD-NORTHERN

RUNIC MONUMENTS

OF SCANDINAVIA AND ENGLAND.

NOW FIRST

COLLECTED AND DECIPHERED

BY

Dr. GEORGE STEPHENS, F. S. A.;

Knight of the Northern Star (Sweden), St. Olaf (Norway) and of the Danebrog (Denmark); Hon. Fellow of the Roy. Hist. Soc. London; of the Soc. Ant. Scotland; of the Roy. Hist. & Archæol. Assoc. of Ireland; and of the Ant. Guilds of Cumberland-Westmoreland, Newcastle-upon-Tyne, Yorkshire, Helsingfors, Christiania, Tronyem, Gotenburg, Stockholm, Upsala, West-Gotland, &c. &c.; Prof. of Old-English and of the English Language and Literature in the University of Cheapinghaven, Denmark.

THE 3 FOLIO VOLUMES RE-ARRANGED WITH SHORT TEXTS, BUT KEEPING ALL THE OLD-NORTHERN CHEMITYPES AND ILLUSTRATIONS.

REPRINTED IN PHOTO–REDUCED FORMAT, LINEAR REDUCTION x 0.7, BY LLANERCH PUBLISHERS, FELINFACH, 1993. ISBN 1 897853 02 5.

WILLIAMS AND NORGATE;

14 Henrietta St., London, 20 S. Frederick St., Edinburgh.

H. H. J. LYNGE;

8 Valkendorfs Str., Cheapinghaven (Kjøbenhavn, Copenhagen).

PRINTED BY THIELE.

1884.

TO

OUR GREAT ENGLISH OLDLORIST,

THE GIFTED AND GENEROUS

AUGUSTUS WOLLASTON FRANKS

IN THANKFUL MINNE.

———

FOREWORD.

I have often been askt to publish in a cheap and handy shape the rune-laves in my great folio volumes, which many cannot well buy or have time to read. And this I have long wisht to do; but I waited for more finds and a better knowledge of this hard science. The day has now come when I can lay this HANDBOOK before all lovers of our Northern mother-tung. sametimely with my *third folio tome*, which holds more than 70 new pieces bearing Old-Northern staves[1]. This additional gathering and the on-flow of runic studies have. of course, thrown fresh light on the monuments already known. I have therefore been able, as I think, here and there to amend a former version or an approximate date, and I give these ameliorations accordingly. Some more of the Bracteates now seem to me barbarized copies, and therefore meaningless. But, as before, all I do is only tentative. The engravings[2] have also been corrected, where any fault has been discovered.

On the whole, my system of transliteration and translation remains, as far as I can see. not only unshaken, but abundantly strengthened and proved by the many *new* finds. We thus clench the conclusion — so probable on the mere ground of Comparative Philology — to which I have pointed again and again, that in the very early period to which these Scando-Anglic remains chiefly belong (say the first 700 years after Christ), the *Northern* dialects here treated were on very much the same footing in essentials as *all the other olden* Scando-Gothic folk-talks. Those peculiar features, (especially the Passive or Middle Verb and Post-article), which *now* stamp the *Scandinavian* branches of the Scando-Gothic tree, are quite simply of *later local Scandian growth*. They were *unknown* when the first great Northern settlements

---

[1] The whole tale of these O. N. rune-bearers is now about 250, of which nearly *1-third* is from ENGLAND ALONE, Scandinavia's oldest colony.

[2] Chiefly drawn and chemityped by Prof. Magnus Petersen, the woodcuts by Hr. J. F. Rosenstand, whom I thank for all their friendly aid.

wrested England from the partly Romanized Kelts, and they were not yet *formed* when *the same* mother-lands sent out their wiking-swarms in the 9th and 10th centuries. Hence they have *never been found in Britain.*

Consequently I see no reason to alter any one of my fundamental opinions, which I should otherwise have been happy to do, and think it best to reprint here, without change, my general conclusions when my second band was printed in 1868. See my Vol. 1, Foreword, pp. VII—XIX:

"1. *That the rune-values I have laid down are really so, and particularly that the Old-Northern stave* Ψ *was always A, certainly no consonant, still less M as in the later Runic Staverow.*

All the oldest and best skinbook futhorcs give to ᚤ (the provincial English substitute for the older Ψ, but which Ψ is also found in England with the same power of A) the sound-value A, and to ᚠ (the common Old-Northern — Scandian and English — Æ, afterwards the provincial-Scandinavian O) the sound-value Æ. But the scholars at the beginning of this century and up to the appearance of my First Part who first tried to read the Old-Northern letters, and who were unanimous in giving to Ψ (really A) the power of M, which it has in the later runic system, *concequently had no A* in their new-made alphabet. Yet an A could not be wanting. Therefore, taking advantage of the well-known fact that A sometimes tends to an Æ-sound in certain districts, and that Æ sometimes tends to an A-sound in certain districts, as is accordingly shown by a couple of the later futhorcs, they followed each other in giving to ᚠ the universal and standing sound-value A. Thus Ψ was M, ᚠ was A. But as it is now evident, from the futhorcs themselves and from *ALL the Old-Northern monuments*, that Ψ is undoubtedly and always A, the simple mistake of giving to ᚠ the power of A should now be at once laid aside. To perpetuate error is foolish, alike highly perplexing and often destructive both of language and of grammar. On one single excessively ancient stone for instance (Sigdal, Norway), we have *in close juxtaposition*, within the compass of the first 28 clear and undeniable letters, ᚠ = Æ 4 times and Ψ = A 6 times. How is it possible to smear them all into one uniform A? What common sense can there be in so doing? What is gained by it? Surely, even learned zeal should not be carried so far as this. *The cause being taken away, the effect ceases.* An A (and the *real A*) being now identified, the Æ should no longer be compelled to do duty both for Æ and A.

I have already referred to and protested against the guess (p. 326) that this Ψ is -R. There are five objections to this theory:

a. It is plainly contrary to all the monuments. This is surely decisive. But also

b. It is plainly contrary to all the ancient parchment alphabets.

c. It can only have even a momentary and mechanical short-lived plausibility with regard to a couple of the inscribed pieces, one in twenty of the whole number, in some of which it is so plainly and precisely and glaringly and decisively contradicted that the whole supposition becomes simply ridiculous.

d. It leads us into endless contradictions. Thus if we read ⟨HᵻꝐUWOLᵻFꝛ⟩ at p. 170 (Stentoften), what shall we do with the ⟨IᵻꝐU (? HᵻꝐU)WOLᵻFᵻ⟩ of the Gommor stone (207)? If we read on the Stentoften block ⟨HᵻRIWOLᵻFꝛ⟩, what shall we do with the HYRIWULÆFÆ of the Istaby pillar? If we read on the Golden Horn (p. 326):

"EK HLEVA-GASTIR HOLTINGAR HORNA TAVIDO"

and on the Tanum stone (p. 197):

"ÞRAWINGAN HAITINAR WAS"

(Thrawingan hight (called) he-was)

(this last as privately proposed to me by a Danish scholar[1] and since printed in Ny Illustrerad Tidning, Stockholm, June 29, 1867, p. 207), what do we get? These pieces are undoubtedly among the very oldest in the whole North, as indeed is admitted on all sides. And yet we are called upon to believe that in "Gothic" times, when the S was still a characteristic, and side by side with such *archaisms* as VAS (for VAR) and such *extra-archaisms* as HORNA (for HORN) and TAVIDO (for TAVIDA, TAVIDE), and such *extra-extra-archaisms* as ÞRAVINGAN ("nom. sing., a weak noun in N, with the N still left" for ÞRAVING) and HAITINAR ("past part. n. s. m. with the AR still left" for HAITIN), — we are to accept such comparative *modernisms* as HAITINAR for HAITINAS and GASTIR for GASTIS and HOLTINGAR for HOLTINGAS! So on the Tune stone (p. 247) we are seriously askt to read DOHTRIR (with R) *close to* the word DALIDUN (3 pl. past. with N still left)! And then we must bow our necks to such "nominatives of some sort" as HAITINAR (p. 197) and HOLTINGAR (p. 326) and VIVAR (p. 247) and IUPINGAR (p. 256) and HALAR (p. 254) and HILIGAR (p. 258) and VARUR (p. 264) and so on, with some charming examples of RUNAR, STAINAR, &c. as in "middle Scandinavian".

e. But the worst is, that in spite of all this self-contradiction and violence and caprice — the whole thing breaks down. Scarcely *one or two* monuments out of all the 60 can in this way be even *plausibly* translated. We are called upon to believe that all our oldest written remains are "unreadable", "unintelligible", "nearly inexplicable", "only here and there a word to be understood", "gibberish", "some outlandish tung", "carved by a foreign slave who had learned the runes", "miscut",

---

[1] Since then Prof. S. Bugge has proposed nearly the same version. But he makes ÞRAWINGAN to be in the genitive sing., and WAS to mean *it became.*

and the like.   And all because people will not abandon their school-creed about
"Icelandic", and their German contempt for the evidence of the monuments themselves!

2.   *That the Runic Alphabet* whether the older (or Old-Northern) or its modification and simplification the younger (or Scandinavian) — in one word THE ART OF
WRITING — *was apparently altogether unknown to the first outflow of the Scando-Gothic
tribes, the Germans*[1]; *equally so to the second, the Saxons or Lowcountry men or Flemings;
and was first brought to Scando-Gothic Europe or early learned or developt therein by the
third* (and latest) *clan-wave, THE NORTHERN OR SCANDINAVIAN*, the facts and monuments
thus absolutely confirming the very oldest Northern and Latin traditions.   Let us
see *why* FOR THE PRESENT, TILL NEW FACTS COMPEL US TO FORM NEW CONCLUSIONS,
we must hold fast this interesting and curious result:

a.   German or Saxon Runes, or *Runes in Germany* (High-Germany) *or in Saxony*
(the real Old Saxony, = Holstein and adjoining cantons in Mecklenburg and Westphalia)
were NEVER HEARD OF TILL IN MODERN TIMES, in the lucubrations of modern German
"annexers" and system-makers.

b.   No hint of or reference to Runic Monuments, direct or indirect *has ever
been found* even in the very oldest German or Saxon chroniclers or historians or
other writers, tho many such mentionings occur in Anglo-Scandic skinbooks.   The
monuments themselves might be destroyed and disappear; but, if they had ever
existed in German or Saxon lands, they would have left some trace behind them in
living words or dead parchments.

*c.   In English and Scandian Boundaries and Charters RUNIC BURIAL-STONES
are repeatedly spoken of as "marks".   In the very oldest similar German and Saxon
documents, some of which go back to semi-heathen times — *no such reference has
ever been found.*   Thus if the Northern lands had lost every single Runic Block, we
could dig them up again out of our ancient bookfells.

*d.   No Runic Alphabet has ever been discovered in any original German or Saxon
manuscript.*   The few codices found abroad containing Runic staverows were either
brought from England by English or Irish missionaries, or copied by German or
Saxon Scribes from English originals for missionary and epistolary purposes.   This
is FRANKLY ADMITTED by Wilhelm Grimm himself, and some other Germans of the
better sort.

*e.   No Runic Stone or other "fast" Runic piece has ever turned up on German
or Saxon soil.*   This also is FRANKLY ADMITTED by Wilhelm Grimm himself, and some
other Germans of the better sort.   The *half-dozen* LOOSE PIECES (Movables, Jewels)

---

[1]   Some think that the Saxons came first to Europe, and then the Germans.   This will nowise affect what i
here stated.

found beyond the present borders of Scandinavia and England — out of *so many thousands* of Runic Remains already known and daily turning up *in the Anglo-Scandic lands* — are therefore clearly WANDERERS, or the Runes upon them were risted by Northmen who were abroad. This is also proved by the details in each separate instance. It would have been A MIRACLE if no single Runic Jewel or any single Rune-writing Northman had ever WANDERED from a Northern country, and we may yet hope to find other such *stray pieces.*

f. No Runic Coin was ever struck in any German or Saxon shire, the HUNDREDS of different runic types were regularly minted in the Northern kingdoms, till these rune-bearers gradually disappeared before Roman-lettered pieces.

g. Runic and non-Runic Golden Bracteates, all which are heathen Jewels and Amulets, have been found BY HUNDREDS in the Northern lands, BY ONES AND TWOES outside the North. Their findstead, their make, their types and patterns, all show that they were struck by heathen Northmen or in the heathen North. They *could not* have been made by tribes WHO HAD NO RUNES. *The half-dozen of these pieces hitherto found outside the North have therefore been carried over the border, are WANDERERS.*

h. As old buildings are repaired or taken down and various diggings made in the Northern lands, RUNIC STONES *are continually turning up.* Under the like circumstances, *NOT ONE ever comes to light in any Saxon or German territory.*

In *German lands*, in woods and fields and out on hills and at crossroads and beside sea and stream and in crypts and churches and cellars and mills and public and private buildings, lying open or buried out of sight or long since used as building-materials — exactly as is the case with our own runic monuments — have been found THOUSANDS of inscribed remains FROM THE FIRST CENTURY DOWNWARDS, and every year new ones are dug up. But what are these pieces? Is ONE SINGLE ONE a runic block? No! They are ALL Roman Tiles and Altars and Funeral Stones and other such. And yet, if ever Germany had runes, it must have been during the first 500 winters after Christ!

i. Rune-clogs (Rune-staves, Runic Calendars), of all sorts of material and of every size, have been known in the Anglo-Scandic lands from the early Christian times to our own day, *those still older having disappeared. Not one such piece has ever been heard of in any Saxon or German folkland.*

j. The language on all hitherto discovered Runic laves is one and the same — OLD NORTHERN in some one or other of its many dialects, *certainly NOT* GERMAN or SAXON.

Each one of these *facts* is a shock to the "German" *theory.* Taken all together they are a wall of bayonets, and no shadow of doubt *can* remain. But I dare say we shall long continue to hear of these so-called "German Runes" and —

as other such archæological fictions and cobwebs *have already been used* for hounding on to the Germanization and annexation of North and South Jutland — so also this new humbug may become a welcome weapon and holy argument for trying to butcher and enslave and "Germanize" and "annex" all the free and noble races yet living in our Anglo-Scandic lands. The free and noble "Saxon" peoples have already been largely overwhelmed and happily "incorporated", and their far superior language annihilated or placed under a High-German ban.

All Northern folksayings agree in this, that the iron-wielding clans of cavalry who swarmed over to Scandinavia from the East, and who obtained supremacy over and gave their impress and culture to the runeless bronze-wielding populations they found in Scandinavia, *brought the Runes with them*. At what era they came, is not known. Grave-finds show that it was at least as early as some time (how long?) *before Christ*. But where and when on their long march from Northern or Central India did they learn or invent these letters? Or did they learn and modify or invent them *after* their arrival in the Scandian lands? We can give no answer. Perhaps all our appliances on this side the Caucasus will never avail to clear up the difficulty. So the band of lore-men must now begin at the other end — in India itself, and slowly trace and test the graves northward and westward. A beginning is already made. In many parts of India great numbers of grave-mounds *from the Iron age*, with weapons and horse-harness and ornaments similar to those in the barrows of the North, and with the like stone-settings raised around them, have been discovered and many of them opened. Several Archæological Societies have been formed to pursue these and kindred studies, and by degrees they may push their enquiries nearer and nearer the Northern lands. Perhaps somewhere on the line RUNES may be met with. But there is here a difficulty. Immense districts on this enormous route are endless plains and steppes where there is *no stone*, consequently, there at least, no *inscribed stones*. Runes on iron and wood soon wear away, runes on hard metals always are mere exceptions. Still fortune may favor us, and perhaps in future years some point east and south of Scandinavia may be found with tombs containing our olden staves — possibly enough not minutely similar but still evidently the same. Then a further link will be added to the chain of this eventful history.

One thing is certain, that the Northern Runes were no mere direct loan or copy or adaptation from the Roman letters. Their *order* is different. The Roman are in ABC, the Runic in FUÞORC. Their *number* is different, the Runic being far more multitudinous than the Roman. Their *shape* in many cases is so unlike, as to show a *different* (tho *common*) origin. Many staves are more or less the same in both. Some of these belong to the Old-Northern alphabet, and therefore should have subsisted (if mere Roman) as the great stream of Roman culture set in. But on the contrary, as Scandinavia became more and more Romanized these particular staves *died out*, and assumed *other forms* in the later Runic staverow. Properly speaking, if they had a Roman source, the Runes should have been more and more "Romanized" as Roman influence grew supreme. But just the contrary took place.

Nor do we know what violent or silent or political or religious revolution led to the gradual simplification of the Old-Northern futhorc, and to the sound-power of ᛘ being changed from A into M, the older M (ᛉ) being altogether laid aside. All this, and a thousand questions mo', wait for "new lights". Some of these "lights" may come when least expected. Let us only go on working, and all our work be honest and true and thoro. The Father of Lights may then reward us with yet other glimpses into the history of the past[2].

3. That — *these Runes and this Northern Tung in which they are written never having been found OUTSIDE the North* all Scandinavia from Lapland to the Eider and all England from Kent to the Firth of Forth, *while they are everywhere the ancient characteristic WITHIN all these Anglo-Scandic lands down to our own day*, and THE MOTHER-TUNG and THE ART OF WRITING being the clearest and most decided of all known and accessible proofs of NATIONALITY — there is no longer a doubt as to that great historical fact (of which we have so many other independent evidences, archæological and historical and linguistical and geographical and topographical and ethnographical, as well as an endless flow of ancient tradition on either side the North Sea that *the old population of Danish South and North Jutland* the old outflowing *Anglic and Jutish and Frisic settlers, mixt with Norse and Swensk adventurers and emigrants, who flockt to England in the 3rd and 4th and 5th and following centuries, were chiefly Scandinavians, Northmen, not Saxons, still less Germans.* Of course all this does not affect the fact that England had an independent mixt population, native Kelts and incoming various-blooded strangers among its Roman cohorts and its mercantile settlers. *Every country has more or less a mixt population,* and always has had. Wise men only speak in the general.

4. That this is so much the clearer, as *THIS RUNIC BRAND, THIS BROAD ARROW, this outstanding mark of a peculiar Culture and Nationality, is not confined to one particular*

---

1 "The extent of the unknown which each discovery exposes is generally larger than its own revelation". — *John Hill Burton,* The History of Scotland from Agricola's Invasion to the Revolution of 1688. 8vo. Vol. 1. Edinburgh 1867, p. 117.

2 Since the above was written, the birth of the Runes has been cleared up. The Rev. Dr. Isaac Taylor has shown that these staves were an independent off-shoot from the old Greek Alphabet in "Scythia" (from Thrace and the Black Sea and the Crimea and Dnieper up towards the Vistula). There numerous and flourishing highly-civilized Greek Colonies were in daily warlike and peaceful contact with the Gothic Clans of Scandia and its nearest marches. See Dr. Taylor's "Greeks and Goths" 8vo. London 1879, the chapter on the Runes in his "The Alphabet." 2 vols. 8vo. London 1883, my Old-N. Run. Mon. Vol. 3. folio. p. 183, 268, and page 10 of my "Studies on Northern Mythology", London 1883. 8vo. The date was some 6 or 7 centuries before Christ.

spot in each Northern land. It was not the special heirloom or invention of one single Northern clan, one conquering Northern tribe, and communicated by war or peace by force or fraud to the other Northern races nearest to them. The Runes meet us in Sweden from the North to the South, in Norway from the North to the South, in Denmark from the North to the South, in England from the North to the South. And everywhere from *the oldest Northern days* and *at one common period.* There is therefore neither time nor place for a certain Runefolk to carry its letters from land to land. *All the Northmen had these staves everywhere, and at the same time.* And so with the gradual modification of the older Runic Futhorc. There can be no "conquest", no "carrying"; for everywhere in Scandinavia we see the older staverow *slowly* — and *at the same time,* from common internal causes — passing over from the more copious and complex to the simpler and fewer-lettered. The same "development", would, as I have said, have taken place in England, and *did partially so,* had not the whole Runic culture there been early stopt by Christianity and the Latin alphabet — which eventually took place in all Scandinavia also. But this *oneness* between the English and the Scandinavians is many times directly asserted on both sides. The time came when the classical "Germania" (which signified "Barbaria", "Non Romania", "Celtic", and what not) came to be misunderstood and to mislead. But the oldest statements all agree — the English came from the North, the Northmen settled in England, and both spoke QNE TUNG. I could add *many* very old and plain Scandinavian testimonies. I will only give two: —

"Vèr erum einnar túngu, þó at greinzt hafi mjök önnur tveggia eða nakkvat báðar".

We are of one tung (we speak the same language), tho that the one of the two, or in somewhat both of them, be now much changed.

Spoken of the Norse-Icelandic and the Old-English talks before the Norman Conquest. — *"Um Stafrofit", written about the year 1140 (see note 1, p. 10), Prose Edda, Vol. 2, Hafniæ 1852, 8vo p. 12.*

"Ein var þá túnga á Einglandi sem í Noregi ok í Danmörku; en þá skiptust túngur í Einglandi er Vilhjalmr Bastarðr vann Eingland".

One was tho (then) the tung on (in) England [in the time of king Ethelred, an. 979—1016] sum (as) in Norway eke (and) in Denmark; an (but) tho shifted (were altered) the-tungs in England as (when) William the-Bastard wan England.

Gunnlaugs Saga Ormstúngu, (Islendínga Sögur, Kjöbenhavn 1847, 8vo. Vol. 2, p. 221).

The above writers *do not* notice the great fact, that the Scandian talks themselves on the one hand, as well as those of Anglia on the other, had — from within and from local causes — greatly altered and developt and separated — each branching off in its own way — BEFORE the Norman Conquest; and they *could not* point out, but *we can*, that the Anglo-Norman was only a passing fashion among the ruling classes, that the speech of the Commons continued to live and thrive, and that in a short time (the old South-English Court-dialect having been broken up by the shock) the olden English folk-speech returned — tho far more Latinized than any of the Scandinavian languages, which on their side became largely Saxonized and Germanized — in the shape of that mighty and noble and thoroly Scandinavian (*Old* Scandinavian) NORTH ENGLISH which is now the birth-tung of England and her colonies.

5. *That the many lettered Runic Alphabet is the forner, the shorter one the later; the former alone being found over the whole North and always on the oldest pieces, the latter being provincially Scandinavian and occurring only on younger monuments.* Hence it is that no objects bearing the multitudinous runes, or Old-Northern staves, have ever appeared in any of the later Scandian colonies (Iceland, Greenland, Færöes, the Ile of Man, &c.) while they abound in England, the oldest Scandian settlement. Hence also is it that every purely Old-Northern piece in Scandinavia, and almost every overgang runic lave there, is — as being so very old — distinctively and decidedly HEATHEN; while, on the contrary, every such Old-Northern piece found in the so rapidly Romanized and Christianized England is (with the exception of the two Sandwich Stones and probably of the Thames Sword) as distinctively and decidedly CHRISTIAN.

6. That, the Northern settlements in England being so very old, *the oldest English dialects give us the best idea of and the best key to what the oldest Scandian folk-talks must have been in the 3rd and 4th and next following yearhundreds*, and will and must be the best help to our understanding the very oldest laves in our Scandinavian homeland. Hence it is that I have been able to read (*if I have redd*) some of these pieces. I have mastered the rune-marks and I am an Englishman. I have no other merit.

7. That *the efforts to translate all the oldest* Scandian Runic pieces *into "Icelandic"* are *futile*, and have everywhere necessarily failed; "Icelandic" being only *one* Northern dialect out of *many* — tho it *afterwards* largely became a *Mandarin lingua franca* in Scandinavia and partly in England among the "educated classes", especially as to bookwriting — and *this one* comparatively *modern*, Iceland itself not having been discovered and *colonized* till the end of the 9th and the beginning of the 10th century, by which time the Old-Northern Runes as a system HAD DIED OUT on the Scandian

main and were followed by the later Runic alphabet. But even this MODERN "Icelandic" of the 10th century *has not come down to us.* FAR FROM IT. If it had, it would be *very different* from what is now vulgarly so called, which is the greatly altered so-called "polisht" and "classical" "Icelandic" of the 13th—14th century. At the best, "Icelandic" is on the face of it a peculiarly develop and artificial local School-tung, largely — even of old — little understonden of the common folk in the rest of Scandinavia. Several of its specific characteristics have never been found outside its own local sphere. The oldest written "Icelandic" known to us is in a couple of pieces said to date from about the year 1200. In one word, to translate the oldest runic inscriptions, written in their local floating dialects from 200 to 700 or 800 years after Christ, into a modern "uniformized" "Icelandic" of the 13th or 14th age, is as reasonable as it would be to read Latin monuments from the times of the Kings and the Republic as if they answered to the "classical" dialect of Florentine Dante!

8. *That the whole modern doctrine of ONE UNIFORM CLASSICAL MORE OR LESS "ICELANDIC" LANGUAGE all over the immense North, from Finland and Halogoland to the Eider and the Thames, in the first 1000 winters after Christ, is an impossible absurdity,* there being then and there, as everywhere else, no unity in government or in race, but scores of independent "states" and "kingdoms", and equally so "tungs" manifold and running into each other and always changing in the various clans and folklands, dialects in various stages of development, tho all were bound together by certain common national characteristics. Time and Commerce and the local influence of other clans or of the remains of far older tribes and greater or less isolation and War and Slavery and a thousand Accidents, NOT RACE, explain *among cognate peoples* the presence or absence of particular forms and words and phrases and idioms and technical terms, here more or less olden and "hoary", there more or less worn and "advanced".

9. *That the Runic and other oldest art remains of our Northern forefathers show that these peoples possest not only the Art of Writing*, in itself a great proof of power and mastership and development, but, generally (in like manner as all the other Scando-Gothic races), *a very high degree of "BARBARIC"* (= NOT GREEK OR ROMAN *civilization and technical skill*, in some things higher than our own, even now, and this for war as for peace, for the home as for out-of-doors, for the family as for the commonweal. *This explains how it was possible for these dauntless clans so largely to remodel and invigorate a considerable part of Europe*, so easily to overrun and overturn the rich but rotten the mighty but marrowless the disciplined but diseased "Roman Empire", that gigantic and heartless and merciless usurpation, that strange conglomeration of hard straightforward materialism and abject overtrow, worldwide grinding

despotism, systematized and relentless Imperial and Proconsular and Fiscal plunder, and of depravity deep as hell.

10. That the thousands of stately Hows — Barrows, Cairns, Gravemounds — from the Iron Age, still found in our Northern lands (altho thousands many mo have been destroyed), and the Inscribed and Uninscribed Standing Stones so often on or near them, and often the very funeral words employed — speaking of PEACE and REST for the departed, *are the best commentary to our own oldest national written descriptions of THE SANCTITY AND REPOSE OF THE DEAD.* I might give ten thousand extracts. I confine myself to 2 or 3. Let us listen to the solemn injunction in the Elder Edda:

"Þat ræð ek þér it níunda,
at þu nám bjargir
　　hvars þu á foldu finnr;
hvárt eru sóttdauðir
eða sædauðir,
　　eða 'ro vápudauðir verar.
"Haug skal göra
hveim er liðinn er,
　　hendr þva ok höfuð;
kemba ok þerra,
áðr i kistu fari,
　　ok biðja sælan sofa".

Rede ninth rede I thee: —
rescue the lifeless,
*　a-field where'er thou find them;*
whether sank he on sick-bed
or sea-dead lieth,
*　or was hewn by hungry weapon.*
O'er the breathless body
a Barrow raise thou.
*　hands and head clean washen;*
comb'd and dried eke
in his kist fare he,
*　and bid him SOFTLY SLUMBER.*

The Elder Edda. Sigrdrífumál, verses 33, 34. ed. P. A. Munch.

And again, that fine picture of raising the grave-mound over the folklord, as found in our noblest English Epic. After his awsome kamp (battle) with the fire-drake — which he slays, but at the cost of his own life — the dying Wægmunding's last words are:

Ne mæg ic her leng wesan.
Hátað heaðo-mære
hlæw gewyrcean,
beorhtne æfter bæle,
æt brimes nosan;
se scel tó ge-myndum
mínum leódum
heáh hlifian
on Hrones næsse;

My life-day's now over.
Bid my good barons
to build me A LOW —
fair after fire-heap —
at the flood-dasht Headland.
A minne shall it stand there
to my mates and landsmen,
high looming
on Hronesness,

þæt hit sǽ-líðend	*so that seafarers*
syððan hátan	*sithance shall call it*
Biówulfes biorh,	*BIOWULF'S BARROW,*
ða ðe brentingas	*as their beak-carv'd galleys*
ofer flóda genipu	*out of hazy distance*
feorran drífað.	*float haughtily by.*

Beowulf. Near the end of Fitte 38.

Accordingly, farther on, after some fragmentary lines describing Beowulf's *lík-brand* (the burning of his body), the lay tells us:

Ge-worhton ðá	*Gan then to make them —*
Wedra leóde	*those Gothic heroes —*
HLÆW on liðe,	*A LOW on the lithe,*
se wæs héah and brád,	*lofty and broad,*
[wæ]g-liðendum	*by the fearless foam-plougher*
wíde g(e)-sýne,	*seen far and wide,*
and be-timbredon	*till on the tenth day*
on tyn dagum	*towering stood there*
beadu-rófes bécn;	*the battle-chief's beacon.*
bronda laſe	*The brand-scorcht floor*
wealle be-worhton	*a mound covered*
swá hyt weorðlícost	*mighty and worshipful,*
fore snotre men	*as found most fitting*
findan mihton:	*their famousest sages.*
hí on beorg dydon	*Within THE BARROW,*
beg and siglu,	*laid they beighs and ornaments,*
eall swylce hyrsta	*and such driven drink-cups*
swylce on horde ǽr	*as in the drake-hoard*
níð-hedige men	*the furious warriors*
ge-numen hæfdon;	*a-fore had taken.*
forleton eorla gestreón	*The earth be-gem they*
eorðan healdan,	*with earl-sprung jewels,*
gold on greóte,	*fling gold on the gravel,*
þær hit nú gen lífað	*where a-gain it shall lie*
eldum swá unnýt	*to all as useless*
swá hit [æro]r wæs.	*as erewhile it was.*
Ða ymbe hlæw riodan	*Round THE HOW rode then*

hildedeóre,
æþelinga bearn
ealra twelfa,
woldon [ceare] cwiðan,
kyning mænan,
wordgyd wrecan
and ymb [Wælhealle] sprecan.

those Hilde-champions,
all the troop
of those twelve athelings,
their Keen raising,
their King mourning,
word-lays chaunting
and of [Walhall] speaking.

Beowulf. Near the end.

And as to the Stone. What says the Edda?

"Sonr er betri
þótt sé síð of alinn
  eptir genginn guma;
sjaldan bautarsteinar
standa brautu nær,
  nema reisi niðr at nið."

Blissful a Son is
tho born but lately,
  his father already fallen;
seldom Bauta-stones
bound the folk-path,
  save raised by kin to kindred!

The Elder Edda. Hávamál, verse 71. Ed. P. A. Munch.

The Bauta-stone (Beaten-one's Stone, Standing Stone in memory of one who had fallen in battle) was mostly runeless. The word is sometimes employed for a Runic Block, or for a Minne-stone in general inscribed or not.

This has been happily applied by a modern Danish poet:

"Ruster Eder! rask, ei seen,
Rister mig en Runesteen!
Runesteen, som reist bestaaer,
Risen lig, i tusind Aar."

Rush to arms with ready tread,
Raise a Rune-stone o'er mine head;
Rune-stone rist, as Ettin strong,
Ringing my fame time's waves along!

A. G. Oehlenslæger, Harald Hildetand.

11. That we have undeniable proofs that many of the Inscribed Runic Stones were, *in the oldest Iron Age*, deposited *inside the cairn*, not *outside*. This is a striking illustration of the same custom in Egyptian and other Oriental tombs, which were often carefully hewn and finely decorated tho more or less invisible to the passer-by, — and of our own *inscribed* rich coffins let down *into* the earth *for the worms to read*. We here see that the grave was a continued House, and that the departed lived a mystic life therein, visiting it at pleasure when they chose to leave their other-land abode.

12. That the heathen runic inscriptions, the formula of REST, and even the occasional invocation of the Gods themselves, all show that our ancestors held

fast the belief of a future state, the ever-life of the soul, Personal Deities, and all the other comforts and joys of faith in the Godhead. Thus Christianity had only to give clearer views and to teach the name of the Great Unknown whom all felt after, to gain a wide and rapid acceptance. As we know, only a part of Scandinavia was "converted by force", and even this was the act of their own Kings. As much "force" was used in carrying out the Reformation in Scandinavia as in introducing Christianity.

13. That, as far as we can see, the monuments before us yield *no single instance of anything like a date* or fixt chronological era, *or of any Time-measure* (name of a Month or Week or Day or Hour), *or of the age of the deceast,* as little as they have *any numerical figures.* Consequently we do not know how they reckoned events or time, or what were their ciphers for numeration (if they had any), in our oldest North. But all these things are also absent on the great mass of *the later* Runic monuments deep down into the Christian period, when the Christian era and Numeral marks were well known. It is *very seldom* that *any* of the Scandinavian-runic stones bear a date, still rarer that the "forthfaren's" age is mentioned on them. Among these few slabs, perhaps the earliest using Christian chronology are found in the ile of Gotland. But no such dated runic grave-stone is older than the 14th century. Dated runic Bells go a hundred years farther back. Runic Coins (with Scandinavian runes appear in Scandinavia at the end of the 10th century, in England (with Old-Northern runes, as early as the 7th. Golden Bracteates (O. N. runes) begun in the 4th or 5th.

Place-names are occasionally found both on Old-Northern and on Scandinavian-runic pieces, those on the oldest monuments being of course — from the enormous lapse of time — very hard to identify. On the later monuments the place-names are often familiar; our own ENGLAND is common enough; nay, on one block we meet with BATH, on another LONDON.

From intermarriage and commerce and travel and military service abroad and "a good education", or from contact even while at home with strangers or Christians or war-prisoners or slaves, and from various other causes, many of the Northmen — even from the earliest times at Rome and Constantinople down to the early middle age — *knew* more tungs than their own, sometimes could *write* them. Hence in their foreign settlements and colonies and subjugated "kingdoms" they often more or less freely and rapidly adopted the language and (Roman letters of the Christian country to which they had come. This would particularly be the case in and near to England, Old English being merely a dialect of their mothertung. We have striking examples of this in Normandy, where the wikings nearly all married French women, so that in one generation the home-speech there became largely French, and in Ireland, where it would soon become largely English. Hence no

Runic Stones or Runic Coins have ever been found in Normandy and Ireland, altho this latter country had coins struck by Scandian princes earlier than Scandinavia itself. All the coins struck by Northern "Earls" and "Kings" *out of the North* (Scandinavia and England) *bear only Roman letters.*

14. That, *as the Northmen* (the Scandinavians and English) *more nearly, and the Scando-Goths* (the Northmen, the Saxons and the Germans) *more generally, are all of one blood and tung*, so they should *all hold together*, love and help and defend each other, avoid every beggarly temptation to hate or plunder or ruin or "annect" each other, nobly taking their stand as brothers and fulfilling their mission as one great folkship with its own local limits and national duties, in necessary providential counterpoise — but in all friendly harmony with — the great Romance and Magyar and Greek and Slavic and other race-groups.

15. That the whole theory of *the Runes being in oldest times "mysterious"*, "secret marks", "used only in magic", "the private staves of the priests and kings", is *utterly unfounded.* On the contrary, we find them everywhere, on gravestones, rocks, weapons, ornaments, tools, and often even in the form of *the Alphabet,* in order that the common people might easily see and quickly learn them. It was only in proportion as they begun to die out (supplanted by the Roman letters) that, like all other "old-fashioned" and "fantastic" characters, they descended to the wizard and the juggler. If, when *first* introduced, these Runes were more or less "magical" and "mysterious" (which may well have been the case), they have left no trace thereof on the oldest monuments, and therefore many centuries must then have elapst between their original invention or adaptation and their *earliest* use AS WE KNOW THEM.

16. That, whatever else we do, *we must not read these monuments by altering them at our pleasure.* All the talk about "miscuttings" is so childish and monstrous, and is so evidently mixt up with the ignorance and insolence of modern know-every-thing-ism, that is of modern sciolism, that we must at once discard it. Should a real uncorrected "mis-hewing" ever be found on these pieces, *which has yet to be proved,* we must cheerfully accept it. In any case it will be *very* exceptional. But we must not cloak our own inability, our own necessary groping among words and dialects and times and creeds and institutions of which we know so little, by treating the oldest remains of our fore-gangers as so much useless granite or old metal, a mere field for everyman's idle and capricious and impudent conjecture. We approach these objects, many of them colossal or costly and often cut with great elegance, as learners, not as masters and tyrants. All our monumental history, Oriental and Classical and Runic, is full of the terrible mistakes, the humiliating blindnesses, the childish blunders, the unheard-of combinations and wild guesses, the endless rash

changes of letters or words, which have resulted from this unhappy school of half-taught "criticism". Let *us*, now at least, steer clear of the shoals markt by so many a disastrous shipwreck. Why should we not now and then be able and willing to say — "this I cannot understand"?

Some of these remarks will be found elsewhere in these pages. But I have been careless of a little repetition[1], partly because in this summing up it could not easily be avoided, and partly because certain things cannot apparently be repeated too often.

Such are my conclusions from *the facts* here before me. But some may be astonisht or offended or disappointed that THESE FACTS THEMSELVES, *the Old-Northern Runic pieces* here collected, are after all *so very few*. Rather should we be surprised that they are *so many*. As to "loose" articles, Arms and Jewels and Tools &c., of course it is and was quite exceptional for an owner to "whittle" his name upon them[2]. And of the few thus inscribed, the majority has been long since melted down — or is still lying undiscovered. Usually everything is smasht or used up after 2 or 3 generations, or remade in accordance with the new fashion[3]. All our European Museums put together can only show *a poor handful* of the Tools and Utensils and precious Ornaments used from the time of William the Bastard to William of Orange; similar things from the days of Julius Cæsar to those of the Norman adventurer — how many are they? — As to "fast" pieces, Memorial Stones &c., we must remember that in all times and countries there have been endless and ever-varying rites of burial, and that only a small fraction of the population ever had or has any decorated grave-minne or other such more or less *expensive* funeral mark. Most people may be thankful if they are *burned or buried at all* with any decent rites. But *written grave-stones* have always been, and still are an exception. In many whole districts, century after century, they are even now almost unknown. In certain folklands the inscribed grave-mark was during certain periods popular, and hence

---

[1] "In the course of this work I have never shunned repetitions of any sort or kind, when I have found repetitions needful. Repetitions are not superfluities: nor is it surplussage to reiterate the same thought or fact under diverse combinations." — *Sir Francis Palgrave*. The History of Normandy and of England. 8vo. Vol. 1, London 1851. p. 353.

[2] And even then, this writing may not at first be observed. Many of these articles are so corroded or encrusted and obscured by rust and dirt that any inscription has been long since altogether eaten away or can only be found after careful handling and patient cleaning. *Several of the stave-bearing jewels in this work* have been for years *exhibited in museums*, some of them even *elegantly engraved* in works publisht by distinguisht archæologists, *without a suspicion that there were letters upon them*. The runes have been discovered quite lately, after more minute examination. Other pieces in public or private collections may yet be found to bear writing. But *thousands* of these objects dug up in the last thousand years, even in the last and present century, have been *lost or destroyed* without being scrutinized by competent persons.

[3] The gold and silver plate preserved at Windsor Castle weighs (as we are informed by *The Guardian* Oct. 2. 1867, p. 1061) nearly *thirty tons*, and is roughly estimated at £ 3.000.000. But very little of it is otherwise than modern and trashy, and most of it was melted down and remodeled by that tasteless prince of profligates — George IV.

hundreds are still extant; in others the uninscribed Bauta-stone (Menhir, Pillar) was preferred, tradition doing the rest; for in olden times the living word was the rule, carving the exception. Add to this the endless destruction during 1800 years from greed, for building, for flooring or hearth-stones or gate-posts, for re-use as palimpsest-stones or as minne-blocks to newly deceased persons after being "nicely painted" or "tooled over", from revenge, from religious or sectarian fanaticism, from accident and the elements and from ROAD- and BRIDGE-MAKING (especially the modern MACAD-AMIZING) — and the wonder is that we have *one such stone* still left![1] *How many grave-stones have we* from the days of even Edward the Confessor? Nay, how many from the times of Queen Elizabeth or even George the First? All our beautiful Sepulchral Brasses, where are they? *Not a tithe* of them is left to us, altho they were fine works of art and preserved IN THE CHURCH, under the special eye as it were, of God and Man! But what can resist the foul love of filthy lucre? They have been broken away and sold as old metal, many scores of them in this "enlightened" 19th century. And consider: the more sparse the population[2] the more sparing the

---

[1] A large stone funeral monument sometimes disappears *in one generation*:

"Un jour, j'avais sept ans, on me conduisit, par je ne sais quel hasard, dans le principal cimetière de Nantes, nouvellement inauguré alors. Le plus remarquable et presque le seul monument qu'il y eût encore, était une pyramide avec un soubassement cubique, portant une épitaphe latine sur une table de marbre noir.

"Il y avait peut-être un mois que j'apprenais le latin — Voyons, latiniste, me dit un camarade, explique-nous cela.

"Comme je ne trouvai dans l'épitaphe ni *Rosa*, ni *Dominus*, ni même *Bonus bona bonum*, je n'y reconnus pas un mot et me retirai confus et raillé.

"Vingt ans après, je passais par Nantes, que j'avais quitté tout jeune, et le hasard encore m'ayant conduit aux environs du cimitière, j'y voulus entrer. Cette fois, l'épitaphe allait toute seule, mais le monument était déjà un peu dégradé, il avait bien vielli.

"Dans ce récent voyage, visitant le magnifique Jardin des Plantes, voisin du même cimitière, j'y suis entré encore. Comme il s'était peuplé!! Quant à ma pyramide, je l'ai cherchée en vain, elle n'existe plus. Je suis sorti pensif et triste J'avais déjà vecu plus qu'un monument." — *A. Carro, Voyage chez les Celtes, ou de Paris au Mont Saint-Michel, par Carnac. 8vo. Paris 1867. pp. 35. 6.*

Some times such things are *given back* to us in a way the most unheard-of. I wend (translate) from "Post-och Inrikes-Tidningar" (the Swedish Official Gazette) for Dec. 13, 1867:

"*A grave-monument in a strange place.* A letter from Vadstena communicates as follows. Among the trees cut down lately in the churchyard of our town was an Ash, certainly very old. After the stem had been sawn over, the root was taken up, when a Grave-stone was found imbedded within it. Probably when the tree was young, a couple of its root-branches shot up so as to clasp the stone. In this way, as the Ash grew the slab was drawn more and more up and within the stem, for it was found within the pith of the tree. The block was originally about 4 feet long and 2 broad, and yet showed an inscription, but no more could be made out than the words:

GYNELA JONSDOTTER 1612.

Where the tree was cut down (which was only a few inches above the place in which the stone was found) were counted about 150 year-rings."

[2] As an illustration, I will only refer to *one single race-group* — the Indians of the United States of North America. With regard to them the evidence is thus pithily summed up in the Annual Report for 1861 of the Smithsonian Institution (Washington 1862. 8vo. p. 392): — "Various methods of disposing of the dead have obtained in different tribes, as burning, burial, deposit in caves, in lodges, beneath piles of stone, and in wooden sepulchres erected above ground, placing on scaffolds or in canoes, and attaching to the trunks of trees. In many instances the bones, after a season, are collected together and brought into common cemeteries [= ossuaries, bone-pits]."

grave-stones. But if we have so few left from the late and comparatively *populous* ages of which we have spoken, how many were raised in the early *thinly-peopled* times of the Runic North?

No competent judge of these things will deem otherwise than that the Old-Runic Harvest here brought together is in fact very great, far greater than any of us dared to dream of or hope for a few years ago."

After this long extract from my first tome I have only to add, that the reader who wishes to follow all the *details*, proofs and arguments, to read the valuable *communications* of distinguisht fellow-workers, and to see the crowd of *additional* explanatory *Chemitypes* and other illustrations, besides nearly 100 Runic *Alphabets* in facsimile, all helping us to understand the Old-Northern Monuments — must of course in some Public Library consult my 3 folios. To their pages exact reference is made under each find. I had no choice *here* but to make the text as *short* as possible, while still giving everything absolutely *necessary*.

The present rage for infallibly fixing everything all at once, is highly to be deprecated. Future finds and the progress of Runish studies will doubtless modify some things here given. We shall know more a hundred years hence, than we do now.

Cheapinghaven, Denmark. Feb. 15, 1884.

GEORGE STEPHENS.

SWEDEN.

TANUM, BOHUSLÄN, SWEDEN.

? DATE ABOUT A. D. 100—200.

Old-Northern Runic Monuments p. 196. 835. 976. XXVII.

ÞRÆWINGÆN HÆI-TINÆ A WÆS!
THRÆWING'S HIGH-TINE (pillar-stone) AYE WÆS (be)!
(= Grave-block, stand here alway, in memory of Thrœwing!)
Som-THRÆWINGS GRAF-PELARE ALLTID STÅ!

This enormous monolith is nearly 10 feet long, about 4 feet 10 inches at broadest, and 9 inches thick. It is still at Tanum. Is quite perfect. Runes reverst. Are redd from right to left. Plate engraved in 1864. Was first found at the beginning of this century.

KINNEVED, WEST-GOTLAND, SWEDEN.

? DATE ABOUT A. D. 200—300.

Old.-N. R. Mon. Vol. 3. p. 21.

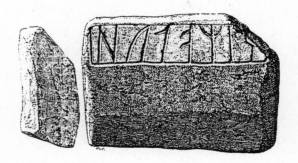

Only the dead man's name,

SIAÆLUH.

Full size. Is of Talcose Slate (Steatite, Soap-stone. Pot-stone). Reverst runes. Was found in 1843, engraved in 1869. In Skara Museum, West Gotland.

SKÅ-ÄNG, SÖDERMANLAND, SWEDEN.

? DATE ABOUT A. D. 200—300.

Old-N. R. Mon. p. 887. Vol. 3. p. 23.

Is twi-writ. Besides the scoring in the old staves, has been used again for death-words in the later runes, maybe in the 11th century. The latter epitaph has long been known; the former was discovered by Dr. Hans O. H. Hildebrand in 1867; we have to thank Archivary Undset for a corrected copy of the runes, whereby I now offer a modification of my former reading:

HÆRING ÆGI LEUGÆ AI!

May-HÆRING OWN (have, hold) his-LOW (grave-hill, tumulus, death-bed. resting-place) AYE (alway)!

Må-HÆRING ÅGA sin-HÖG (hvilo-bädd) Å (alltid)!

The later snake-wind inscription says:

SKANMALS AUK OLAUF ÞAU LETU KIARA MERKI ÞAUSI EFTIR SUAIN, FAÞUR SIN.   GUÞ HIALBI SALU HANS.

SKANMALS (= SKAM-HALS) EKE (and) his-sister-OLAUF THEY LET GARE (make, raise) MARKS (grave-marks) THESE AFTER SUAIN, FATHER SIN (their).   May-GOD HELP SOUL HIS!

SKANMALS OCH hans-syster-OLAUF DE LÅTO GÖRA MÄRKEN DESSA EFTER SUAIN, FADER SIN.   GUD HJELPE
SJÄL HANS!

About 5 feet 3 inches high, greatest breadth about 3 feet, average thickness a little over 1 foot. — As runish staves are often taken twice, we may also read HÆRINGÆ ÆGI. We might also divide Æ GILEUGÆ.

SKÄRKIND, EAST-GOTLAND, SWEDEN.

? DATE ABOUT A. D. 200—300.

Old-N. R. Mon. Vol. 3, p. 26.

Found in the summer of 1876 by Director C. F. Nordenskjöld, who kindly forwarded a drawing and paper cast. Is of reddish granite, about 5 feet 8 inches high. Was the base on which stood an old sandstone Font.

SCIDÆ LEUWÆ.

SKITH'S LOW (grave-mound).

SKID'S GRAF-HÖG.

VANGA, WEST-GOTLAND, SWEDEN.

? DATE ABOUT A. D. 200—300.

Old-N. R. Mon. p. 241, 835, and Vol. 3. p. 27. Re-engraved here from the stone itself, which I visited in July 1873.

May be one word; the Dead Man's name, in the nominative. But I prefer the usual formula, 2 names, a nom. and a dative:

HÆUC ODUA.

HÆUC (? = *HÆUNC*) *raised-this-stone-to-OTHU.*

HÆUC reste-till-OTHU.

Greatest height about 3 feet 5 inches, greatest breadth about 2 feet. Turned runes. First noticed in 1791.

BERGA, SÖDERMANLAND, SWEDEN.

? DATE ABOUT A. D. 300—400.

Old-N. R. Mon. p. 176, 886, XXVII. Vol. 3, p. 29.

The only Old-Northern stone known to me which bears two words, cut far apart and running in different directions. I would therefore now suggest that the one name is carved *later* than the other. Perhaps the Husband or Wife died first, and shortly after the Partner was called away. Thus they most likely lay in the same grave, and were remembered on the same block. So I now propose:

FINO.

The-lord-FINO.

SÆLIGÆSTIA.

The-lady-SÆLIGÆSTIA.

Seven feet 2 inches high, 2 feet 4 inches broad above and 3 feet below. First engraved in 1830.

So the Fjellerad stone, North Jutland, Denmark, has a long inscription in the later runes to a chief named ABI and a lady TUFA, and says of them:

DAU LIKA BADI I DAUM HAUKI.

THEY LIE BOTH IN THIS HOW (grave-mound).

MÖJEBRO, UPLAND, SWEDEN.

? DATE ABOUT A. D. 300—400.

Old-N. R. Mon. p. 178, 900, XXVIII. Vol. 3. p. 30.

As drawn about the middle of the 17th century and publisht in Göransson's Bautil in 1750.

For several reasons (among others, the common one of there being here no stops, and the consequent doubt how we are to divide the words) this risting is *very* hard to read. Abandoning my former attempts with the first line, I am now inclined to look upon it as containing only *names* — perhaps those of the dead Chief and of his 2 Sons and Daughter, or 3 of his nearest kin. I therefore, with great diffidence, would offer:

ÆNÆHÆ, HÆISLÆ, GINIA, FRÆWÆRÆDÆA.

Sir-ÆNÆHÆ, Sir-HÆISLÆ, the-lady-GINIA, raised-this-stone-to-the-lord-FRÆWÆRÆD.

2*

Nearly 8 feet 3 inches high. Reverst staves. I here, once for all, make a remark, which will often apply more or less: Out of 14 vowels, no less than 9 are Æ, an evident proof of local dialect. As to the 2nd name, 5 brothers named HOISLI are mentioned on the Rök stone, 9th century, which see. — The stone is hard red quartz and feldspar.

As drawn by Prof. Carl Säve, of Upsala, in 1862.

ETELHEM, GOTLAND, SWEDEN.

? DATE ABOUT A. D. 400—500.

Old-N. R. Mon. p. 182.

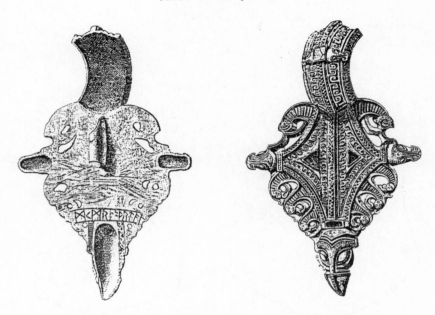

MC (= MIC) MRLÆ (= MIRILÆ or MERILÆ) WRTÆ (= WORTÆ).
ME MIRILÆ WROUGHT (= Merilæ made me).
MIG MIRILÆ GJORDE.

Engraved full size.   Silver-gilt Brooch, found in 1846.   On the front, the raised rands and upstanding carved ridges have their original white glitter.   The zigzags were filled with a bluish niello, as were the runes.   The rest richly gilt.   The square red stone or fluor-spar or glass still remains, tho broken.   The two triangular stones in the centre, and the oblong one lower down, have fallen out.   As we see, to save space, the less weighty vowels are omitted, as often.   There was no room for them.

KROGSTAD, UPLAND, SWEDEN.

? DATE ABOUT A. D. 400—500.

Old-N. R. Mon. p. 184, 967, XXVII. Vol. 3, p. 31.

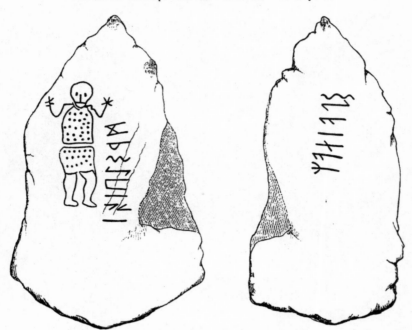

As drawn in middle of 17 cent. and publisht in Bautil 1750. but corrected by Baron J. Nordenfalk in 1858.

Runes as they were in 1869. from tracings by Prof. C. Säve and Docent N. Linder,
here Photoxylographt 1—6th of the size.

But, according to Dr. H. Hildebrand and Prof. Bugge, the ᴜ should lean a little at the left top, the right leg being also a trifle longer than the left.

ᴍᴡꜱʏᴏᴜɪɴɢɪ ꜱʏᴏᴁɪɴᴁᴀ.

ᴍᴡꜱʏᴏᴜɪɴɢɪ (Musowingi, Mysing) to-ꜱʏᴏᴁɪɴ (in memory of Swain).

ᴍᴡꜱʏᴏᴜɪɴɢ (skref dessa runor) till-ꜱʏᴏᴁɪɴ (Sven).

This grave-stone is upwards of 6 feet high. The dots I take to be conventional for ·ring-mail, and the open band for *the belt*. As a curiosity, I add *the oldest* drawing of this stone, by ᴊ. ᴛ. ᴀ. ʙᴜʀᴇ, made about 1620—40, full size:

KONGHELL, BOHUSLÄN, SWEDEN.

? DATE ABOUT A. D. 500—600.

Old-N. R. Mon. p. 208, 835.

Runes as they stand on the Staff:

H F Ú K Ú U Þ F Ú A H

Runes (of course reverst) engraved from a photograph:

HAUFÞUÚKÚFH

ᶠ I take to stand for FUR and H for BARI, and read:
HAUFÐUÓKÚ F(ur) H(ari).
The |HEADING| (Headman, Chief, Leader, Commander) FOR (of) the-HÆR (army,
navy, forces, troops).
(= This is the General's Baton of Command).
HÖFDINGEN FÖR HÄREN.

A Staff or Baton, of Heart of Yew, now very dark in color, 33¹⁄₂
Danish inches long, here engraved 1-fourth the size. Found in the ruins of the
old Konungahella, between Gotenburg and Kongelf, at Kastellgården in 1864.

In my folio text I have many arguments and engravings to show that
this was a General's Staff, and I think that there can be no doubt of it. I here
add a drawing of WILLIAM OF NORMANDY encouraging his troops before the battle
of Hastings, taken from the Bayeux Tapestry:

BJÖRKETORP, BLEKING, SWEDEN.

? DATE ABOUT A. D. 600—700.

Old.-N. R. Mon. p. 165. Vol. 3, p. 32.

My plates, August 1864.

SÆAÞ ÆT BÆRUTA UT I ÆAWELÆ DÆUDE.

H.EER.E MÆLE USA GINÆ-RUNÆA ÆRE GEU.

F.ÆLE HÆLHÆDA OÆG.

HÆIDAR‿RUNO‿O RO NU.

UÞÆR, ÆBÆ SBÆ.

SÆATH AT the-BARRATRY (battle, campaign) OUT IN ÆAWEL DIED.

HERE MELL (tell) of-US the-GIN-RUNES (our power-staves) his-ARE (fame) YEA (truly).

FELE (many) of-HELTS (heroes) he-WOOG (slew).

HADOR- (that honor's) RUNA (friend) OWES (hath, takes) his-ROO (rest) NOW.

UTHÆR and-ÆBÆ the-SPAE (Wise) (= raised these stones and carved these runes).

SÆATH I KAMP UT I ÆAWEL DÖDDE (dog).

HÄR MÅLA (förtälja) VÅRA MAGT-RUNOR hans-ÅRA JO.

MÅNGA HJELTAR han-VOG (slog han).

HEDERS-RUNI (vän), han-ÅGER sin-RO NU.

UTHÆR och-ÆBÆ SPÅ (den kloke) (= reste desse stenar och högg dessa runor).

Rune-pillar more than 13 feet high, the two other blocks upwards of 10. Nearby have been found a Stone-kist and a Stone-circle (Doom-ring). First copy is Worm's, in 1636. ,BÆRUTA maybe a place-name, as well as ÆAWELÆ. See the Stentofte stone, further on.

From Worsaae's lithographs, drawn in 1844.

My plate. August 1864.

GOMMOR, BLEKING, SWEDEN.

? DATE ABOUT A. D. 600—700.

Old-N. R. Mon. p. 206, 835, XXVIII.   Vol. 3, p. 32.

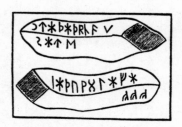

Sent to Cheapinghaven, Denmark, in 1652 or thereabout, and perisht in the great fire of 1728. This curious grave-stone was about 2 feet long, 2 feet all round, undrest, of a purple color, and inscribed on all the 4 sides. As we see, Worm's woodcut (Dan. Mon. 1643) is barbarous, and any reading is only approximative.

I now take the 1st stave to have been an s, the 4th an N, the 8th an L, the 10th an F, and the 1st in the 3rd line an H, and propose:

STÆNÆ ÞRLÆF (= ÞORLÆF) SÆTE H.EÐUWOLÆFÆ.

F F F.

*This-*STONE THORLÆF SET *to-*HÆTHUWOLF.

F. F*s-son* FAWED *(carved).*

Denne-STEN THORLÆF SATTE till-HÆTHULF.

F. F's-son SKREF-runorna.

Apparently the HÆÐWOLF of the Stentofte and Istaby stones. ÞORLÆF may have been his son or foster-brother.

ISTABY, BLEKING, SWEDEN.

? DATE ABOUT A. D. 600—700.

Old-N. R. Mon. p. 173.   Vol. 3. p. 33.

My plate. September 1864.

My plate, September 1864.

YFÆTA HYRIWULÆFÆ, HYÐUWULÆFA,
HYERUWULÆFIA WÆRYIT RUNYA ÐYIYA.

AFTER (in memory of) HYRIWOLF and-HYTHUWOLF
the-lady-HYERUWOLFIA WROTE (let-write) RUNES THESE.
EFTER (till minne af) HYRULF och-HYTHULF
HYERULFIA SKREF RUNOR DESSA.

I now take HYERUWULÆFIA to be a womansname. She was probably *the sister* of the two warriors. — This will then be the family-stone, the public (official) block being at Sten-tofte, which see. The Gommor stone seems raised to one of the brothers.

About 4 feet 6 inches above ground, and 2 feet 6 at broadest. First made public in 1748.

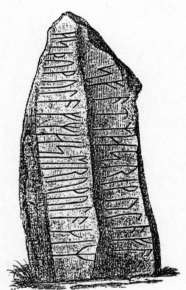

From Worsaae's lithographs, drawn in 1844.

LINDHOLM, SKANE, SWEDEN.

? DATE ABOUT A. D. 600—700.

Old-N. R. Mon. Vol. 1, p. 219. Vol. 3, p. 33.

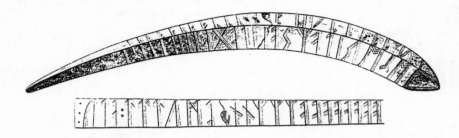

Nov. 1876. Prof. S. Bugge and Archivary I. Undset both decide that this piece (which I have never seen) has at the break ᚨ (Æ) not ᚺ (N). I have corrected the block accordingly.

Of bone. Full size. Found deep in Lindholm Moss in 1840. Runes reverst, and therefore redd from right to left. Very difficult as not divided by word-points, and also because we do not know whether the piece was made for an Amulet, or as Witch-gear, or a Tool or some Game. Another such, found in 1761 in Flemlöse Moss, Fyn, was destroyed without being copied!

The *repeated* letters were perhaps not magical, but to fill up, making the one line as long as the other. If so, we get ÆANB, may be = ÆANP = ÆAMP, nearly the N. I. JAPR (? JANPR, JAMPR), a kind of snake mentioned in the Prose-Edda. The next word, in the same way, would be MUT (MÓT). — Whether ÆLA (or ÆLLA) was a person (the owner), or a Witch or Wizard (the user), or a Serpent-chief or House-god (the being invoked), we cannot tell.

The late discovery (summer of 1877) of the Kragehul Lance-shaft (Denmark) and the Fonnås Brooch (Norway), with their remarkable inscriptions, have now suggested to me another reading:

EC, ERILÆA SÆ IILÆ, GÆA HÆTEC Æ, ÆANB, MUT ÆLU.

I, ERILÆA (= *JARL, EARL*) *SE* (the) *ILL* (*foe-crushing, fierce*), — ʿGOʾ, *HIGHT-I* (*I command, I bid*). ʿAYE, O-SNAKE, AGAINST ÆLA!*

JAG, ERILÆA, HIN ILLE, ʿGÅ', BJUDER-JAG. ʿÅ (= alltid) O-ORM, MOT ÆLA!ʾ

In this case ERILÆA was the name of the owner, just as an ERILÆA owned the Kragehul Lance. On these pieces, therefore, *the owner speaks* (I) to his amulet or weapon, while on the Gilton Sword (England) the *Sword speaks* (I) to his master. — Further finds may perhaps help us to amend the above. The actual characters are, as they stand:

ECERILÆASÆIILÆGÆAHÆTECÆ ⋮

ÆÆÆÆÆÆÆAANNNBMUTTT:ÆLU ⋮

STENTOFTE, BLEKING. SWEDEN.

? DATE ABOUT A. D. 600—700.

Old · N. R. Mon. p. 167. Vol. 3, p. 34.

My plate, September 1864.

My plate. September 1864.

The first (bad) drawing was made early in this century. The first *publisht* drawing is the careful one by Worsaae. As on this stone ✶ is the usual Æ and ⋏ the usual O, ᚠ I now take to be here transitional for Œ. When ⋏ altogether died out, this ᚠ (in its many varieties) became O. It here only occurs once, in the word HŒGES. I now agree with Bugge, that the stave after GÆF is more like the variously-modified ING-mark than the S-mark, and therefore read GÆFNG, = GÆFING.

From Worsaae's lithographs, drawn in 1844.

My present, ameliorated, reading is:

> ÆIU HÆBO RUMA,
>
> NIU HŒGES TUMA,
>
> HÆDUWOLÆFA GÆFING,
>
> HÆRIWOLÆFA MÆ,
>
> > HIDEAR-RUNGNO.
>
> HERÆ MÆLÆ SÆA ÆRÆ GEUW.
>
> MUCNU HELÆHDDUÆ (W)UGO.
>
> > ÆBÆ RIUTI
>
> > DERÆ GINO-RONOA.

AYE shall-they-HAVE ROME (lustre, praise),
in-the-NEW of-their-HOW TOOM (space, chamber, = on the fresh floor of their tumulus).
HÆTHUWOLF GÆFING (of the Gæf-clan, or, Gæf's-son),
and-HÆRIWOLF MÆ (called the Mœ),
> *HADOR- (those-honor's) REGEN (lords, = those honor-crowned chiefs).*
HERE MELL (speak) THESE-runes their-ARE (fame) YEA (truly).
a-MUCKLE (multitude) of-BELTS (braves) they-WOOG (slew).
> *ÆBÆ WROTE (carved)*
> *TBEIR GIN-RUNES (mighty letters).*

4*

ALLTID skola-de-HAFVA BERÖM

i-den-NYA af-deras-HÖG KAMMARE (= i deras grafhögs nya hvalf),

HÆTHULF GÆFING,

och-HÆRIULF MÆ,

HEDERNS-HÖFDINGAR.

HÄR MÄLA (omtala) DESSA-runor deras-ÄRA JO.

en-MYCKENHET (skara) af-HJELTAR de-VOGO (dödade).

ÆBÆ RITADE (inristade)

DERAS GIN-RUNOR (kraft-runor).

About 4½ feet above ground and 2 feet 4 inches broad. This seems the official (public) pillar, the family block being at Istaby. See also Gommor and Björketorp.

UPSALA, UPLAND, SWEDEN.

? DATE ABOUT A. D. 600—700.

Old-N. R. Mon. p. 204. Vol. 3, p. 36.

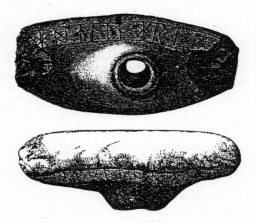

ÆH OLDA ÖKISI.

OWES (owns, possesses) OLTHA this-AXE.

ÄGER OLTHA denna-YXA.

Engraved full size.   Stone Axe, found in the beginning of the last century.   OLDA is probably a female name.

VARNUM, VERMLAND, SWEDEN.

? DATE ABOUT A. D. 600—700.

Old-N. R. Mon. p. 216. Vol. 3, p. 36.

Found in 1862 by Herr J. W. Alsterlund in the ruins of a grave-low at Järsberg,
Varnum Parish, near Christinehamn Unhappily the top is broken away, and we shall therefore
never be quite sure of the reading. Hence the many different interpretations. I adhere to

the one I originally gave. I take it to read *oxgang-wise*, first from the top on the right and turning up at the ET, after the 3 dots, — and then concluding with the rune-cutter's epigraph (as so often), beginning with the smaller staves (RUNOA) and bending round; the last word, the large-carved name of the artist, ending before the 3 dots. We have many other examples of reverst and not reverst runes intermixt, as here, partly depending on their position. I now restore to ᛆ here, as an O. N. letter, its usual power of ᴀ. Supposing the lost top bit — as it may have been longer or shorter — to have borne, as *the beginning* of the one line and *the end* of the other, something like:

Stæinæ ræis- (*or* Stæinæ þænsi ræis-)

ætæ sinæ (*or* ætæ sinæ kuþan),

my reading was and is:

[Stæinæ (þænsi) ræis]TI ÆHECER I LÆA ET IHAÆ, B(U)[ætæ sinæ (kuþan)].   RUNOA WÆRITÆ

UANÆBÆRÆH.

[Stone (this) rais]ED ÆHECER IN LÆA AT (to) IHAI (= INGE). BO[nde (husband) her (good)].   *These*
RUNES WROTE UANÆBÆRÆU.

[Sten (denne) res]TE ÆHEKER I LÆ ÅT (till minne af) IHAI (= INGE). BO[nde (man) sin (god)]|.

Dessa-RUNOR RITADE (högg) UANÆBERG.

Nearly 8 feet long, 5 above ground. WANNBERG is still a Swedish family-name.

WEST-THORP, SKONE, SWEDEN.

? DATE ABOUT A. D. 700—800.

Old-N. R. Mon. p. 222.   Vol. 3, p. 36.

IIT HIUK UNBOÆU.

IIT HEWED (made this) for-UNBOA.

IIT HÖGG (skar dette) för-UNBOA.

Of bone, probably the tooth of the Walrus. Full size. Found in 1823 deep down in a moss at West-Thorp in Vemmenhögs Härad. Several Combs inscribed with olden and later runes have been found in Scandinavia and England. The name may be that of a female.

RÆFSAL, BOHUSLÆN, SWEDEN.

? DATE ABOUT A. D. 800—900.

Old-N. R. Mon. Vol. 3, p. 38.

Down to the time of Holmberg (1845), of whose rude woodcut I give a facsimile, the stone remained unbroken and the last runes were perfect. They were first copied in 1746.

HOLMBERG'S WOODCUT, 1845.

HARIWULFS STAINAR.

HARIWULFS STONES (grave-marks).

(These stones were raised in memory of Hariwulf.)

As it stands now, this block is about 5 feet 7 inches high.

RÖK, EAST-GOTLAND. SWEDEN.

? DATE ABOUT A. D. 800—900.

Old-N. R. Mon. p. 228, LVIII, Vol. 3, p. 41.

Fresh finds have thrown fresh light on this difficult text. Prof. S. Bugge's labors have also cleared up the meaning of several lines. Add to this, that the copy used by me was very far from correct. I therefore now venture on a new version.

Greatest height about 13 feet, greatest breadth about 4 feet 8 inches. Bears more than 770 runes. Thus stands alone *as a Runish Stone-book.* First side engraved as early as 1660. Stone uncovered and the other runes discovered in 1843. Here given from photographs and blocks kindly forwarded me by the Royal Swedish Academy of Hist. and Antiquities. The stone itself I have never seen.

FRONT (FIRST SIDE) OF THE BLOCK.

I now take the runes in the following order:

a. Foreside or front, 8 standing lines.

b. Foreside, 2 flat lines.

c. Foreside. Edge or narrow side.

d. Back. Edge or narrow side. *In cipher.*

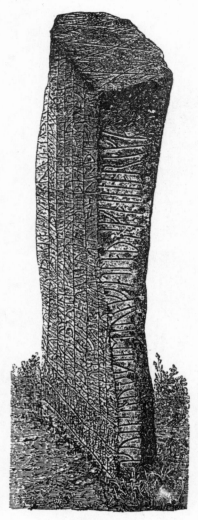

SECOND SIDE OF THE BLOCK.   FOURTH SIDE OF THE BLOCK.

e. Back. Top cross-line. *In cipher; d.* and *e.* first redd by Prof. Bugge.

f. Back. Second cross-line, to the stop.

g. Back. Rest of second top line. *In cipher.*

h. Back. Third top line, to the stop.

i. Back. Rest of the line, frame-line below and frame-line to the left, all in *chiefly* OLD-NORTHERN RUNES. These I take to be in *cipher or contraction,* and to contain some Prayer or Grave-formula or Lament.

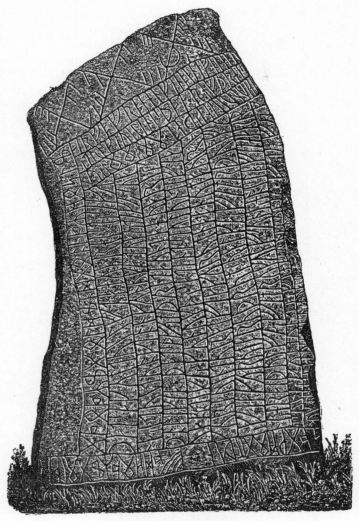

THIRD SIDE OF THE BLOCK.

j.   Back.   The 9 standing lines.

k.   Back.   Top.   *Tree-runes.*   Right to left.   First redd by Bugge.

l.   Back.   Top: 2 plain staves.

m.   Front.   Top; 5 plain staves.

n.   Front.   Top.   *Tree-runes.*

A. To whom the stone was raised.

AFT UAMUD STONTA RUNAR DAR.

After (in memory of) Uamuth stand runes these.

B. By whom the stone was raised.

IN UARIN FADI. FADIR.

AFT FAIKION SUNU.

But Uarin fawed (made. raised-this). the-father.
after his-fey (deceast) son.

C. What the Father says about his Son.

SAKUM, UK MINI DAT:

     HUAR I AR-UAL

     RAUBAR UARIN

     TUA, DAR'S UA_AD

     TUALF SINUM

     UARINUM NART,

     UAL-RAUBR

     BAD, AR SOMO,

     NOUMIS_SU-MONOM.

DAT SAKUM ONART:

     HUAR FUR NIU ALTUM

     ON_NURDI-FIARU MIR;

     HRAID-KUTUM AUK TUM_

     MIR ON UBS AKAR.

     RAID_DURMUDI

     STILIR FLUTNA,

     STRONTU HRAID-MARAR.

     SITIR NU KARUR_

     ROK_KUTA SINUM,

     SKIALTI UB-FATLADR,

     SKATI MARIKA.

         RU DI NIMR FLUOI!

SAKUM, UK MINI_:

     I UAIMSI BURIN_NIDR TROKI?

       UILIN IS DAT.

     OKR UOKNAI AI UN;

       UILIN IS DAT.

We-saw. and remember-thou that:
Where in yore-fight
booty's Warin (hero, = WAMUTH)
two — where he battled ón
with-twelve his
Warins bravely —

war-spoils
gained. Thane of Glory.
from-Noumi's sea-men.

That saw-we next:
 Where he-swept with-nine war-bands
 on the north-coast with-me;
 to-the-Hraith-Goths added-he fresh-rule.
 that-mighty-one on Ul's Acre (= the Ocean).
 Swayed illustrious,
 he the-daring
 prince of deck-braves,
 the-strand of Hraith-mere.
 Sitteth-he now ready-equipt
 by-war-steed his,
 with-shield tight-belted,
 that-lord of-the-Marings [1].
   His-rest, so, taketh-he in-his-Galley!

We-saw, and remember-thou:
 In whom born-is an-heir to-that-warrior?
   Wilin is that (= it is).
 For-us-both may-he-redden alway the-billow!
   Wilin is that (= his name is Wilin).

D. What the Father says about himself.

ÞAT SAKUM TUALFTA:
 HUAR HIST*R* SIKUNA*R*
 IT, UIT-UOKI ON,
 KUNUKA*R* TUAI*R*;
 TIKI*R* (= TIKI*R*) SUA ÞO LIKIA.

ÞAT SAKUM ÞRITAUNTA:
 HUARI*R* TUAI*R* TIKI*R* (= TIGI*R*) KUNUKA*R*
 SATINT SIULUNT I
 FIAKURA UINTU*R*,
 AT FIAKURUM NABNUM,
   BURNI*R* FIAKURUM BRUÞRUM:
 UALKA*R* FIM, RAÞULFS SUNI*R*;
 HRAIÞULFA*R* FIM, RUKULFS SUNI*R*;
 HOISLA*R* FIM, HARU(a)ÞS SUNI*R*;
 KUNMUNTA*R* FIM, AIRNA*R* SUNI*R*.
FTI*R* (= IFTI*R*) FRA NUK MO(NA U)ALUI(RK)I;
AINHUA*R* I Þ(aim uik)I (fial).

---

[1] I now translate MARIKA as a Clan-name, *of the Marings*, not *of the Illustrious*. and in this I adopt the suggestion of Docent Leffler in the Letterstedt Tidskrift. No. 2, Stockholm 1878, p. 165—9.

That saw-we. I-the-twelfth:
> *Where the-horse of-Sigun (= the Wolf)*
> *ate, Uit-wong on.*
> *kings two;*
> *tikes so they lie (= like dead dogs lie they).*

That saw-we. I-the-thirteenth:
> *Which two tens (= 20) kings*
> *were-sitting Sealand in*
> *four winters,*
> *at (with) four names,*
> > *born of-four brothers:*
>
> *Ualks five, Rathulf's sons:*
> *Hraithulfs five, Rukulf's sons:*
> *Hoisles five, Haruath's sons:*
> *Kunmunts five, Airn's sons.*

Thereafter learned-I manifold of-those-men's war-deeds:
each-one-of-them in that [struggle fell]!

E. What the Father said to the stone-cutter.

RUNI BODR
BIARI HUHUAN.

These-runes he-biddeth
Biar to-hew.

Let us now take the whole more freely and poetically:

A. *The name of the dead.*

AFTER WAMUTH STAND RUNES THESE.

B. *The raiser of the stone.*

BUT WARIN FAW'D, his-FATHER,
AFTER his-FEY SON.

C. *The Father sings his dead son's exploits.*

I.

WE SAW, FORGET IT NEVER!
> WHERE, IN FIRST FIELD
> FRESH SPOILS SEEKING, —
> WITH HIS WARINS TWELVE
> WARRING BRAVELY —
> TWOFOLD VICTORY,
> HARD-EARN'D TRIUMPHS,
> THE STRIPLING GAIN'D
> O'ER SEAMEN OF NOUMI.

II.

WE SAW THEREAFTER:

WHERE, NINE SHIPS NEARING

FAR NORTH-SHORES WITH ME,

THE MATCHLESS WAVE-RIDER

GAVE MIGHT TO THE HRAITH-GOTHS.

FIRM AND FEARLESS,

FOLK-LORD, SHIP-LORD,

the-STRANDS BY HRAITH-MERE

STRUCK HE WITH AWE.

BIDES NOW, BELTED,

BATTLE-STEED HOLDING,

SHIELD ON HIS SHOULDER,

THAT SHOOT OF THE MARINGS.

REST HE SO THERE IN HIS GALLEY!

III.

WE SAW, FORGET IT NEVER!

IN WHOM UP-SPRINGETH ANOTHER WAMUTH;

WILIN IS HE!

LIKE US BOTH, THE BILLOW SHALL HE REDDEN.

WILIN IS HE!

D. *The old king speaks of himself.*

I.

THAT SAW WE, TWELVE OF US:

WHERE SIGUN'S HELL-FOAL (= the Wolf)

SCOUR'D THE WIT-WONG,

KINGS TWAIN CRUNCHING —

CURS AS THEY WERE!

II.

SAW WE, THIRTEEN OF US:

WHERE SAT KINGS TWENTY,

IN CAMP ON SEALAND

FOUR LONG WINTERS.

FOUR NAMES BEARING,

SONS OF FOUR BROTHERS;

WALKS FIVE, RATHULF'S SONS;

HRAITHULFS FIVE, ROGULF'S SONS;

HOISLS FIVE, HARWATH'S SONS;

GUNMUNDS FIVE, AIRN'S SONS.

THEIR WAR-DEEDS MANY AFTERWARD HEARD I. —

TILL WEAPON-DRUNK sunk they ALL at last!

E. *Whom the King chose as Rune-cutter:*
THESE RUNES BIDS HE
BIAR TO CHISEL.

The scald — perhaps king Warin himself — was a great lay-smith. Some of these lines might have stood in the Edda itself. May this monolith long stand at Rök, to tell us of the gallant Hraith-Goths and of Olden Swethland in the later Iron Age!

Fragments of a heathen grave-slab have lately been found at Ekeby in Gotland which, besides Scandian-runic minne-words to the dead, has also borne a formula (now lost) in the Old-Northern staves.

The chiefly O. N. staves mentioned under letter *i* must be studied on side 3.

SÖLVESBORG, BLEKING, SWEDEN.

? DATE ABOUT A. D. 800—900.

Old-N. R. Mon. p. 192. Vol. 3. p. 64.

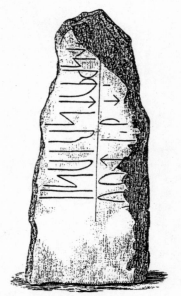

Worsaae's copy in 1844.

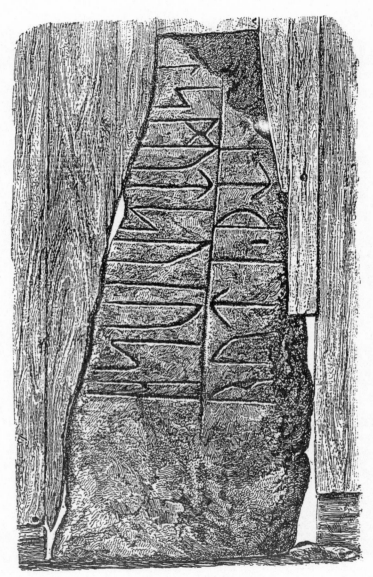

My copy in Sept. 1864.

ÆSMUTS RIUSII.

RUTI WTI (= WRAITI).

ÆSMUTS (= ÆSMUND'S) RUSE *(stone-heap, barrow, stone-mound).*

RUTI WROTE *(these runes).*

ÆSMUTS (= ASMUNDS) RÖSE (sten-hög).

RUTI RITADE (skref dessa runor).

Height about 4 feet 6 inches, breadth a little more than 18 inches. First engraved (barbarously) in 1748. Whitish granite.

HOGA, BOHUSLÄN, SWEDEN.

? DATE ABOUT A. D. 900—1000.

Old-N. R. Mon. Vol. 3, p. 65.

As the stone has suffered so much, it is very possible that the first II were originally an O. N. H, and the name was HÆURI. But we can only give what now stands:

IIÆURI ÆA TÆEN ÞÖNLE ROAUL.

IIÆURI HEWED (carved) TINE (grave-pillar) THIS to-ROAUL (= ROAULF, HROTHWULF = our RALPH, ROLF, ROLL, RAF, &c.).

This graystone TINE or "tall token" is about 12 feet high, including the part in the ground. The first publisht (very bad) drawing is that by Worm in 1643.

ÖSBY. EAST-GOTLAND, SWEDEN.

? DATE ABOUT A. D. 1000—1100.

Old-N. R. Mon. Vol. 3. p. 68.

No. 1124 in Liljegren, but barbarous there. Has the old rune for G. More than 6 feet above ground. The 2 ball-stones at the foot are old grave-memorials.

HALSTUN RISTI STUN ÞANSI YUIR (or ÐUIR) FAÐR SIN SIGI.

HALSTUN RAISED STONE THIS OVER (in memory of) FATHER SIN (his) SIGI (= SIGGE).

Drawn by Director Carl Fr. Nordenskjöld in 1876 and 1877. Of granite, about 6 feet high, nearly 2½ feet thick.

INGELSTAD, EAST-GOTLAND, SWEDEN.

? DATE ABOUT A. D. 1200—1300.

Old-N. R. Mon. p. 837.

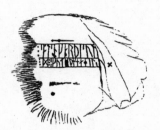

Copy in Liljegren's papers.

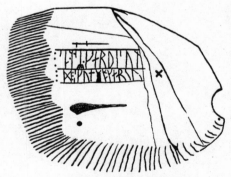

Lector L. Wiede's copy.

SAMSI KARÐI SUL DIK, UENA MARIU.

SAMSI GARED (made) this-SILL (ground-frame, earth-timber work) for-THEE, WENE (fair) MARIA.

Cut on a small rock; now covered over. Has commemorated the building of some small house or chapel. Only *one* O. N. rune, the D. — The runes first observed about 1840. Neither of the above copies seems absolutely correct. The translation may give the meaning.

MÖRBYLÅNGA, ÖLAND, SWEDEN.

? DATE ABOUT A. D. 1200—1300.

Old-N. R. Mon. p. 243.

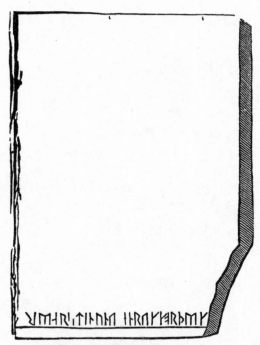

Facsimile of the woodcut in Göransson's Bautil, 1750, but copied nearly a century earlier.

KEARSTIN UNU. ENRUK KORÞE K . . . .

KEARSTIN (= KRISTINA) UNA'S-*daughter-lies-here.*   ENRUK (= HENRIK) GARED *(made) this-*KUMBEL
(grave-mark).

KEARSTIN (= KERSTIN) UNAS-dotter-ligger-här.   ENRUK (HENRIK) GJORDE dette-KUMMEL (graf-märke).

This grave-slab was about 6 feet 11 inches long, by about 4 feet 9 broad. Observe the interesting variant of the O. N. E. — UNU may *perhaps* be the family-name in the genitive, frozen into a compound nominative.

NORWAY.

VALSFJORD, FOSEN, NORTH TRONYEM, NORWAY.

? DATE ABOUT A. D. 1—100.

Old-N. R. Mon. Vol. 3, p. 73.

HÆGUSTÆLDIA ÞEWÆA GODÆGÆS.

To-the-HAGUSTALD (Lord, Captain) THEWÆ GODÆGÆS (= GOODDAY)-wrote-these-runes.

The most northerly O. N. inscription yet found. On a sea-bluff at the Firth of Val. about from 16 to 20 feet above the highest water-flow, and some 40 feet from the nearest sea. But it could only have been carved from ship-deck. The land has gradually risen in this locality to so great an extent. — These death-runes were first remarkt about 1870. — See a Chief of the same name (ÞEWÆ) under Thorsbjerg Moss, Denmark.

50

LEKTOR KARL RYGH'S 2nd AND REVISED TRACING. About ¹⁄₅ th.

LEKTOR K. RYGH'S 1st TRACING. HELIOTYPE FROM BUGGE'S LITHOGRAPH.

UNDSET'S NORMALIZED COPY. HELIOTYPE AFTER BUGGE.

BÖ, STAVANGER AMT, NORWAY.

? DATE ABOUT A. D. 200—300.

Old.-N. R. Mon. p. 846.

HNÆBMÆS (or HNÆBDÆS) HLEIWÆ.

HNÆBMÆ(W)S (? HNÆBDÆS) LOW (grave-mound, hillock).

    7 feet high above ground, 22 inches broad below, from 4 to 5 inches thick. — First discovered in 1865.

STENSTAD, THELEMARK, NORWAY.

? DATE ABOUT A. D. 200—300.

Old-N. R. Mon. p. 254. 839.

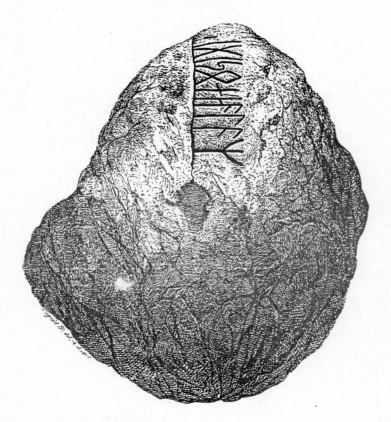

    I now read and translate:

IGINGON HÆLÆA.

IGINGA'S LOW (grave-mound, how, tumulus, cairn).

Found in 1781 inside a stone-kist in Holden Parish, and sent to Denmark, where it now is (at Jægerspris in Sealand). With it were several curious grave-articles. Is of grayish Norse marble. Greatest height about 23 inches.

Bugge and Wimmer have both suggested that IGINGON is a *woman's* name in the genitive, and this is possible but by no means certain.

EINANG. VALDERS, CHRISTIANS-AMT, NORWAY.

? DATE ABOUT A. D. 200—300.

Old-N. R. Mon. Vol. 3, p. 79.

BUGGE AND LORANGE'S FACSIMILE, COPIED HALF SIZE.

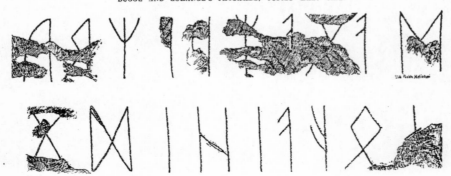

DÆGÆ ADÆA RUNO FÆIHIDO.

DÆG (= DAY) to-ATHÆ these-RUNES FAWED (carved).

The first old grave-minne found in Norway yet standing on its ancient funeral mound. This barrow is nearly circular, and about 50 feet in diameter. The block is about 5 feet 8 inches above ground, upwards of 3 feet broad, from 7 to 9 inches thick. — Stone (lime-stone slate) discovered in 1871.

EINANG, VALDERS, CHRISTIANS-AMT, NORWAY.

? DATE ABOUT A. D. 200—300.

Old-N. R. Mon. Vol. 3, p. 86.

Apparently a bind, making the mansname

HAO.

From 12 to 18 inches all round, lightish gneissose granite. — Found in a stone-heap out on a field, about 70 yards from the large Einang stone. Like many other such memorials, had doubtless been placed inside the barrow. Taken up in 1871.

TUNE, SMÅLENENE, NORWAY..

? DATE ABOUT A. D. 200—300.

Old-N. R. Mon. p. 247, 904.

Very slightly modifying my former version, I now propose:

ECWIWÆA ÆFTER WODURIDE, WITÆI GÆHÆLÆIBÆN, WORÆHTO R(unæ).

ÆRBINGÆS INGOST, LIA, ÆRBINGÆ NODUINGOA, DOHTR, IA DÆLIDUN (SET)A WODURIDE STÆINÆ.

ECWIWÆA AFTER *(in memory of)* WODURID, her-*WITTY (wise, high, mighty, illustrious)* LOAFFELLOW *(partner, mate, husband),* WROUGHT *(carved, = let carve)* these-R*(unes).*

The-HEIRS *(sons)* INGOST *and-*LIA, *and-the-*HEIRESS NOTHUINGOA, *his-*DAUGHTER, HIA *(they)* DEALED *to-*SET *(shared in setting up) to-*WODURID *this-*STONE.

ECWIWÆA EFTER WODURID, sin-VISE (mäktige, högädle) MAKE (husbonde, man) GJORDE (skar, lät rista) dessa-R(unor).

Hans-ARFVINGAR (söner) INGOST och-LIA, och-hans-ARFTAGERSKA NOTHUINGOA, hans-DOTTER, DE DELTE (deltogo i) att-SÄTTA till-WODURID denne-STEN.

This monolith (red granite) rises 6 feet 7 inches, and at its widest part is 2 feet 4 inches broad. — First publisht by Worm (very incorrectly) in 1636.

VÆBLUNGSNÆS, ROMSDAL, NORWAY.

? DATE ABOUT A. D. 200—300.
Old-N. R. Mon. p. 274.   Vol. 3. p. 90.

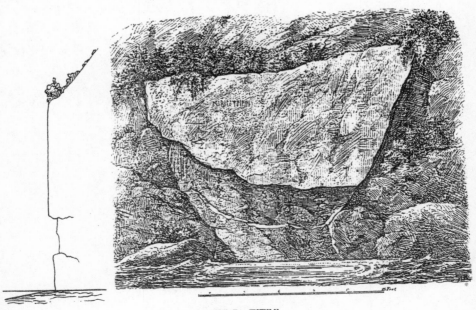

MIRILÆA WIWILN.
*To-*MIRILÆ *WIWIL'N-carved-these-runes.*

Runes about 1—7th of the natural size:

ᛗ I R I ᛚ ᛊ ᚠ Y Þ I Þ I ᛗ

A rune-carved Rock or Bluff in the innermost or easterly end of the wide and deep and far-stretching sea-like Romdals-firth. Cliff-side almost perpendicular. The letters over 11 feet above the highest water-mark, and when carved the land must have been much lower here than now. WIWIL'N is a formative of WIWIL, the local magnate who probably gave his name to what is *now* pronounced VÆBLUNGS-næs. Schöning first publisht a (bad) copy of this inscription. in 1778.

ELGESEM, LARVIK'S FOGDERI, NORWAY.

? DATE ABOUT A. D. 300—400.

Old-N. R. Mon. Vol. 3. p. 95.

Only the mansname:

ÆLU.

Found in 1870 deep down *inside* the grave-how.   Is 5 feet 7 inches long by 2 feet 9 broad, and from 5 to 6 inches thick.   Coarse granite.

FRÖHAUG, ROMERIKE, NORWAY.

? DATE ABOUT A. D. 300—400.

Old-N. R. Mon. p. 250.

The 4th rune, on the spectator's left, is nearly obliterated by the knife of the finder. Prof. Rygh thought it must have been Ⲩ (ᴀ), but it may have been Æ or ɪ.   Perhaps:

SÆG(? ᴀ).
For-SEGE (victory!).
För-SEGER!

Full size. Bronze. Probably Amulet or Talisman, intended to be fixt on a Belt. The freehold FRÖHAUG (Frey-hof) had doubtless once a temple dedicated to the God FREY. This piece was found in 1865.

NORWAY; BUT FOUND AT CHARNAY, BURGUNDY, FRANCE.

? DATE ABOUT A. D. 400—500.
Old-N. R. Mon. p. 587.   Vol. 3. p. 97.

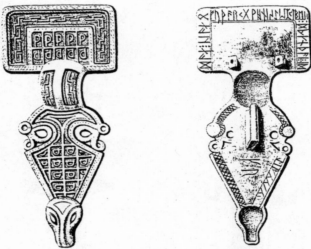

M. Baudot's own facsimile, as corrected by himself.

Re-engraved from Dr. Wimmer's Chemitype, by Prof. Magnus Petersen, from fresh facsimile-drawing (1874) by M. Baudot and M. Beauvois.

As both these copies by the accomplisht owner *differ*, I cannot say which is correct. But the latter is doubtless superior to the former. Probably we shall never get a facsimile more exact. I therefore modify my first attempt accordingly.

First, along the upper long line, we have the beginning of the O. N. Runic Alphabet:

F, U, Þ, Æ, R, C, G, W, H, N, I, Y, YO, P, A, S, T, B, E, (M).

Thereafter, starting from the top of the right side and ending with the top of the left and with the 3 runes on the right low down:

UÞ FYÞÆI IDDÆN CLÆGO (or CLÆNGO) YOLÆ.

UTH FAWED (made) for-IDDÆ KEENG (brooch) THIS.

UTH GJORDE för-IDDÆ SPÄNNE DETTA.

Found in 1857. Of silver, parcel-gilt. Engraved full size. *Norwegian.* No other than the Norse-Icelandic dialects have — or, as far as we know, in any *historical* time ever had — KENG for Fibula. In a nearly allied meaning it is found in Sweden and England.

The 7th stave on the left has the straight N-shank but the leaning G-stroke, and may be a bind for NG; if not, I take it to be G. The plain KR, below the point of the tung, are a contraction, of what word or words I do not know. — See Dr. Wimmer, Runeskriftens Oprindelse (Aarb. f. N. Oldk. 1874), p. 265 and Pl. 3, fig. 2.

ORSTAD, STAVANGER AMT, NORWAY.

? DATE ABOUT A. D. 400—500.

Old-N. R. Mon. p. 258.

HILIGÆA SÆRÆLU.

A RÆW HÆR(Æ).

To-HILIGÆ (= HILGE, HELGE) SÆRÆLU (= SÖRLI-carved).

He-OWES (owns, enjoys) ROO (rest) HERE.

Till-HILIGÆ SÆRULU-skref-dessa-runor.

ÄGER-han RO HÄR.

Light-gray granite. Found inside a grave-kist in 1855. Is 3 feet 9 inches high, 2 feet 7 broad below, 5 inches at the top and 4½ inches thick. Whether from the sour earth or accidental damage, the runes have suffered, especially the lowest line. The frequent Æ is here evidently dialectic, as often on these pieces. Now in the Christiania Museum.

REIDSTAD, LISTER, NORWAY.

? DATE ABOUT A. D. 400—500.

Old.-N. R. Mon. p. 256.   Vol. 3, p. 99.

IUÞINGÆA ICWÆSUNA UNNBO WRÆITÆ.

To-IUTHING ICWÆSON (= INCWÆSON) UNNBO WROTE-these-runes.

Till-IUTHING ICWÆSON UNNBO SKAR-dessa-runor.

Found in 1857 in Hiterön.   About 2 feet each way.   Is now in the University Collection, Christiania.

SIGDAL, AGGERSHUS SHIRE, NORWAY.

? DATE ABOUT A. D. 400—500.

Old-N. R. Mon. p. 271. 841.   Vol. 3. p. 100.

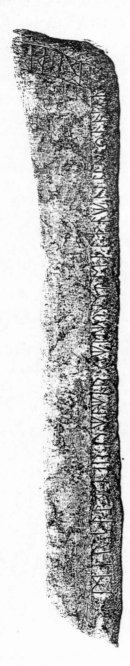

MIRILÆ AH ROAÆ, AH ROAE AO, UTE ÞÆTÆA HÆLDÆO [or HÆLDO] LÆEWE [or LÆIWÆI].

R M Þ L.

O-MIRILÆ, OWE *(own, have, take)* ROO *(thy-rest)*, OWE *(enjoy) thy-*ROO *(repose)* AYE *(ever, endless)*, OUT-IN *(in, within)* THIS of-HELTS LOW *(this hero-tomb)*.

[? *These-Runes Markt* TH . . L . . .].

O-MIRILÆ, ÅG (njut) RO, ÅG din-RO ALLTID (evig) UTI DENNE HJELTE-HÖG.

[? Dessa-Runor Märkte (skar) TH . . L . . .].

First drawn in 1744. Sandstone. Is 5 feet 4 inches high on the narrow where the runes are, 3 feet 2 broad on the broad side. and about 9 inches thick. Is now in Christiania.

At p. 841 I translated AH as 3 s. pr. = *has, enjoys*; I now prefer it as 2 s. imperative, = *have-thou, enjoy-thou*, taking MIRILÆ as a vocative. Perhaps the change was needless.

BELLAND, LISTER, NORWAY.

? DATE ABOUT A. D. 500—600.

Old-N. R. Mon. p. 261.

About 5 feet long by 3 broad. and from 9 to 10 inches thick. First seen by Engineer Kielland about 1850. While lying as above, a spang over a beck which divides the farm at Belland, it was drawn by Hr. H. C. Kielland in 1865. The runes are from the paper squeeze of Prof. S. Bugge in 1865, 1-third the bigness. Bears simply the name of the forthfaren:

ACEÐÆN.

This chief had thus gotten his name (AKÉ-THANE, the Driving or CAR-THANE) from chiefly driving, or from being the owner of some exceptionally new or costly vehicle. Stone apparently granite.

BRATSBERG, TRONYEM, NORWAY.

? DATE ABOUT A. D. 500—600.

Old-N. R. Mon. p. 267. 841.   Vol. 3. p. 100.

The whole slab. engraved 1818, from Klüwer's Norske Mindesmærker, 1823, p. 44. Pl. 10, fig. C.

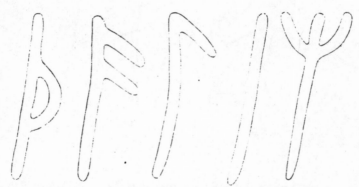

The runes alone, from rubbing by M. F. Arendt, 1806.

Thus the womans-name:

DÆLIA.

Found in an immense grave-how; now lost or broken. Was about 22 inches square·
and 3 to 4 inches thick.   An iron Spear-head was taken from the mound.   But of old lived
many a famous Shield-may (Battle-chieftainess).   See p. 290 (Vol. 1) the Old-English silver
Shield-boss. whose writ distinctly states that it belonged to the War-lady ÆDUWEN. — Earliest
copy is Arendt's.

FONNÅS, HEDEMARKENS AMT, NORWAY.

? DATE ABOUT A. D. 500—600. *Old-N. R. Mon. Vol. 3, p. 101.*

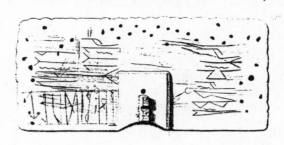

This Silver Brooch, the costliest yet met with of this kind in all the North, was found in July 1877 in the loose earth, 2 feet below the surface. Strongly gilt, with niello and garnets. Here given full size. Old-North-English work. Has belonged to an English lady who apparently became the wife of a Norwegian chieftain. Bears 2 runic legends, probably carved at different times and by different persons.

The first, in the Old-North-English dialect:

IH BIM ULTYO.

I BE (am) ULTIA's-brooch.

The second, 3 lines, seemingly in Old-Norse:

WAS HU INGLSK, LAING, ASPING, R . . . ing, B . . . ing, S . . . ing, E . . . ing.

WAS HU (she was) ENGLISH (an Englishwoman), LAING (La's-daughter), ASPING (who was Asp's-son), R...ing (the son of R...), B...ing (the son of B...), S...ing (the son of S...), E...ing (the son of E...).

Now in the Christiania Museum, to which it was given by the owner, H. T. Tronnæs.

FÖRDE, SÖNDFJORD, N. BERGENHUS, NORWAY.

? DATE ABOUT A. D. 500—600.

Old.-N. R. Mon. Vol. 3, p. 106.

Either one word, the mansname ÆLUAO, or, as I prefer,

ÆLUA O.

ÆLUA OWNS-me.

Of steatite. Full size. May have been a Dog-collar, or an owner's mark for something else. Found in 1874.

TOMSTAD, LISTER AND MANDAL, NORWAY.

? DATE ABOUT A. D. 500—600.

Old-N. R. Mon. p. 264, 841.

The lower part, where the grave-formula begins, is lost. It has apparently consisted of 2 words, divided by 3 dots. The first was, I think, in the nom., as the 2nd seems to be in the dative. Tomstad being in the same Shire as Belland, and nominatives in ÆN being scarce, I think it very likely that the damaged name was originally ACEÞÆN, who thus, ere he himself died, may have raised this block to his friend or kinsman WÆRU.

..... ÆN WÆRUA.

(⁝ aceth)ÆN-carved-these-runes to-WÆRU.

(? aceth)ÆN-skref-dessa-runor till-WÆRU.

Found in 1852 in a ruined barrow. Undrest. Length taken at centre about 2 feet 3 inches, breadth about 1 foot 6 inches.

NORWAY; BUT FOUND AT FREI-LAUBERSHEIM, RHEIN-HESSEN, GERMANY.

? DATE ABOUT A. D. 600—700.

Old-N. R. Mon. Vol. 3, p. 109.

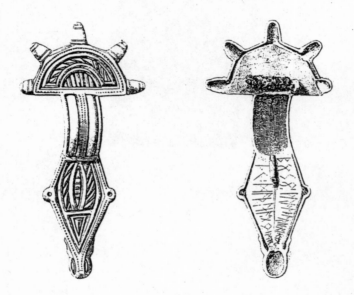

BOSO WRÆET RUNÆ, IOD (O)DC(U), DÆDYONÆ GOIDU.

BOSO WROTE these-RUNES, YOUTH (son) of-(O)THCA, of-the-DÆTHES (= of the Dœthe-clan) the-PRIESTESS.

Found in 1873, with many other valuables and ornaments, in a Lady's grave. Silver, parcel-gilt; border decoration filled-in with niello. Engraved full size.

SEUDE, THELEMARK, NORWAY.

? DATE ABOUT A. D. 700—800.

Old-N. R. Mon. p. 273.

A. WORM's Literatura Runica, 4to, 1636, p. 68:

PFᎢᎢFᎢ2F⋈F⧢

B. WORM's Literatura Runica, fol., 1651, p. 66:

PFᎢᎢFᎢZF⋈F⧢

The real staves may possibly have been:

ᛈᚦᛁᛁᚠᛁ᛭ᚠᛈᚠᛣ

WÆTTÆT SÆMÆNG

WIþANT SÆMING (WITHANT SAM'S-SON). — Or perhaps,

WÆTTÆ⌣ÆT SÆMÆNG

WÆTTÆ AT (to, in memory of) SÆMING.

Lost. Size of this grave-stone not given by Worm, the first to engrave the runes, in 1636.

VATN, VERNES PARISH, S. TRONYEM, NORWAY.

? DATE ABOUT A. D. 750—800.

Old-N. R. Mon. Vol. 3. p. 115.

Bears only the mansname

RHOÆL(T)R.

Of gray slate. which has partly peeled off; 2 feet 7 inches long. 1 foot 2 inches broad. Now only about 2 inches thick. Found in 1871 by Archivary I. Undset.

WEST TANEM, TRONYEM, NORWAY.

? DATE ABOUT A. D. 700—800.

Old-N. R. Mon. p. 269.

From Klüwer's engraving in 1818 (publisht 1823).

Runes full size. from Prof. O. Rygh's paper cast. 1865.

Thus no doubt of what the inscription was. I divide and translate:

MÆNIS LAU.

MÆN'S (= MAN'S, MÆNI'S) LOW (*Grave-heap, Tumulus*).

MÆNS (eller MÆNIS) GRAF-HÖG.

Found in 1813 inside a kemp-how. Length about 3 feet. Is now in the Christiania Museum. but is deplorably injured.

GJEVEDAL, OMLID, NORWAY.

? DATE ABOUT A. D. 1050—1150.
Old-N. R. Mon. p. 276. Vol. 3, p. 116.

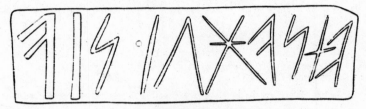

ÆNSÆGUI SIÆ.

To-ÆNSÆGU THESE-memorial-runes.

Till-ÆNSÆGU DESSA-minne-runor.

From a paper cast by M. F. Arendt, dated Aug. 11, 1805. Original — probably of wood, unknown whether Christian or Heathen — now *lost*. Size not stated. The assumed date is the lowest possible; the piece may have been centuries older.

HOLMEN, SIGDAL, NORWAY.

? DATE ABOUT A. D. 1150—1250.
Old-N. R. Mon. p. 278. Vol. 3, p. 117.

† ꝺissa kloko leto stýða aluer, prestr i sikktale. ok ꝺort bonte aa auik; uk stýðpte toue
ꝺorr-son(r).

† *this clock (bell) let steep (yote, cast) aluer, priest in sikktal (Sigdal), and thort (Thord)
bonde (yeoman) on (at) auik; eke (and) steept (cast it) toue thorr-son.*

† denna klocka läto stöpa aluer, prest i sigdal, och thord bonde å auik; och stöpte-den
tove thorson.

Unhappily this late overgang piece is lost, that is, long since re-cast. Engraved
from a drawing by Rev. P. Haslef, dated Dec. 1810. Height, exclusive of ears, was 19 inches,
greatest diameter about 2 feet.

WEST STENVIK, N. TRONYEM, NORWAY.

In 1858 an O. N. rune-stone was found in a how, and cast away by the brutal finder.

AUDA, JÆDEREN, NORWAY.

About 1870 was taken out of a grave-chamber an O. N. monolith with runes and
ornaments. It was used in a fence and is lost.

THORGÅRD, TILLER, NORWAY.

In 1870 a stone with the olden runes was destroyed at Thorgård.

VOREIM, MÆRE, N. TRONYEM, NORWAY.

A slab with 4 runes in a square cartouche was found inside a barrow some years
ago, placed in a foundation-wall, and could not be discovered in 1871.

DENMARK.

THANKFULLY INSCRIBED

TO

JOHANNES C. H. R. STEENSTRUP,

CHEAPINGHAVEN, DENMARK.

———

THORSBJERG MOSS, SOUTH JUTLAND, DENMARK.

? DATE ABOUT A. D. 200—250.

Old-N. R. Mon. p. 285, LIV. Vol. 3, p. 121.

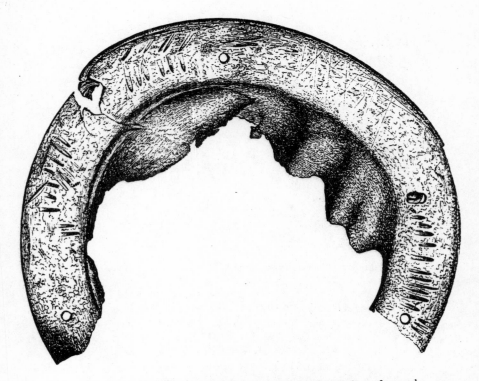

The runes on the back have been very clearly cut with a sharp fine tool:

ÆISG AH.

ÆISG OWES (owns, possesses me).

ÆISG ÅGER-mig.

Full size. Found in 1858. Bronze or Brass Shield-boss, rather thin, of Barbarian not Roman make. But it has on its front the well-known circular line betraying the lathe, as we can see by the following engraving, half-size:

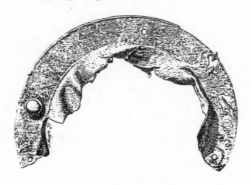

THORSBJERG, S. JUTLAND, DENMARK.

? DATE ABOUT A. D. 200—250.

Old-N. R. Mon. p. 295. Vol. 3. p. 121.

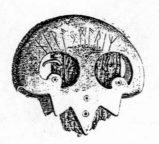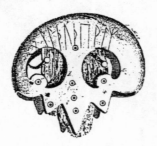

I now adopt the view of Thomsen and Bugge, that OWLÞU is a lisp for WOLÞU, and propose:

NIWÆNG-MÆRIA OWLÞU-DEWÆA.

NIWÆNG-MÆRIA-gives-this-sword to-her-friend-OWLÞU-ÞEWÆ.

Bronze end-clasp or chape of a Sword-sheath. Blade and Sheath probably a keepsake from a lady to her lover or kinsman. Full size. Most of the 45 Sword-chapes found in this bog-hoard were of bronze, only a few of silver. Various in form. Some quite round.

Apparently this lady was MÆRIA of the NIWÆNGS. There were clans of the NĪWÍNGAS settled in England in 6 different Counties. See Kemble, S. in Engl. 1, p. 470. — Dug up in 1860. DEWÆ is also on the Valsfjord cliff, Norway.

.. (I)L(I)ᴀ.

End of a mansname. — Found in 1874 by the Norwegian Archæologist Adjunkt
Bendixen in the Kiel Museum, where these Danish Remains, dug up in 1858—60, now are.
Possibly part of a wooden Bow. Above 7 Danish inches long. — Sept. 1879. Docent
Dr. Wimmer and Prof. M. Petersen have examined this piece, and think the marks only
accidental impressions. This may be. I have not seen the bit.

BALKEMARK, NEXØ, BORNHOLM, DENMARK.

? DATE ABOUT A. D. 200—300.

Old-N. R. Mon. Vol. 3, p. 122.

TUNBA.

Only 18 inches high, about 8 broad and 5 thick, dark heavy stone. Found in
1866. — This mansname is of excessive antiquity.

DALBY, SOUTH JUTLAND, DENMARK.

? DATE ABOUT A. D. 200—300.

Old-N. R. Mon. p. 283.   Vol. 3, p. 123.

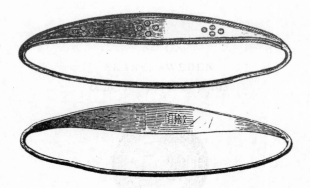

LUÐRO (may also be redd LEÐRO).

This name, whether masc. or fem., may, of course, be divided, L. O. *L OWNS-me*. At the right corner, still more lightly cut, is what seems to be a double-rune, ⊥Ḷ. If a letter-sign, apparently L and O. — Golden Diadem or Head-wreath. Half-size. Found in 1840.

HIMLINGØIE, SEALAND, DENMARK.

? DATE ABOUT A. D. 250—300.

Old-N. R. Mon. p. 297, 857.

The name of the buried, probably masculine:

HÆRISO.

Parcel-gilt fibula. Full size. Is of mixt metal, a kind of bronze, overlaid with thin plates of silver riveted with silver nails. The 3 round beads are of blue fluor-spar, or some such material. A central ornament has fallen away. — Taken from the grave in 1835.

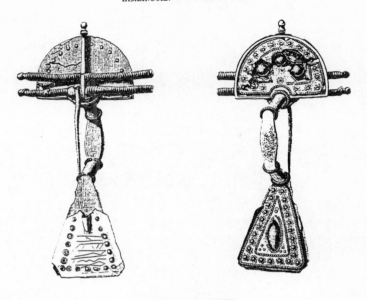

NYDAM MOSS, SOUTH JUTLAND, DENMARK.

? DATE ABOUT A. D. 250—300.

Old-N. R. Mon. p. 299.

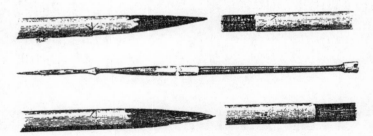

All doubtless marks of ownership. Are on some of the many wooden Arrows found. One has a plain A, another a kind of bind-rune, a third a reverst L, a 4th a reverst LUÆ, probably a mansname. There were various other such marks, as well as zigzags, a half-moon, and so on. Thus each could at once recognize his own weapon. Engraved full size. The moss-finds were dug up in 1859. 1862, 1863.

VI MOSS, ALLESØ, FYN, DENMARK.

1. Old-N. R. Mon. p. 301.

Clasp of a Sword-sheath. Silver ornamented with gold. Rust-film covers a part of the staves. which may only have been idly scratcht. Those visible are meaningless. Full size. — Dug up in 1853.

2. Old-N. R. Mon. p. 305.

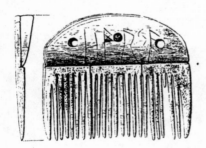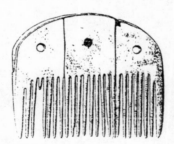

HÆRINGÆ.

The owner's name. — Bone Comb. Full size. Some dozens of Combs came to light, some of them ornamented, but only this one was a rune-bearer. — Found in 1865.

3. Old-N. R. Mon. p. 307, LV.

Of ash-wood. Full size. Oldest Plane existing in the world. Dug up in 1865.

TOP.

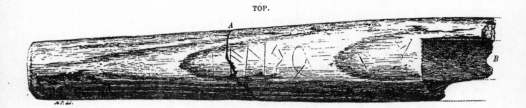

SECTION AT A.

A

SECTION AT B.

B

SIDE.

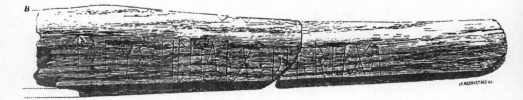

The 1st of these workshop scribbles is:

TÆLING O.

TÆLING OWNS-me.

TÆLING ÅGER-mig.

There are, now faint, dividing dots between the NG and the O. If, notwithstanding this, we make the whole one word, it is a mansname.

The 2nd, unhappily, wants some letters (probably LOCER) at the end, which have mouldered away:

GISLIONG-WILI ÅH LÆ-ORB(Æ) [? locer].

GISLIONG-WILI OWNS this-LEA-STAFF (sithe-shaft) [loker = plane].

GISLIONG-WILI ÅGER denne-LI-ORF- [höfvel].

The 3rd, on the side, I now take to mean:

TIÞAS HLEUNG, ÞE RIIGU.

TITHAS HLEUNG (= HLE-SON), THEOW (slave or servant) of-the-lady-RIIGA.

The inscriptions are in 3 different "hands", perhaps *many* years between each. — Cutting-irons gone. The cutting section being concave, this was a Hollow Smooth Plane or Fork-staff Plane, to make Sithe-shafts, Lance-poles, &c.

Another, *runeless*, Plane was found. Its cutting-iron has perisht, but the section shows that this Plane was for making Arrow-shafts, &c.

In 1877, among the tools of a farmer-carpenter at Ekeby in Gotland, OLE OLS-SON by name, were found 2 wooden Planes with date and initials, in the letters he was most familiar with, thus:

1 7 8 6 .

ᛁ·ᛁ·ᚼ·∴

O. O. S. (= OLE OLS-SON).

His son gave one to the Visby Museum, and the other to my collection.

---

4.   Old-N. R. Mon. Vol. 3, p. 125.

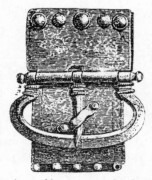 

As it would seem, merely the name of the owner:

ÆÐÆGÆS(LI) LÆÆSÆUWINGÆ.

= EDGISLI LESSING (= LES-SON).

Brass Buckle, silver ornamented, for a Belt. Full size. Dug up in 1851.

GALLEHUS, NORTH JUTLAND, DENMARK.

? DATE ABOUT A. D. 300—400.

Old-N. R. Mon. p. 321. Vol. 3. p. 128.

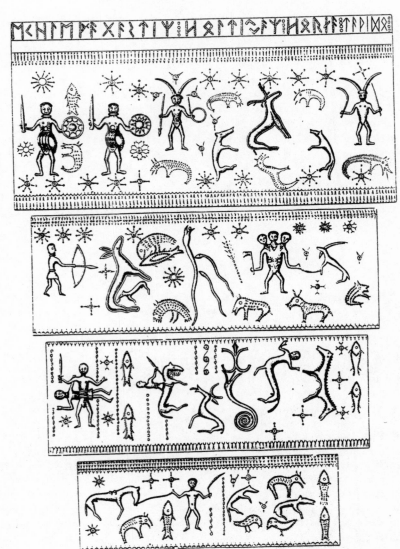

ECHLEW ÆGÆSTIA HOLTINGÆA HORNÆ TÆWIDO.

ECHLEW for-the-AWEST (most-awful, most-dread, supreme, most-mighty) HOLT-INGI (Holt-King,
Wood-prince, Woodland-god) this-HORN TAWED (made).
(= To the ever-to-be-feared Forest-God, Echlew offered this Horn!).
ECHLEW till-den-högst-FRUKTANSVÄRDE SKOG-GUDEN dette-HORN GJORDE (offrade).

This Golden Horn was found in 1734, was about 20 inches long and weighed about
8 English Pounds. With its fellow, found in 1639 and 33 inches long, it wandered to the
melting-pot, the prey of a rascally thief, in 1802.

YNGI or ÝNGVI was the especial epithet of the Danish FROE, the Old-English FREA, the
Norse-Icelandic FREY, the Woodland- and Harvest-God. To his Temple I believe this offer-
horn was given by ECHLEW, a name (as ECGLAF) in the Old-English Epical legend *Beowulf.*
The famous forest FARRIS SKOW was not far from Gallehus, with a separate "Herred" (Hundred)
called after FROE. All this can scarcely be accidental.

First copy of the staves on the Runic Golden Horn.

Photoxylographic transcript, full size, by J. F. ROSENSTAND, of the large facsimile made
with his own hand by Med. Doct. GEORGE KRYSING of Flensborg, in 1734, from the Horn itself,
a few weeks after it was found at Gallehus:

ᛗ᛫ᚺᛁᚠᛘᛈᚹᚨᚠ᚜ᚨᛈ᛫᛬ᛏᛁᛁᚤ᛬

ᚺᛟᛈᛏᛏᛁ᛬᛭ᛖᛈᚤᚺᛟᛈᛈᛏᚱ᛬ᛏᚠᚹᛁᚷᛟ᛬

From the excessively rare double-folio engraving "Cornu Aurei Typus", an impression
of which is in my own bookhoard; another is in the Danish National Library. Here these
runes are *twice given,* in their place at the mouth of the Horn, and separately *on a still larger
scale* lower down on the plate. It is *this latter line* which is here photographt, full size, direct
on to the wood, and carefully cut in. In both places Krysing gives a plain separating mark
(<) between the words ECHLEW and ÆGÆSTIA. The runes in his copy of the Horn itself begin
with ECHLEW and end with TÆWIDO. But below, he has "corrected" the order, begins with

TÆWIDO and ends with HORNÆ. In a unique copy of the same plate however, a kind of second edition in the same year, in my collection, from a volume of "Runica" brought together by ALARIK VON WITKEN ZU WITTENHEIM in 1734, Dr. Krysing has *erased* the TÆWIDO at the beginning of the long line and placed it at the end, as it had stood in his drawing at the mouth of the Horn, *preserving* the *divisional mark* between the ECHLEW and the ÆGÆSTIA, which he has in *both* places also in his first edition of this large plate. In my facsimile I have restored the .order. But whether we take TÆWIDO first or last, the meaning is the same. In the old Ms. Essay on this Horn by the learned Icelander JON OLAFSON of Grunnavik (Danish National Library), the mark between the w and the Æ is *plainly given*. But PAULLI, who says he was purposely careless about small things, omits it, and later drawings follow PAULLI. We thus see: — that the Horn bore marks of division between *every word*, — and that *each letter-group between* these separating stops was *one word*.

THE RUNELESS GOLDEN HORN.

here given. was quite complete. with 13
broad rings. . Like the rune-bearer. it was found
in the earth near Gallehus, somewhat to the
north. near Mogel-Tonder. about 5 Danish miles
from the North-Jutland border, an enclave at-
tacht to the diocese of Ribe.

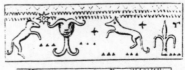

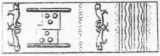

KRAGEHUL MOSS, FYN, DENMARK.

? DATE ABOUT A. D. 300—400.

No. 1. Old-N. R. Mon. p. 317—319.

.....NÆU (or ÆÆU)..

....UMÆ BERÆ.

I do not pretend to translate these fragments. Full size. Of ash-wood. A knife-handle or small box or amulet or something such. Uneartht in 1865.

No. 2. A BONE-SNAKE. bearing O. N. Runes, *lost.* Found in 1750. See Vol. 1. p. 319.

No. 3. A WOODEN LID, bearing O. N. Runes. *lost.* Found in 1750. See Vol. 1. p. 319.

No. 4. Old-N. R. Mon. Vol. 3, p. 133.

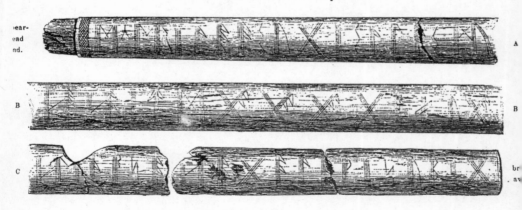

Full size. Ashen Lance-shaft. Found in 1877. As I take it, in verse, the Ban on casting the war-spear over the enemy's border. See Bracteate No. 57. Permission to copy their clichées kindly given by the Roy. Soc. of North. Ant. The Lance-hurler's name was = EARL, JARL.

EC, ERILÆA, ÆS-UGIS
ÆLÆ SMUHÆ HÆITE : —
'GÆ, GÆ,
GÆGIN UGÆ;
HE NIYÆ
HÆGÆLÆ,
WIYU-BIGI (? æ
wapnbautin).'
I, ERIL, ANS-UGG'S (= Woden's)
IRON-STORM PIERCER (= this Lance)
BID: — 'GO, GO,
GAINST the-SAVAGE;
HENCE HURRY
HÆGÆL QUICK,
on-GORY WAR-BED
gash him thro!'

VALLOBY, KOGE, EAST OF SEALAND, DENMARK.

? DATE ABOUT A. D. 300—400.

Old-N. R. Mon. Vol. 3. p. 136.

Roman Bronze vessel, with many other Roman and barbarian pieces and jewels, found in 1872 in a skeleton mans-grave. Here given half size:

Underneath is the owner's name, 5 runes, on the bottom of the vessel, of which all that is left is — half bigness:

I add the runic part full size:

Doubtless the common mansname WIIS(A), or WIIS(Æ) or WIIS(I).

GLOSTRUP, SEALAND, DENMARK.

? DATE ABOUT A. D. 500—600.

Old-N. R. Mon. p. 858.

TU.

Apparently TU (= TIU) the Heathen God, the Mars of the Old North, to whom TUES-DAY was given.

Doubtless an Amulet. Full size. Is the spike of an Echinite (fossil). — Found in 1846.

VEILE, NORTH JUTLAND, DENMARK.

? DATE ABOUT A. D. 600—700.

Old-N. R. Mon. p. 332.

ΨΛdCΙξΙΙ†✕:

Stone lost. Copy of the inscription is in P. Syv's Ms. Collec. in P. F. Suhm's "Samlinger til den Danske Historie", 4to, Vol. 1, Part 2, Kjobenhavn 1779, p. 117. But we cannot depend on such old transcripts. Any restoration is only a guess. I propose, reversing the wend-runes:

:✕†ΙΙξΙ○þϜΨ

ÆNI ISINGTHÆA.

ÆNI-carved these-runes to-ISINGTHÆW.

Perhaps the 7th rune was ◊. I cannot help such guesses being unsatisfactory. Why did not the old school take *paper casts*?

VOLDTOFTE, FYN, DENMARK.

? DATE ABOUT A. D. 600—700.

Old-N. R. Mon. p. 333, LVII.

Is now at the Palace of Jægerspris in Sealand. Bears only one word, the name of the deceast warrior:

RUULFASTS.

About 5 feet 4 inches high, 3 feet broad. — Found about 1840—45. Granite.

VORDINGBORG, SEALAND, DENMARK.

? DATE ABOUT A. D. 600—700.

Old-N. R. Mon. p. 335, 857. LVII. Vol. 3, p. 139.

ÆFT ÆÐISL, FAÐUR. TRŮBU KÆRÐI ÐIÆU ÐRUI.

AFTER (in memory of) ÆTHISL, his-FATHER, TRŮBU GARED (made) THIS THRUCH (stone-kist).

EFTER ÆTHISL, sin-FAÐER, TRŮBU GJORDE DETTA TRÅG (sten-kista).

Lower down is the bind-rune ʜᴡ, probably a mansname beginning with ʜ. and ᴡ the first letter of ᴡʀᴀɪᴛ (or something such); thus ʜ..... ᴡʀᴏᴛᴇ-the-runes.   Still lower, is ᴜɪ, perhaps short for: *May-Thur-wɪʜ (bless)-these-runes!*

Height about 4 feet 5 inches, breadth (both the runic sides) about 3 feet 1 inch.

During its removal to the Old-Northern Museum, this granite block fell and was broken. It has been restored, but is not now so legible as when my engraving was made. — Worm's bad engraving, anno 1643, is the earliest known.

KALLERUP, SEALAND, DENMARK.

? DATE ABOUT A. D. 700—800.

Old-N. R. Mon. p. 342.

HURNBURÆ STÆIN, SUIÐIKS.

HURNBURE'S STONE, SWITHING (= SWITHE'S-SON).

6 feet long, 1 foot 6 broad, 2 feet thick. — Ploughed up in 1828.

SEALAND, DENMARK.

? DATE ABOUT A. D. 700—800. *Old-N. R. Mon. Vol. 3. p. 140.*

UDÆICT.

DISFAVOR (= BADI The Bad Throw!)

Perhaps the mark on the 2-side means UEL, VEL. *(WELL, FAVOR, the Good Throw).*

4. DÅLIGA KASTET. — 2. ? GODA KASTET.

Of soap-stone (steatite). A "barbaric" Danish runic Die. Full size. — Found in 1865.

FREDERIKSBERG, SEALAND, DENMARK.

? DATE ABOUT A. D. 750—800.

Old-N. R. Mon. p. 861. Vol. 3, p. 141.

Amulet: I believe. for finding out a Thief. Such pieces were used with water and a small looking-glass. or otherwise. that the Thief's image might appear. I take the risting to be:

DIWByO-FUNDR.

THIEF-FIND. (For finding a Thief).

The end-R seems written below for symmetry. — This little stone was pickt up in 1866. Full size.

HELNÆS, FYN, DENMARK.

? DATE ABOUT A. D. 750—800.

Old-N. R. Mon. p. 338. Vol. 3, p. 141.

RHUULFR SATI STAIN, NURA-KUDI. AFT KUDUMUT, BRUDUR-SUNU SIN. TRUKNADU (? Hanum alir).

ÆUAIR FADI.

RHUULF SET this-STONE, of-the-NUR-men (or, of the NUR district) the GUTHI (Temple-chief and Magistrate). AFTER KUTHUMUT (= GUDMUND), BROTHER-SON (nephew) SIN (his). DROWNED (were drowned, perisht at sea) (with-him all. = himself and all his men). ÆUAIR FAYED (raised this stone and carved these runes).

RHUULF SATTE denne-STEN, af-NUR-männen (eller, af NUR landet) GUTHI (Tempel-föreståndare och Domare), EFTER (till minne af) KUTHMUT (= GUDMUND), BRODER-SON SIN. DRUNKNADE (omkomno på hafvet) (med-honom alla, = han sjelf och alla hans män).

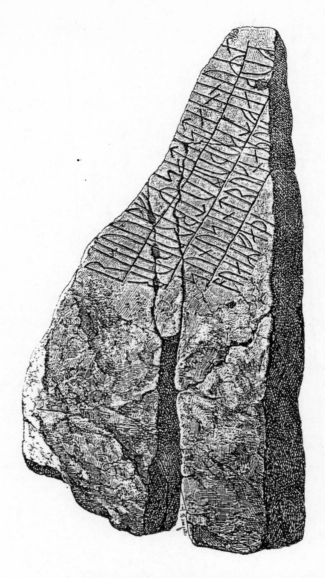

Now in the Old-Northern Museum, Cheapinghaven.   Height about 6 feet 10 inches, greatest thickness about 2 feet.   Was much broader before it was so barbarously cloven. Found in 1860. — Overgang. only the H, Æ and M being Old-Northern letters.

FREERSLEV, SEALAND, DENMARK.

? DATE ABOUT A. D. 800—850.

Old-N. R. Mon. Vol. 3, p. 142.

Found in April 1876. Softish sandstone, about 4 feet 6 inches high, 2 feet broad and 2 thick. Has several letters *understood*, to save labor, as often. I divide and translate:

ÆSLAIKIR RAISTI STAIN,

IKR (= IKUR), AFAI SINÆR;

IN UK UNITR,

SKWLFS (= SIKWULFS) A(Rfik)I,

IWKA (= IWIKA) AFTA

ÆR-RNR (= RUNAR) (Þ)ISI.

ÆSLAIK RAISED this-STONE,

INGA'S, HIS GRANDMOTHER'S;

IN (but) SET UNID,

SON of-SIGWULF,

EVER AFTER-her

ORE-RUNES (honor-words) THESE.

Grandfather: SIGWULF — INGA, *Grandmother.*

UNID, *Son.*

ÆSLAIK, *Grandson.*

JYDERUP, SEALAND, DENMARK.

? DATE ABOUT A. D.: A, — 800—900; B, — 1200—1300.

Old-N. R. Mon. p. 859. Vol. 3, p. 146.

Side A.   Side B.

? TYW AL! — *O-TYW, ELE (help)!*

? TYW AL! WXYZ.

Doubtless an amulet.   Full size.   Of glimmer sandstone. — Dug up in 1866.

SNOLDELEV, SEALAND, DENMARK.

? DATE ABOUT A. D. 800—900.

Old-N. R. Mon. p. 345, 857.   Vol. 3. p. 146.

KUNUÆLTS___STÆIN. SUNAR RUHALTS. ÞULAR O SALHAUKU(M).

KUNUÆLT'S STONE. SON of-RUHALT, THYLE (Speaker. Priest) ON the-SALHOWS.

The 3 Horns form the mark of Thor. To the right is the mark of Woden. (ON) o
SALHAUKUM is the present hamlet of SALLOW. in the parish of Snoldelev.   On the top of the
stone is a Cup-hole from the Stone Age. — About 4 feet long. 2 feet 3 inches broad. 21
inches deep. Now in the Old-Northern Museum. Cheapinghaven. — Found at the end of the
last century.

BÅRSE. SEALAND, DENMARK.

? DATE ABOUT A. D. 1000—1100.

Old-N. R. Mon. p. 862.

. . . . ÞES (? i).

ʜᴡ.

Stone smasht and lost. Only this bit (here given ᴉ-fourth) found on the highway. in 1822.

MAGLEKILDE, SEALAND, DENMARK.

? DATE ABOUT A. D. 1000—1100.

Old-N. R. Mon. p. 864.

First side. among other staves, the mansname SIƲARÐ.

Second -   -   -   -   -   -   OLUFR.

     Bronze. Seems to have hung at the belt, and to have been an amulet. Full size. — Dug up in a field in 1866.

SÆDING, NORTH JUTLAND, DENMARK.

? DATE ABOUT A. D. 1100—1200.

Old-N. R. Mon. p. 351.

Elling's drawing, 1797:   Kruse's drawing, 1857:

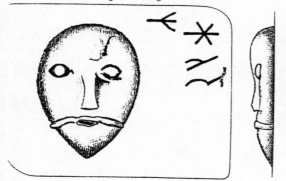 

? YKÆ R.

? YKÆ (INGE) RISTED (*carved; or RAISED. built*).

     2 feet long by 16 inches broad. About 5 feet above ground in the northern outside wall of the church at Sæding, Bolling Herred, Ringkjobing Amt. Bears no O. N. letter and. therefore *goes out*, if, as I now think, the whole must be redd as the mansname:

SKÆR.

THISTED, NORTH JUTLAND, DENMARK.

? DATE ABOUT A. D. 1100—1200.

Old-N. R. Mon. p. 355.   Vol. 3, p. 147.

ÞORÆ, TADIS SOL, HUILER HÆRÆ.

THORÆ, TAD'S (= TAND'S) SOL (sun) WHILES (reposes) HERE.

(Here rests Thoræ, the Sun of Tand).

THORÆ, TAND'S SOL, HVILER HÄR.

Size of the Slab 4 feet 2 by 1 foot 8. — First copied early in this century.

TØMMERUP, SEALAND, DENMARK.

? DATE ABOUT A. D. 1227.

Old-N. R. Mon. Vol. 3. p. 148.

Found in Jan. 1876 in digging a grave in the Churchyard of Tommerup, Holbæk Amt. Is a Priest's Sacramental Cup, of silver. Engraved full size:

Has been buried on the breast of the corpse. On the rim of the Chalice is an overgang-alphabet of 21 letters, of which only 2 are distinctively later or Scandinavian. The 19 are Old-Northern or in common to both Futhorks. I add the line of runes and marks in facsimile, beneath them the normal shapes of the unworn and uninjured characters, and beneath these their usual powers. The marks I take to be the date, MCCo27, or 1227.

F. U.D. O, R, K, H,N.I.A.S. T, B, M. L. E. D. YO.NG.,Æ,Œ

ENGLAND AND SCOTLAND.

THANKFULLY INSCRIBED

TO

THE REV. WALTER W. SKEAT, M. A.,

CAMBRIDGE, ENGLAND.

———

ENGLAND; BUT FOUND AT NORDENDORF, AUGSBURG, BAVARIA.

? DATE ABOUT A. D. 400—500.

Old-N. R. Mon. p. 574. Vol. 3. p. 157.

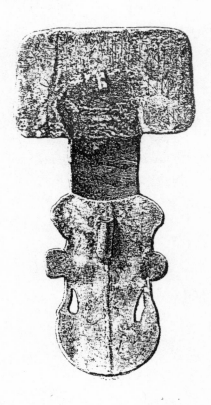

Full size. Silver-gilt fibula with niello. Bears 3 runish scribbles. The *first*, at the top of the back, the mansname:

ÆLEUBWINI.

= *Æleubwini owns this Brooch.*

The *second*, at the opposite corner, the mansname:

LONÆWORE.

The *third* below this, in 2 lines:

WODÆN WINIWONÆWYO.

WODÆN-gives-this to-the-lady-WINIWONÆW.

Found, with other treasures, in a lady's grave in 1844. Inscription is in Old North English.

ENGLAND; BUT FOUND AT NORDENDORF, AUGSBURG, BAVARIA.

? DATE ABOUT A. D. 400—500.

Old-N. R. Mon. Vol. 3. p. 158.

BIRLNIO ELS

To-the-lady-BIRLINIA ELS-gave-this.

Or, *For* ..... *made.* Full size. Silver, with gilding and niello, &c. Found some years back in a grave at Nordendorf. The inscription is in Old North English.

ENGLAND; BUT FOUND AT OSTHOFEN, RHEINHESSEN.

? DATE ABOUT A. D. 400—500.
Old-N. R. Mon. p. 585. Vol. 3, p. 159.

 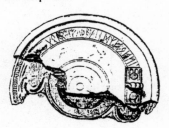

The runes for D and M being distinctly differenced, I now read:

GONRAT FUÞE MIC. DAH OH MIC.

GONRAT (= *GUNDRAD, CONRAD*) *FAYED (made) ME. DAH* (= *DAY*) *OWES (owns) ME.*

GONRAT GJORDE MIG. DAH ÄGER MIG.

If we take the O in OH twice, in the runish fashion, the name will be DAHO. — Brooch of gilt bronze. Full size. Doubtless English. If not, then Scandinavian. It is therefore I have removed this piece from the Wanderers. We know of no German or Saxon talk that said FUÞE for *made* and OH for *has*. — Came to the Mainz Museum in 1854.

THAMES, LONDON, ENGLAND.

? DATE ABOUT A. D. 400—500.
Old-N. R. Mon. p. 361. Vol. 3, p. 159.

Large Iron Knife or Small Sword (Scramasax), found in the Thames in 1857. Present length 2 feet 4½ inches. Characters and ornaments of gold and silver wire twisted together, cut into proper lengths, and beaten into incisions in the metal.

First comes the Futhorc or Alphabet, of 28 letters:

F, U, Þ, O, R, C, G, W, H, N, I, Y, YO, P, A, S, T, B, E, NG,
D, L, M, Œ, Á, Æ, C, EA.

Then ornamentations and the name of the owner (or maker):

BEAGNOTH.

Now in the British Museum.

SANDWICH. KENT. ENGLAND.

? DATE ABOUT A. D. 428—597.

Old-N. R. Mon. p. 367.

Found ab. 1830. Stone: 16 in. high by 4 × 4 at top. 6 × 6 below. Only *the name* now legible:

RÆHÆBUL.

SANDWICH, KENT, ENGLAND.

? DATE ABOUT A. D. 428—597.

Old-N. R. Mon. p. 363.

Runes defaced. — Found ab. 1830. Of hard stone. About 17 inches high, by 5 × 5 where broadest.

CLEOBURY MORTIMER, SHROPSHIRE, ENGLAND.

? DATE ABOUT A. D. 500—600.

Old-N. R. Mon. Vol. 3. p. 160.

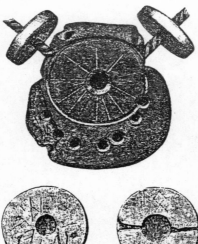

Engraved ²/₃ of the original size from the woodcuts of the Rev. D. H. Haigh in "The Yorkshire Arch. & Top. Journal", Pts. 17, 18. London 1877, p. 201, foll. Ploughed up in 1816. Of shell sandstone; the one disk of sandstone, the other of limestone. A portable Sun-dial, the chief side thus restored (as to its intention) by Mr. Haigh:

The holes on the other side are as follows:

and the hole-groups are supposed by Mr. Haigh to have rudely represented the Constellations Woden's or Ceorl's Wain and the Ship. The runes on the disk apparently mean, the whole being probably a gift:

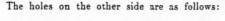

CLAÆO IWI

Let-the-CLAW (pointer) EYE (show you)!

GILTON, KENT, ENGLAND.

? DATE ABOUT A. D. 500—600.

Old-N. R. Mon. p. 370. Vol. 3, p. 163.

Silver Pommel of an Iron Sword, now in the Liverpool Museum. What is left is thus given by Mr. Akerman:

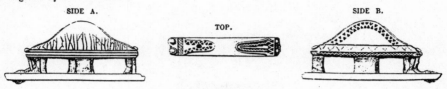

SIDE A.　　TOP.　　SIDE B.

Runes re-engraved, from squeezes by Mr. Haigh:

With Haigh I suppose the last letter on A to have been ᚠ (Æ), the arms now worn away; his dotted (guest) ᛙ on B I would take to have been the bind-rune ᚱ (UN). My proposal is as follows:

YCE IK SIGI. MERGE MIK WISÆ, DÆGMUND!

EKE (increase) I SIGE (victory). MERRILY ME WISS (show, brandish, bare), O-DÆGMUND.'

ÖKER JAG SEGERN. MUNTERT MIG VIS, DÆGMUND.

Engraved full size. — Found at the beginning of this century.

ST. ANDREWS, FIFE, SCOTLAND.

? DATE ABOUT A. D. 500—600.

Old-N. R. Mon. p. 371.

Bronze Finger-ring. Full size. Probably a Signet, for the letters are sunk. As on a wax impression, reads ISAH. If taken as they appear to the eye the staves are HASI, in either case a common mansname. — Found in 1849.

TRURO, CORNWALL, ENGLAND.

? DATE ABOUT A. D. 500—600.

Old-N. R. Mon. p. 372, 865.

Pig of Tin, found in the last century; about 2 feet 11 long, 11 inches broad, and 3 inches high. The stamp (of the maker), which it bears, is well known in the Old-English Runic Futhorc. It has the power of ST and is called by the name

STAN.

Stamp full size:

BROUGH, WESTMORELAND, ENGLAND.

? DATE ABOUT A. D. 550—600.

Old-N. R. Mon. Vol. 3, p. 169.

Apparently the central slab of a grave-cross to a Christian Lady, most likely a Christian Martyr. The excessively old Double-Cross above, the Palmbrauch on each side — the earliest Christian symbol of triumph over death —, and the still half-Scandian dialect in 12 lines of stave-rime verse, together with the olden runes the HOW and the CUMBEL-BOO announce the overgang from heathendom. Several of the runes rare and peculiar variants. Most of the letters are well preserved, but some are worn and damaged and doubtful. They were *rubbed-in* with some tool.

IKKALACGC I BUCIAEHOM

BECKCTO CUOMBIL-BIO

CIMOKOMS. ALH'S COINU,

OC. TIMD I ECBI,

O ACLIHCG

AILIC I RAIRA WOLC.

HOUH OSCIL, OSBIOL,
CUHL. OEKI FAIDU.
LAICIAM ALWIN KRIST
IUKC RECS IFT BROK.
OC EC CEARUNGIA WOP
AICI COEC(AS MEC more).

INGALANG IN BUCKenHOME
BIGGED (built) this-the-CUMBLE-BOO (grave-kist)
of-CIMOKOM, ALH'S QUENE (wife);
OK (but), TEEMED (born) IN ECBY.
ON ACLEIGH
HOLY INTO (to) RYRE (ruin, destruction) she-WALKT (went).
Her-HOW (grave-mound) OSCIL, OSBIOL.
CUHL and-OEKI FAWED (made).
My-LEGEM (body) the-ALL-WINE (all-friend, all loving) CHRIST
YOUNG-again REACHES (leads forth, shall renew) AFTER BROOK (death),
OK EKE (but indeed, and truly) CARING'S WOOP (care's tear-flow)
NEVER QUETCHES (shall move, shall afflict) (me more).

      INGALANG I BOCKEHEM
      BYGGDE detta-KUMBEL-BO (grafkammare),
      CIMOKOM'S, ALH'S QVINNA'S (hustrus);
      MEN, FÖDD I ECBY,
      Å (på, vid) ACLEIGH
      HELIG I (till) DÖDEN hon-GICK.
      Hennes-graf-HÖG OSCIL, OSBIOL,
      CUHL och-OEKI GJORDE (uppkastade).
      Min-LEKAMEN (kropp) ALL-VÄNNEN KRIST
      UNG-igen RÄCKER-fram (uppväcker) EFTER BRÅK (döden),
      OCH SÅ ÅNGSLANS TÅRAR
      ALDRIG SKOLA-PINA (mig mera).

Engraved 1-third of the size, from Casts generously forwarded by the Cumberland and Westmoreland Archæological Society. Found in October 1879 in the foundations of the old Church-porch. Carboniferous sandstone. Among other sculptured slabs dug up at the same time, was a fragment of a Roman stone beginning IMP. CÆSAR. This is not surprising, as Brough was a Roman military station.

WHITBY, YORKSHIRE, ENGLAND.

? DATE ABOUT A. D. 600—650.

Old-N. R. Mon. Vol. 3. p. 180.

(go)D USMÆ US! GOD ALUWALUDO HELIPÆ CUN(niæs ussæs)!
May-GOD ON-SMEE (look on, regard, bless) US! May-GOD ALL-WALD (Almighty) HELP KIN (family, house) our!
GUD SIGNE OSS! GUD ALLSMÄGTIG HJELPE HUS VÅRT.

Full size. Bone Comb. Found with other old things in 1867, in the kitchen-midden belonging to the old monastic family (house) at Whitby.

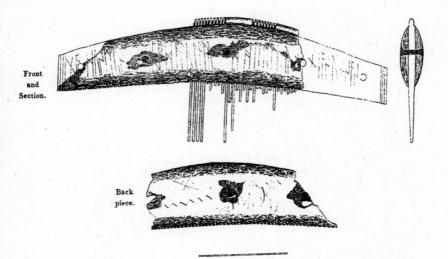

Front and Section.

Back piece.

NORTHUMBRIA, ENGLAND;
BUT NOW IN THE DUCAL MUSEUM, BRUNSWICK.

? DATE ABOUT A. D. 620—650.

Old-N. R. Mon. p. 378, 865.

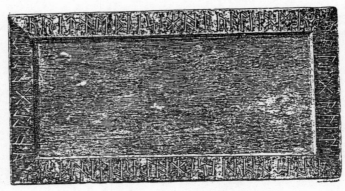

URIT NEÞII SIGHYOR ÆLI, IN MUNGPÆLYO GÆLIeA.

WROTE (carved this) NETHII for-the-SIG-HERRA (victory-lord, most noble) ÆLI, IN MUNGPÆLyO (Montpellier) of-GAUL.

RITADE (skar detta) NETHII for-SEGER-HERREN (den ädle) ÆLI, I MONTPELLIER af-GALLIA.

Inscription carved twice over. Material, thin plates of the ivory of the Walrus with settings of yellowish Bronze. Bottom-plate *(as given p. 119)* also of Walrus- or Morse-ivory, fixt in slips of Bronze on which the runes are cut. Chemityped full size. Runes first pointed out by our English rune-master J. M. Kemble. — The front, both ends, and back follow.

COLLINGHAM, YORKSHIRE, ENGLAND.

? DATE ABOUT A. D. 651.

Old-N. R. Mon. p. 390.

All now really left is:

ÆFTAR ONSWINI, CU(ning) — — —

— — — — — — — —

AFTER ONSWINI, KING — — —

— — — — — — — —

Upper stones do not belong to the lower. This base is 2 feet 9 inches high. — Found in 1841.

KIRKDALE, YORKSHIRE, ENGLAND.

? DATE ABOUT A. D. 660.

Old-N. R. Mon. Vol. 3. p. 184.

A fragment of a grave-slab, bearing O. English runes, was found some years ago, and Mr. Haigh thought he could read the name of ŒTHILWALD, king of Deira (Yorkshire), 651—660. But the letters are now so gone that we are sure of nothing. So I pass this piece by.

BAKEWELL, DERBYSHIRE, ENGLAND.

? DATE ABOUT A. D. 600—700.

Old-N. R. Mon. p. 373.

— — — (M)INGH(O) — — —

— — — HELG — — —

The first line may have been part of a Place- or a Mans-name. the second a fragment of the word HOLY ("HELIG"), or of a name.

Size about 12 inches by 9. — Found about the middle of this century.

LANCASTER. LANCASHIRE. ENGLAND.

? DATE ABOUT A. D. 600—700.

Old-N. R. Mon. p. 375. Vol. 3. p. 184.

Cross from the drawings of Mr. M. Jones. in Arch. Journal.

Runes from a Cast by Dr. Hibbert. in the Danish Museum.

After having myself examined the stone, now in the British Museum, I agree with the last suggestion of Mr. Haigh, that at the close the letter was an H, half gone, that next came a T, of which there is only a trace, and that the rune for ING is *quite* broken away. This *substantially* coincides with our great Kemble's idea — in my eyes an additional recommendation. I therefore now divide and translate:

GI-BIDÆD FORÆ CŪNIBALÞ CUÞBŒRE(Hting).

BID (pray-ye) FOR CŪNIBALTH CUTHBŒREHTING (= CŬTHBERT-SON).[!]

This sepulchral cross is 3 feet high. It was found in 1807.

NORTHUMBRIA, ENGLAND.

? DATE ABOUT A. D. 600—700.

Old-N. R. Mon. p. 386.

Nothing known of this Old-English (? Silver) Brooch but the inscription:

ᚠᚢᚻᚱᚻ ᚻᛗᚤ ᚹᚩᚱᚻ[ᛏ]
ᛗ ᚠᛁᚤᚾᚹᚱᛁᛏᚻ ᚻᛗᚤ ᚱ[ᚼ]

GUDRD MEC WORH(T)E. ÆLCHFRITH MEC A(H).

GUDRĬD ME WROUGHT. ÆLCHFRITH ME OWETH (owns).

Lost or mislaid. Size and material not given. Last seen by Mr. Kemble, our great rune-smith, in 1847.

CROWLE, LINCOLNSHIRE, ENGLAND.

? DATE ABOUT A. D. 650—750.

Old-N. R. Mon. Vol. 3, p. 185.

Part of a Runic Grave-Cross, made use of as a lintel in the doorway leading from the tower to the nave in the Church of S. Oswald at Crowle. I here show its original position.
Sculpture on runic side: the Hermit-saints Antony and Paul meet in the wilderness. — Below, probably: the Flight into Egypt. Lower down, what is left of the grave-words:

. . . . (AP)Æ LIC-BÆCUN B(eAFTÆ)r . . . . . .

(Set . . .)APÆ this-LIK-BEACON (grave-shaft) AFTER . . . . . .

The stone is 7 feet long, 18 inches across at the widest. 7 to 8 inches thick. — First really made known by the Rev. J. T. Fowler in 1868.

Section of wall at East face.

Section of wall at West face.

HARTLEPOOL, DURHAM, ENGLAND.

? DATE ABOUT A. D. 650—700.

Old-N. R. Mon. p. 392.

Besides the common ancient Christian grave-formula (A)lpha and (O)mega — CHRIST
THE EVERLASTING. THOU ART MINE HELP! — has only the woman's-name BILDITHRCTH.

A   O

HILDIÐRÚÐ.

Pillow-stone.   From grave of a Nun.   Size 11½ inches.   Found in 1833.

HARTLEPOOL, DURHAM, ENGLAND.

? DATE ABOUT A. D. 650—700.

Old-N. R. Mon. p. 396, 865.

Bears only the woman's-name HILDDI(G)ÚTH.
Pillow-stone.   From grave of a Nun.   Size 7¾ inches by 6½. — Found in 1833.

BEWCASTLE, CUMBERLAND, ENGLAND.

? DATE ABOUT A. D. 670.

Old-N. R. Mon. p. 398.

EAST SIDE (no runes). — WEST SIDE:

A.   ᴋ..s..s (Doubtless the Holy Name *KRISTUS*).
B.   † GESSUS KRISTTUS († *JESUS CHRISTUS*).

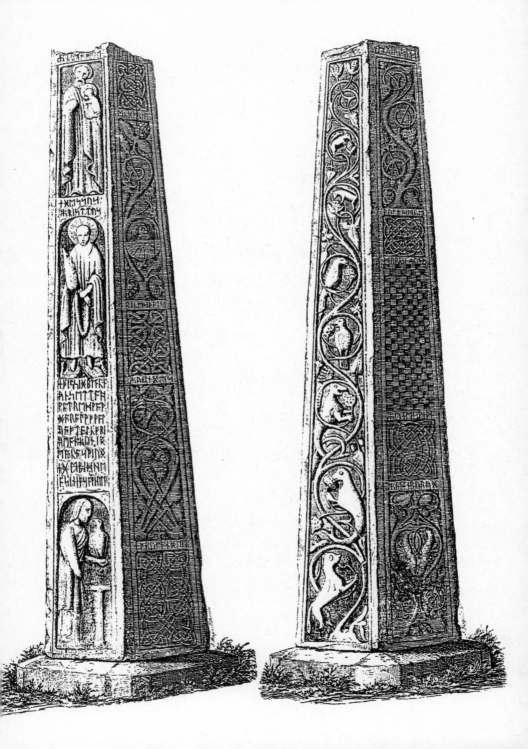

C.　† DIS SIG-BECN ÐUN　　　　　† *THIS SPIRING SIGN-PILLAR*
　　SETTON HWÆTRED,　　　　　　　*SET WAS BY HWÆTRED,*
　　WODGAR, OLWFWOLDU,　　　　　*WOTHGAR, OLUFWOLTH,*
　　AFT ALCFRIDU,　　　　　　　　*AFTER ALCFRITH,*
　　EAN KÚNING　　　　　　　　　*SOMETIME KING*
　　EAC OSWIUNG.　　　　　　　　*AND SON OF OSWI.*
　　† GEBID HEO-SINNA SOWHULA.　† *PRAY FOR HIS SOUL'S GREAT SIN!*

SOUTH SIDE:

† FRUMAN GEAR KÚNINGES RICES ÐÆES, ECGFRIDU. LICE (? he friþes).

† *In-the-FIRST YEAR of-the-KING of-RIC (realm) THIS, ECGFRITH. — LIE (he = may Alcfrith lie,*
in frith, in peace).

NORTH SIDE:

A.　KÚNNBURUG = The Queen of Alcfrith.
B.　KÚNESWIÐA = Her Sister.
C.　MYRCNA KÚNG} = Wulfhere, King of the Mercians, son of Penda and brother
D.　WULFHERE　}　　　　　　　　　　of Kúnnburug.
E.　† † † GESSUS = *JESUS.*

Originally 20 feet high. Now, the Cross-shaft broken away, only 14½ feet above the pedestal.

Partly handled in 1607, and often later. Present materials chiefly supplied by the late Rev. J. Maughan in 1857 and following years.

RUTHWELL, NORTHUMBRIA, ENGLAND.

? DATE ABOUT A. D. 680.

Old- N. R. Mon. p. 405, 865. Vol. 3, p. 189.

EAST SIDE.

A.　Top-stone. Bird (Dove or Eagle).
B.　Arm-piece. *Modern.*
C.　Lower limb of Cross. Two half-figures.
D.　St. John Baptist with Agnus Dei. Letters, nearly effaced, end with .....(a)DORAMVS.
E.　The Lord Christ and the miracle of the Swine. Inscription:

† IHS XPS IVDEX AEQVITATIS. BESTIAE ET DRACONES COGNOUERVNT IN DESERTO SALVATOREM MVNDI.

F.　St. Paul the Hermit and St. Antony break a loaf of bread in the desert. Words:
　　SCS PAVLVS ET A(ntonius eremitae) FREGER(vn)T PANEM IN DESERTO.

G.　Flight into Egypt. Broken words: † MARIA ET IO(sephus .....).

H.　Lowest compartment. Defaced.

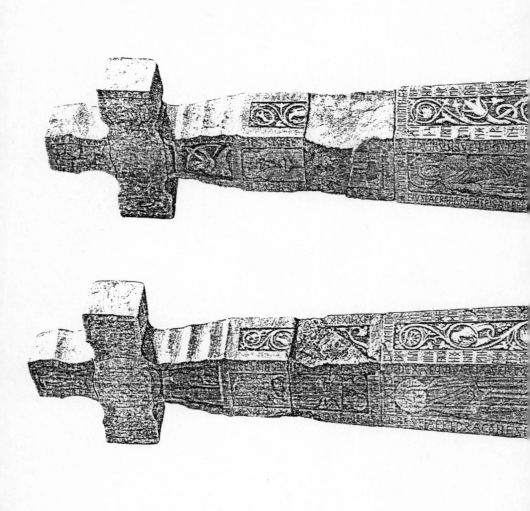

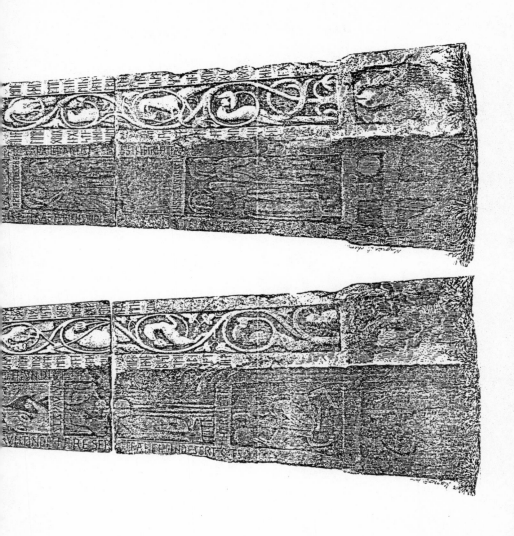

WEST SIDE.

A. Top-stone. ? St. John Evangelist and his Eagle.

B. Arm-piece. *Modern.*

C. Bowman taking aim.

D. The Visitation. St. Mary and St. Elizabeth. Fragmentary Latin letters.

E. St. Mary Magdalene. Risting:

† ATTVLIT AL(ab)ASTRVM VNGVENTI & STANS RETROSECVS PEDES EIVS LACRIMIS COEPIT RIGARE PEDES EIVS ET CAPILLIS CAPITIS SVI TERGEBAT.

F. Christ heals the man born blind. Legend:

† ET PRETERIENS VIDI(t hominem coecvm) A NATIBITATE ET S(anavit evm a)B INFIRMITA(te).

G. The Annunciation. Both heads have the glory. Words:

† INGRESSVS ANGELVS (ad eam dixit, Ave gratia plena, Dominvs) TE(cvm) BE(nedicta tv in mvlieribvs).

H. Crucifixion. Nearly gone.

NORTH SIDE.

Christ the Vine; and so, the Vine as the Church.

SOUTH SIDE.

Here we have *the Runes.* All that now can be made out is:

(ON)GEREDÆ HINÆ	*GIRDED HIM THEN*
GOD ALMEYOTTIG.	*GOD ALMIGHTY,*
ÞA HE WALDE	*WHEN HE WOULD*
ON GALGU GI-STIGA.	*STEP ON THE GALLOWS,*
MODIG FORE	*FORE ALL MANKIND*
(ALE) MEN.	*MINDFAST, FEARLESS.*
(B)UG(A IC NI DARS)TE :	*BOW ME DURST I NOT;*
. . . .	. . . .
. . . .	. . . .
(AHOF) IC RIICNÆ CÜNINGC,	*RICH KING HEAVING,*
HEAFUNÆS HLAFARD;	*THE LORD OF LIGHT-REALMS;*
HÆLDA IC (N)I DARSTÆ.	*LEAN ME I DURST NOT.*
BISMÆRÆDU UNGCET MEN BA ÆT-GAD(R)E;	*US BOTH THEY BASELY MOCKT AND HANDLED;*
IC (WÆS) MID BLODÆ BISTEMID,	*WAS I THERE WITH BLOOD BEDABBLED,*
BI(G)OT(E)N O(F)	*BE-SPINKLED FROM . . . .*
. . . .	. . . .
. . . .	. . . .
KRIST WÆS ON RODI.	*CHRIST WAS ON ROOD-TREE.*
HWEÞRÆ ÞER FUSÆ	*BUT FAST, FROM AFAR,*
FEARRAN KWOMU	*HIS FRIENDS HURRIED*
ÆÞÞILÆ TI LANUM:	*ATHEL (noble) TO THE SUFFERER.*
IC ÞÆT AL BI(H)EAL(D).	*EVERYTHING I SAW THERE.*
S(ARE) IC WÆS	*SORELY WAS I*
MI(Þ) SORGU(M) GI-(Þ)RŒ(FE)D.	*WITH SORROWS HARROW'D;*

H(ɴ)ᴀɢ (ɪᴄ)	STOOPT I . . . .
. . . .	. . . .
. . . .	. . . .
. . . .	. . . .
ᴍɪ𝐃 ꜱᴛʀᴇʟᴜᴍ ɢɪ-ᴡᴜɴᴅᴀᴅ.	WITH STREALS (missiles) ALL WOUNDED.
ᴀ-ʟᴇɢᴅᴜɴ ʜɪᴀᴇ ʜɪɴᴀᴇ ʟɪᴍᴡᴏᴇʀɪɢɴᴇ,	DOWN LAY THEY HIM LIMB-WEARY.
ɢɪ-ꜱᴛᴏᴅᴅᴜɴ ʜɪᴍ (ᴀᴇᴛ) ʜ(ɪꜱ ʟ)ɪᴄᴀᴇꜱ (ʜ)ᴇᴀꜰ(ᴅᴜ)ᴍ,	O'ER HIS LIFELESS HEAD THEN STOOD THEY,
(ʙɪ-)ʜᴇᴀ(ʟ)ᴅᴜ(ɴ̇) ʜɪ(ᴀᴇ) ᴅᴇ̇(ʀ) ʜ(ᴇᴀꜰᴜɴ) . . .	HEAVILY GAZING AT HEAVEN'S . . . .
. . . .	. . . .
. . . .	. . . .

ᴛᴏᴘ-ꜱᴛᴏɴᴇ (wrongly placed by Dr. Duncan, should have been turned round) bears on its Latin side:

ɪɴ ᴘʀɪɴ(ᴄɪᴘɪᴏ ᴇʀᴀᴛ) ᴠᴇʀʙᴠᴍ.

On the Runic side is the costly carving:

ᴄᴀᴅᴍᴏɴ ᴍᴀᴇ ꜰᴀᴜᴏᴇᴅᴏ.

CADMON (= CÆDMON) ME FAWED (made, composed).

Was in Pennant's time 20 feet high, besides capital and base. Is now about 17 feet 6 inches high. First mentioned in 1703. Best later handling that by Mr. Kemble. — The illustrious North-English Poet ᴄᴀᴇᴅᴍᴏɴ or ᴄᴀᴅᴍᴏɴ fell asleep about the year 680, or shortly after.

YARM, YORKSHIRE, ENGLAND.

? DATE ABOUT A. D. 684—700.

Old-N. R. Mon. Vol. 3, p. 189.

[✝ orate	
ᴘʀᴏ tru]	
ᴍʙᴇʀᴇʜᴄ	
ᴛ ✝ ꜱᴀ̇ᴄ ✝	*[✝ pray FOR tru]MBEREHCT ✝ BISHOP ✝*
ᴀʟʟᴀ ✝ ꜱɪɢɴ	*ALLA this-SIGN (beacon, memorial) AFTER*
ᴜᴍᴀᴇꜰᴛᴇʀ	*HIS BROTHER SET ✝*
ʜɪꜱʙʀᴇᴏᴅᴇʀᴀ	
ẏꜱᴇᴛᴀᴇ ✝	

Sandstone, 2 feet 2 inches high, 1 f. ³/₄ of an inch wide and 7¹/₄ i. thick. Found in 1877 doing duty as a weight in an old mangle. Fragment of a large Grave-cross. Both the narrow sides having the same pattern, only one is here engraved. Not in runes, but equal in value for the dialect and formula — Minne-stone of ᴛʀᴜᴍʙᴇʀʜᴛ, Bishop of Hexham from 681 to 684, when he was deposed. Date of his death not known. — ꜱᴀ̇ᴄ is the usual contraction for ꜱᴀᴄᴇʀᴅᴏᴛɪ, at this time the word for ʙɪꜱʜᴏᴘ.

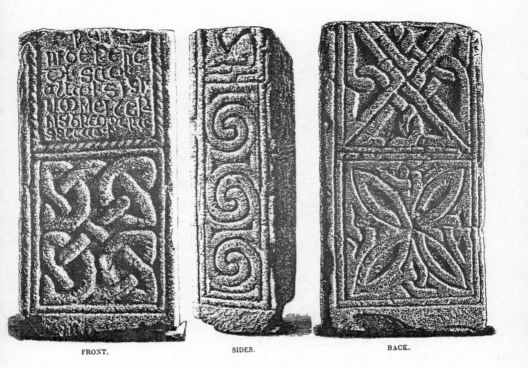

FRONT.   SIDES.   BACK.

LINDISFARNE, AFTERWARDS DURHAM, NORTHUMBRIA.

? DATE ABOUT A. D. 698.

Old-N. R. Mon. p. 449.

CARVINGS ON THE COFFIN OF ST. CUTHBERT.

After the name and bild of ST. JOHN. we have:

THOMAS   PETRVS

= ST. THOMAS.   = ST. PETRVS.

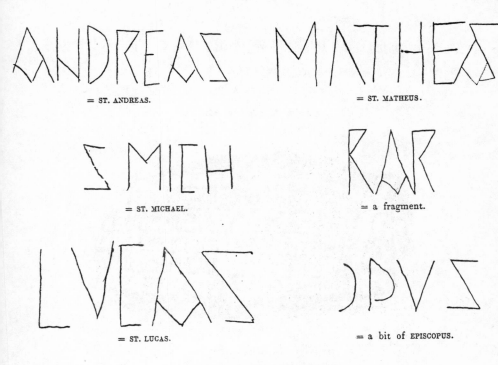

= ST. ANDREAS.

= ST. MATHEUS.

= ST. MICHAEL.

= a fragment.

= ST. LUCAS.

= a bit of EPISCOPUS.

AND THE LATIN INSCRIPTION IN RUNES:

= (IHESUS) SANCTUS

Of the word which preceded this SCS, and which was of 3 letters, only the last was clear. It was a similar old-runic S to the above. The second was apparently H, the first must have been I. Thus this costly old-Runic and old-Roman S was carved at least *thrice* on the coffin. This is so much the more interesting as we know that this lik-kist cannot date *later* than 698. — Found in 1827.

FALSTONE, NORTHUMBERLAND, ENGLAND.

? DATE ABOUT A. D. 700.

Old-N. R. Mon. p. 456.

TWAY-STAVED (RUNIC AND ROMAN).

Roman Staves.	Runic Staves.
† EOMAER THE SETTAE	† EOMÆR ÞŒ SŒTTŒ
AEFTAER HROETHBERHTÆ,	ÆFTÆR ROETBERHTÆ.
BECUN AEFTAER EOMAE.	BECUN ÆFTÆR EOMÆ.
GE-BIDAED DER SAULE.	GEBIDÆD DER SAULE.

EOMÆR THIS SET
AFTER HROETBERT,
this-BEACON (mark, memorial) AFTER his-EME (uncle).
BEDE (bid, pray-ye) for-THE (his) SOUL!

A graystone fragment, about a foot long and 5¹/₂ inches broad, broken away from a Runic Cross or grave-pillar. — First publisht in 1822. Here engraved from a cast in the Danish Museum.

Similar biliteral (Scandinavian-runish and Roman) grave-stones from olden Christian times also exist in Sweden.

BINGLEY, YORKSHIRE, ENGLAND.

? DATE ABOUT A. D. 768—770.

Old-N. R. Mon. p. 486.   Vol. 3. p. 194.

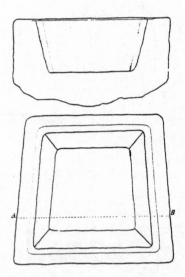

The stone, originally very simply tooled, has suffered fearfully from ill-usage and the elements. The runes, which are carved *on the front*, are almost illegible. What is left of them has been variously deciphered. Mr. Haigh's transcript (see my Vol. 3) I believe to be highly incorrect. After long and careful examination of a Cast, Rubbings and Photographs, I beg — with all deference — to submit my own reading of this doubtful inscription:

> EADBIERHT CŪNŪNG
> HET HIEAWAN DŒP-STAN US.
> (G)IBID FŪR HIS SAULE.

> *EADBIERHT, KING,*
> *HOTE (ordered, bade) to-HEW this-DIP-STONE (font) for-US.*
> *BID (pray-thou) FOR HIS SOUL!*

Should this reading be substantially correct, it can only refer to EADBERT, who was king of Northumberland from 737 to 757, when he became a priest, giving up his kingdom to his son Oswulf. He died as Canon of York in 768, and doubtless ordered several pious gifts to Church and Clergy in the usual way for the good of his soul. Among these was also

this BAPTISMAL FONT, of strong gritstone. It is about $2\frac{1}{2}$ feet square by $1\frac{1}{4}$ high and 10 inches deep. The under-part is quite rough, as if it had never been workt. It has a drain, to let out the water.

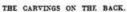

THE CARVINGS ON THE BACK.

THE CARVINGS ON THE RIGHT SIDE.

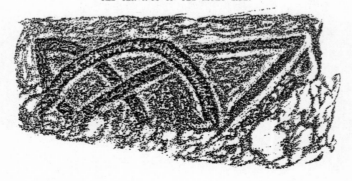

THE CARVINGS ON THE LEFT SIDE.

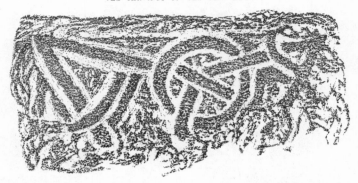

Long known, and as long neglected. For my materials I am indebted to the Rev. J. T. Fowler, F. S. A., in 1869, 70.

ÆTHRED'S FINGER-RING, ENGLAND.

? DATE ABOUT A. D. 700—800.

Old-N. R. Mon. p. 463.

ÆÐRED MEC AH. EANRED MEC A-GROF.
ÆTHRED ME OWNS. EANRED ME A-GROOF (engraved).
ÆTHRED MIG ÄGER. EANRED MIG GRAVERADE.

Mixt Roman and Runish letters in gold. Ground a dark niello. — First publisht, badly, by Hickes in 1705.

DEWSBURY, YORKSHIRE, ENGLAND.

? DATE ABOUT A. D. 700—800.

Old-N. R. Mon. p. 464. Vol. 3, p. 200.

Full size. Fragment of a sandstone memorial Cross, found about 1830. Not in runes, but in the same olden dialect. Mr. Haigh's restoration is:

[. . . . . . ðis settae	[. . . . . . *this set*
aefter EdilBE]RHTAE.	*after EdilBE]RHT.*
BECUN AEFTER BEORNAE.	*a-BEACON AFTER the-BERN (prince).*
GIBIDDAD DAER SAULE.	*BID-ye (pray) for-THE SOUL!*

DOVER, KENT, ENGLAND.

? DATE ABOUT A. D. 700—800.

Old-N. R. Mon. p. 465, 865.

Inscription as *corrected* from a rubbing by the Rev. John Puckle, M. A., Vicar of Dover. Given 1-fifth of the size; only the name of the dead man,

ᛏᛉᛋᛁᚷᚾᛏᚱᚻ᛬

GYOSLHEARD.

Breadth of stone at broadest, 2 feet 1 inch; length, 5 feet 11 inches. — Found about 1825.

IRTON, CUMBERLAND, ENGLAND.

? DATE ABOUT A. D. 700—800.

Old-N. R. Mon. p. 469. Vol. 3, p. 200.

Defaced Cross. Letters nearly gone. Mr. Haigh proposed:

†ᚷᛁᛒᛁᛞᚫᚦ	GIBIDÆÐ	*BID-ye (pray)*
ᚠᚩᚱᚫ	FORÆ	*FOR ....*

But J. R. Allen, Esq., C. E., F. S. A. Sc., who visited the cross in 1879, could find no traces of runes left.

NORTHUMBRIA, ENGLAND;

BUT BOUGHT IN AUZON, BRIONDE, HAUTE-LOIRE, FRANCE.

? DATE ABOUT A. D. 700—800.

Old-N. R. Mon. p. 470, LXIX. Vol. 3. p. 200.

LEFT SIDE.

The tale about Romulus and Remus.

ODLÆ UNNEG ROMWALUS AND REUMWALUS, TWŒGEN GIBRODÆRA; FŒDDE HIÆ WÜLIF IN ROMÆCÆSTRI.

Their-OTHEL (home-land, birth-place) UN-NIGH (far away from) were-ROMWALUS (= ROMULUS) AND REUMWALUS (= REMUS), TWAIN (two) BROTHERS; FED (nourisht, suckled) HI (them) a-WYLF (she-wolf) IN ROMECASTER (Rome-city).

Sin-ODEL (hem) ICKE-NÄRA voro-ROMULUS OCH REMUS, TVENNE BRÖDER; uppFÖDDE DEM en-ULF-hona I ROMA-BY.

Back. The tale of Titus and the Jews.

HER FEGTAD TITUS END GIUDEASU. HIC FUGIANT HIERUSALIM AFITATORES (= HABITATORES).

DOM.   GISL.

HERE FIGHT TITUS AND THE JEWS. HERE FLY-from JERUSALEM its-INHABITANTS.
DOOM (Court, Judgment of Jewish rebels).   GISL (Hostages given to the Romans).

Partly in Runes, and partly in Romanesque letters. The DOM and GISL *may possibly* be taken as one word, the artist's name, DOMGISL. — Or, can the DOM compartment be the Condemnation of Christ, Pilate washing his hands?

Front. The tale whence came the Casket.

HRONÆS BAN FISC-FLODU
A-HOF ON FERGEN-BERIG:
WARD GASRIC GRORN,
DÆR HE ON GREUT GI-SWOM.

Of-the-Hrone (= Whale) the-bones the-fishes'-flood (= the Sea) hove (lifted, raised) on Fergen-berg (Fergen-hill, on the coast of Durham); worth (became, was-he) gas-rich (playing, gamboling) groren (crusht, pasht to pieces, killed) there (there-where, where) he on the-grit (shingles, shore, coast) swam.

THE WHALE'S BONES THE FISHES' FLOOD
LIFTED ON FERGEN-HILL:
HE WAS GASHT TO DEATH IN HIS GAMBOLS,
AS A-GROUND HE SWAM IN THE SHALLOWS.

HVALENS BEN FISK-FLODEN (hafvet) UPPLYFTADE PÅ FERGEN-BERG: HAN-BLEF I-SIN-LEK KROSSAD. DER HAN IN-PÅ STRAND-GRUSET SAMM.

Left front scene.   *The tale of the weapon-smith Wéland.*

Right front scene.   *The tale of the MAGI (in runes MÆGI) offering to Christ.*

BACK OF THE CASKET.

FRONT OF THE CASKET.

Right side.

All the rest
broken away.

? Some tale from the Wéland-saga.

DRYGYÐ SWI(K) ....

DREETH (suffers, bears; or, does, performs) SWIK (deceit).

LIDER (el. GÖR) SVEK ....

TOP OF THE CASKET.

Top. Another tale from the Wéland-saga, doubtless about his brother ÆGIL. His name is written in runes, ÆGILI. He is attackt in his stronghold. But no known ÆGIL-legend can explain to us the details here carved.

THE FRANKS CASKET, bought in France by Augustus Wollaston Franks, Esq., F. S. A., in 1857, and generously given by him to the British Museum. — Full size. Of whalebone. One of the oldest and costliest treasures of ancient English art now in existence. The tenons were doubtless once covered with corner pieces of metal, perhaps bronze. The lock is torn out.

THAMES FITTING, ENGLAND.

? DATE ABOUT A. D. 700—800.

Old-N. R. Mon. Vol. 3. p. 204.

? (Her Jonas) SBERÆDH TYO BŪA I ERHA DÆBS.

? (*Here Jonah*) SPEIRETH (*asks*) TO BO (*bide, be cast*) IN the-ARG (*waves, trough*) of-the-DEEP.

Full size. Only a fragment, as I suppose of a Shrine or Casket. Of lightish Bronze, once gilt. I suppose the Casket to have borne Biblical symbols of the Uprising of Christ, among them the story of Jonah in the Whale's Belly, *so often* used as a type of the Resurrection. See Book of Jonah, Ch. 1, v. 12, S. Matthew, Ch. 12, v. 39, 40. Such applications abound on old ecclesiastical works of art. I add one example from the Catacombs in Rome (Bosio, Roma Sott. Roma 1632, p. 431). Here Jonah is literally asking to be cast forth into the sea:

Dredged out of the Thames, London, in 1866.

THORNHILL, YORKSHIRE, ENGLAND.

? DATE ABOUT A. D. 700—800.

Old-N. R. Mon. Vol. 3, p. 209.

Found, with other grave-cross fragments, during alterations of the church at the close of 1875 and beginning of 1876. Of sandstone. About 1-fifth. Part of the shaft of a funeral pillar.

† EÐELBERHT SETTÆ	*ETHELBERHT SET-up-this*
ÆFTER EÐELWINI DERING(æ).	*AFTER ETHELWINI DERING.*

THORNHILL, YORKSHIRE, ENGLAND.

? DATE ABOUT A. D. 700—800.

Old-N. R. Mon. Vol. 3, p. 210.

Found at same time and place. Sandstone. Scale about 1—5th. Shaft of a Grave-Cross. A Calvary-cross, followed by the words:

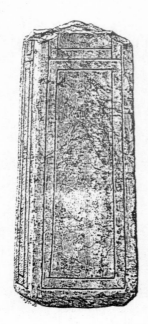 

EADRED SETE ÆFTE EATEYONNE.

EADRED SET-up-this AFTER the-lady-EATEyA.

WYCLIFFE, NORTHUMBRIA, ENGLAND.

? DATE ABOUT A. D. 700—800.

Old-N. R. Mon. Vol. 1, p. 476, E.

BAEDA (? the se)T(tæ)	*BAEDA THIS SET*
AEFTER BERCHTVINI,	*AFTER BERCHTVINI,*
BECVN AEFTER F(? aþoræ.	*a-BEACON (grave-mark) AFTER his-Father.*
ge-bidæd der saule).	*bid-ye (pray) for-the-soul!*

Lost. Not in runes. Fragment of a Grave-Cross. found in 1778.

THORNHILL, YORKSHIRE, ENGLAND.

? DATE. ABOUT A. D. 867.

Old-N. R. Mon. Vol. 3, p. 212.

From Haigh's Thornhill Inscriptions, p. 4. Scale not given. Found at Thornhill with the other fragments. Sandstone. Not in runes, but in the same costly dialect. Only a small part of the center remains, apparently to be restored:

(÷ ecgbe

rcht . ðis

set)E . AEFT

(er.) OSBER

(ch)TAE . BEC

(un . o)SBER

(chtaes . ge

biddað . ða

er . saule.)

Thus 4 lines of stave-rime verse:

ECGBERCHT ÐIS SETE	ECGBERCHT THIS SET
AEFTER OSBERCHTAE,	AFTER OSBERCHT,
BECUN OSBERCHTAES.	the-BEACON of-OSBERCHT.
GEBIDDAÐ ÐAER SAULE.	BID-ye for-THE SOUL.

OSBERCHT fell in the battle at York against the Danes March 21, 867. He was succeeded in his Northumbrian kingdom by ECGBERCHT.

COQUET ILAND, NORTHUMBERLAND, ENGLAND.

? DATE ABOUT A. D. 800—900.

Old-N. R. Mon. Vol. 1. p. 480.

† DIS IS SICILFUR(N).

THIS IS SILVER(N) = of silver.

Lead — but was once silvered and made to pass for silver. Full size. — Found about 1860.

ENGLAND; BUT UNKNOWN WHERE.

? DATE ABOUT A. D. 800—900.

Old-N. R. Mon. Vol. 3. p. 213.

For the present lost. and material unknown. Bears, in O. E. runes, the common olden mansname

OWI.

As we know nothing of the original or its setting. date only approximative.

HODDAM, NORTHUMBRIA, ENGLAND.

? DATE ABOUT A. D. 800—900.

Old-N. R. Mon. Vol. 1, p. 483.

Part of a Runic Cross, now lost. No copy was ever made of the runes. This fragment measured 2 feet in height, 9 inches in greatest breadth, 6 inches at the sides. — Found some time before 1815.

KIRKDALE, YORKSHIRE, ENGLAND.

? DATE ABOUT A. D. 800—900.

Old-N. R. Mon. Vol. 3. p. 214.

Ruined Cross. Has traces of runes. One only, ᛝ (NG), is distinct.

MAESHOWE, STENNES, MAINLAND, ORKNEYS.

? DATE ABOUT A. D. 800—900.

Old-N. R. Mon. Vol. 1, p. 485, Vol. 3, p. 214.

Two scribbles, probably by the same hand. The latter has one Old-Northern letter, the o. From the famous rune-rich Picts-house, long a Wiking rendezvous.

ÞORNR SÆRÐ.

THORN (or javelin) SORETH.

HÆLBI RÆISTO.

HÆLBI RISTED (carved-this).

The stone here engraved 1-third the size of the original. — Found in 1861.

MONK WEARMOUTH, DURHAM, ENGLAND.

? DATE ABOUT A. D. 822.

Old-N. R. Mon. Vol. 1, p. 477.

Runes
full size.

TIDFIRÐ.

This TIDFIRTH or TIDFERTH was the last bishop of Hexham. Stone apparently the base of a small grave-cross, the arms and top being lost. It is 12½ inches high by 8 inches where broadest. — Found about 1860.

LEEDS, YORKSHIRE, ENGLAND.

? DATE ABOUT A. D. 872.

Old-N. R. Mon. Vol. 1. p. 487. Vol. 3. p. 215.

CUN(unc)	KING.
ONLAF.	ONLAF.

According to Mr. Haigh, the ANLAF or OLAF, son of a Danish king, who with his brothers Sitric and Ivar went to Ireland in 853, invaded Britain in 866—7, and probably died there in 872. — Fragment of a Runic Cross, 11½ inches by about 10 inches in height. — Found in 1837.

HACKNESS, YORKSHIRE, ENGLAND.

? DATE ABOUT A. D. 850—950.

Old-N. R. Mon. Vol. 1, p. 467. Vol. 3, p. 215.

For the Photograph, which cannot be repeated here, see p. 467. The stone has suffered too much to bear sharp engraving. But the runes, which are English-Northern, can pretty clearly be made out. They are:

ᚦᛗᛗᚼᛁᚻᛉᛦ
ᛦᛁᚠᛀᛒᛦᚠ

EMUNDR O ON ÆSBOA. *EMUND OWNS-me ON (at) ASBY.*

(*This is the grave of Emund at Asby*).

Below this we have 3½ lines of the rare Twig- or Tree-runes, but so injured as to give no clear meaning. The 6th line closes with one word, in early Roman uncials, the verb ORA (*PRAY for the soul!*). The other side bears the head of a female figure, and above this, in Latin letters, BVGGA VIRGO. — Originally this piece has perhaps been the central slab of a funeral Cross. It is about 16 inches high and 14 broad.

As this is a palimpsest stone, is in the Scandinavian-Wiking dialect, and yet is Christian, I now think it cannot be earlier than the 9th century, or perhaps the first half of the 10th. — Found early in this century.

CRAMOND, EDINBURGHSHIRE, NORTHUMBRIA.

? DATE ABOUT A. D. 900—1000.

Old-N. R. Mon. Vol. 3, p. 215.

Full size. Bronze finger-ring. The letters have suffered so much that I cannot read them. — Found about 1869.

ALNMOUTH, NORTHUMBERLAND, ENGLAND.

? DATE ABOUT A. D. 913.

Old-N. R. Mon. p. 461, 865.

ᛁᛁᛖ Vᛟᛈᛋᚳᚻᚻᛖᚻᚠᛖᚷᛁ

. ADVLFES Đ	? (þis is cyning e)ADULFES Đ(RUH).
. . . . . SAV . .	(gebiddad þære) SAU(le).
MYREDAH MEH WO	MRYEDAH MEH WO(rhte).
(HL)VDWYG MEH FEG . .	BLUDWYG MEH FEG(de).

(This is king e)ADULFS TH(ruh. = grave-kist).

Bid-ye (pray) for-the SOUL

MYREDAH ME WROUGHT (made).

BLUDWYG ME FAYED (inscribed).

Fragments of a partly-runic funeral Cross. Height of what is now left about 3 feet. Given by Haigh to king EADULF of Bamborough, died in 913. — Found in 1790, in the ruins of St. Woden's Church.

AMULET RINGS, ENGLAND.

? DATE ABOUT A. D. 1000—1100.

Old-N. R. Mon. p. 492, Vol. 3, p. 216.

No. 1.

GREYMOOR HILL, CUMBERLAND.

Of gold. Full size. — Found in 1817.

No. 2.

ENGLAND.

Of electrum. Letters on a ground of niello. Full size. Was in Denmark about 1740—50, when it was thus copied by Johan Olafsson:

No. 3.

BRAMHAM MOOR, YORKSHIRE.

Of gold. Found in 1733 or 1734. For the present lost or unknown. The runes were copied in 1805 by Francis Douce.

20*

No. 4.

WEST OF ENGLAND.

Of pinkish Agate. Was lost. Is found, and now, thanks to Mr. Franks, in the British Museum. Full size.

No. 5.

NORTH OF ENGLAND.

Copper. Full size. About 1869 came into the hands of Robert Ferguson, Esq., of Carlisle, who has generously given it to the British Museum.

Thus all these Rings bear, substantially, the same inscription:

No. 1.   ÆRŪRIUFLT ŪRIURIÐON GLÆSTÆPONTOL.

„ 2.   ÆRŪRIUFLT ŪRIURIÐON GLÆSTÆPONTOL.

„ 3.   ÆRŪRIUFLT ŪRIURIÐON GLÆSTÆPONTOL.

„ 4.   ERŪRIUFDOL ŪRIURIÐOL WLESTEPOTENOL.

„ 5.   ÆRŪRIUFLT ŪRIURIÐON GLÆSTÆPANTOL.

I still regard them all as connected with some secret sect or society, and as meaningless — a mere abracadabra; or as a cabbala of mystical origin or for mystical use as a Charm against some sickness or an Amulet or Pass.

ENGLISH (? OR NORWEGIAN) RUNIC CALENDAR.

? DATE ABOUT A. D. 1000—1100.

Old-N. R. Mon. Vol. 2, p. 866. Vol. 3, p. 219.

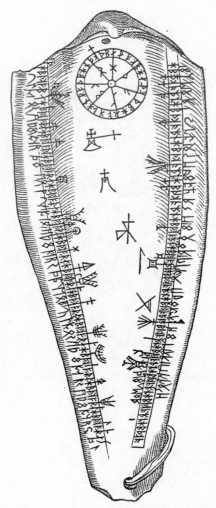

Made of the jawbone of the Porpoise.   Engraved full size from Worm's woodcut.
Bears several Old-Northern and specially provincial English runes. — Found early in the
17th century.

BRIDEKIRK, CUMBERLAND, ENGLAND.

? DATE ABOUT A. D. 1100—1200.

Old-N. R. Mon. Vol. 2, p. 489.   Vol. 3, p. 221.

A strange intermixture of Old-Northern and Scandinavian and Old-English staves and bind-runes. The dialect is also mixt. Early North-English, with a touch of Early Scandinavian. The words are in rimed verse:

WEST SIDE.

EAST SIDE.

ST. JOHN BAPTIZING CHRIST.

SUBJECT AS YET UNKNOWN.

RIKARTH HE ME IWROKTE

AND TO THIS MERTHE ƷERNR ME BROKTE.

RICHARD HE ME I-WROUGHT (made),

AND TO THIS MIRTH (beauty) YERN (glad) ME BROUGHT.

RICHARD HAN MIG GJORDE,

OCH TILL DENNE SKÖNHET GJERNA MIG BRAGTE.

Should my idea be correct, that this RICHARD was the well-known Architect RICARDUS who was Master of the Works to Bishop Pudsey during his improvements at Norham Castle, the date of this stone Font will be about 1150—1170. — The lowermost panel shows RICHARD at work!

The runic inscription is engraved above separately *half size*, from a rubbing by the Rev. D. H. Haigh. — Otherwise the engravings are copied from those publisht by Mr. H. Howard. See his essay, redd in the Soc. of Ant. of London in 1801.

BRACTEATES, &c.

THANKFULLY INSCRIBED

TO

Dr. OSCAR MONTELIUS,

STOCKHOLM, SWEDEN.

———

———

Hundreds of these *Golden Ornaments* — Rank-decorations, Family Medals, Gift-pieces, Amulets, or whatever else they may have been — have no letters at all, either runish or otherwise. Others bear plain staves, but these are only more or less half-runish *blind* imitations of the writing on their prototypes, Classical monies, and are here omitted. Some, here given for the sake of completeness (taking too many rather than too few, as they may be instructive) are doubtless chiefly barbarized imitations or copies' copies of semi-classical or better runish pieces, and till their sources are found can give no sure meaning. After the fresh experience of the last 15 years, I now think that several of my attempts at their translation were failures. But I expressly said of all the Bracteates that my readings were only feelers in the dark, and that "somebody must begin". The majority however of these inscribed golden roundlets are really and seriously intended to be deciphered in the usual way, and my translations of these I think likely or certain. But we learn more and more every day, and some may have to be modified or rejected. *Special* difficulties are connected with all olden *Coin* pieces from the words often not being divided (so that we do not know where to begin), from helpless cuttings, and from mixt and borrowed shapes and up or down turnings of the characters as the object is supposed to be held, — so that the most skilled numismatists are often at fault, even where the pieces are not absolutely "barbarous" and unreadable. Just the same thing holds good with many of the *Bracteates.* Other letters, again, are evidently only contractions, a rune or two standing for a whole word. Add hereto the additional hindrance of so many Holy Symbols and Ornament-marks, which sometimes may be mistaken for letters. So we shall never master many of these beautiful blinks. But of those whose meaning we can reasonably reach — how costly is the word-hoard!

Besides many fresh *runeless* Bracteates from time to time dug up in Scandinavia, two have lately been found in English graves at Faversham in Kent. The one, which turned up in 1873, is a plain disk of gold with a raised ring, internally enclosing a garnet or bloodstone. The other, exhumed in 1874, bears circles of beaded lines, and an open cross workt in the center.

In the Hindostanee Playing-Cards engraved in W. A. Chatto's "Facts and Speculations on the Origin and History of Playing-Cards" (8vo, London 1848, Plates 1 and 2), a kind of Horn or Ornament (*one* not *two*) is borne by the Horses and even by the Elephant. This Horn-like decoration is affixt to the head, or perhaps the head-harness, by the *narrow* end.

One word more. Whatever some linguists may papally lay down, it is *absolutely impossible* for any one *surely to know* whether many of the names on these pieces are *masc.* or *fem.* and in the *nom.* or *gen.* or *dat.* or *abl.* The variations in sound and form of old and unknown dialects are endless. Many (especially in N. English) had *masc.* nom. in -ʊ, while by degrees there grew up regular *feminines* in -ᴀ (gen. dat. ac. abl., especially in Scandinavia, otherwise commonly -ʊ or -o). Consequently where a Bracteate bears *only one word*, apparently the name of the Owner or Maker or Giver, for instance ᴁʟ-ʊ, this *may* have been a mans-name, nominative absolute. But it *may* have been a woman's-name, gen. *ᴁʟᴀ'ꜱ*, or dat. *to-ᴁʟᴀ*, or abl. *from-ᴁʟᴀ*. And so with other words and combinations, sometimes where we have 2 words. Let us ɴᴇᴠᴇʀ believe ɪɴꜰᴀʟʟɪʙʟᴇ philologists. Let us hold these things in suspense.

I offer my own readings with this express proviso. We *must* choose *some one* reading. Now and then some happy find may fix some particular formula for us. Otherwise, opinions may differ. — In combination with his labors on the Golden Horns, the Chamberlain Worsaae thinks (1880) he can now identify the various Holy Symbols on the Bracteates. His important work hereon will appear in due time. — The number of these runed pieces is now (Feb. 1881) 95, but often several *duplicate* copies of *the same* type (and struck from the same die) have been found. And where *one* such blink has been saved, *hundreds* have perisht!

<hr />

No. 1.

BROHOLM, FYN, DENMARK.

O. N. R. M. Vol. 2, p. 519.

Found in 1832. A half-runic *meaningless* imitation of a Roman epigraph. In 1867 I suggested:

KIÞUNK HAG TU OIW HUG.

KITHUNG HEWED (cut-this) TO EVER-during HOW (memory).

<hr />

No. 2.

MIDT-MJELDE. HAUG PARISH, SOUTH BERGENHUS, NORWAY.

O. N. R. M. Vol. 2, p. 520.

Found in 1827. Certainly meaningless.

No. 3.

FIND-PLACE UNKNOWN, POSSIBLY BOHEMIA.

O. N. R. M. Vol. 2, p. 520.

Runes and Latin Uncials. Not known when found.

CUN (= CUNUNG or CUNING) DASCO (or DUSCO).

KING THASCO (or THUSCO).

No. 4.

BOHUSLÄN, QVILLE PARISH, SWEDEN.

O. N. R. M. Vol. 2, p. 521.

Found in 1817. I now read only the mansname: HUTHU.

No. 5.

FIND-STEAD UNKNOWN, PROBABLY SCANDINAVIA.

O. N. R. M. Vol. 2, p. 521.

Found in last half of 17th cent.   Runes and Uncials.   The mansname: ECMC.

No. 6.

MAGLEMOSE, VALLERSLØV, SEALAND, DENMARK.

O. N. R. M. Vol. 2, p. 522.

? SEHS-CUNÆ ÆOAHÆE.
To-the-SIGE-KEEN (triumph-daring. victorious) HORSEMAN.
Till-den-SEGERSÄLLE RYTTAREN.

Most likely refers here not to success in battle but to victory in some great Horse-race. perhaps at Constantinople.   But ÆOAHÆÆ *may* be a mansname.   Found in 1852, with 3 others of same type, and Nos. 39 and 55.

No. 7.

NEBENSTEDT, DANNENBERG, HANNOVER.

O. N. R. M. Vol. 2, p. 523. Vol. 3, p. 227.

? GAL GLYOÆU-GIAUYOU.

GAL to-the-lady-GLYOÆU-GIAUYOA.

GLEE-GIFT or GLEE-GIVERESS is a very fine womans-name. Found in 1859, together with Nos. 8 and 9.

No. 8.

NEBENSTEDT, DANNENBERG, HANNOVER.

O. N. R. M. Vol. 2. p. 524.

Found in 1859, with Nos. 7 and 9. Doubtful or barbarized. Possibly, considering this a careless copy of a better original, we may guess:

TO AULILYOÆ ÞAM TILLE.

TO AULILYO THE TILL (good).

No. 9.

NEBENSTEDT, DANNENBERG, HANNOVER.

O. N. R. M. Vol. 2. p. 524.

Found in 1859, with Nos. 7 and 8. I would now read the staves from below upwards, taking the TA as a clear bind. This gives us the mansname:

TALLWE.

No. 10.

DENMARK, UNKNOWN WHERE.

O. N. R. M. Vol. 2, p. 525.

Not known when found. Meaningless. My guess in 1867 was:

TO GLWK. YOLW HAC.

TO LUCK! YOLW HEWED (carved).

No. 11.

RANDLEV, VIBORG SEE, DENMARK.

O. N. R. M. Vol. 2, p. 525.

Found about 1820. Meaningless. My guess in 1867 was:

TU LUCGWN!

TO LUCK! (Luck to you!)

Nos. 12, 13.

DENMARK, UNKNOWN WHERE.

O. N. R. M. Vol. 2, p. 526.

No. 12, Find-tide unknown. — No. 13, found in the last half of the 17th century. Barbarous. My guess in 1867 was:

TU HIL.

TO HELE! (To Luck!, Hail to thee!)

No. 14.

FAXØ. SEALAND, DENMARK.

O. N. R. M. Vol. 2, p. 527.

Found in 1827. I now take this as the mansname:

FOSLÆU.

•

Nos. 15. 16.

15 SLANGERUP, SEALAND. — 16. SLESVIG or HOLSTEIN.

O. N. R. M. Vol. 2, p. 528.

See No. 18. — No. 15 found before 1817, No. 16 before 1852. Both bear the same mansname:

ÆLU.

No. 17.

DENMARK, UNKNOWN WHERE.

O. N. R. M. Vol. 2, p. 529.

172

Find-tide unknown. Doubtless barbarous. My guess in 1867 was:

ᚣOLSURU HUᚣOC COLLD ÆEÐÐLEO ELOÆ.

ᵧOLSURU HEWED (struck) this-GOLD-piece for-the-ATHEL (noble) ELO.

No. 18.

SNYDSTRUP, HADERSLEV, S. JUTLAND, DENMARK.

O. N. R. M. Vol. 2, p. 529. Vol. 3, p. 228.

See Nos. 15, 16 & 71. Found in 1841. — As remarkt by Prof. Bugge (Aarb. 1871, p. 183), the R in ÆRU was my woodcutter's error for L (ÆLU). Accordingly it is here rectified. I also agree with him (p. 199) in taking the 4th rune in 2nd word as a bind, c and æ. I therefore now read (nom. masc. and dat. masc.):

ÆLU LÆUCÆA.

ÆLU to-LÆUCÆ.

No. 19.

SKÅNE, SWEDEN.

O. N. R. M. Vol. 2, p. 530.

Found about 1840. Bugge, Om Runeindskr. på Guldbrak. p. 199, says rightly that the 8th rune is a bind, c and æ. The 2nd stave in next word has doubtless the same value. So I now read (dat. masc. and nom. masc.):

LÆWULOUCÆA GÆÆCALLU.

To- or for-LÆWULOUCÆ GÆÆCALLU (gave or made).

No. 20.

LELLINGE, SEALAND, DENMARK.

O. N. R. M. Vol. 2. p. 531.

SÆLU SÆLU.

SEEL! SEEL! (= Joy! Joy!, Health and Happiness!)
LYCKA! LYCKA!

Found in 1845.

No. 21.

HADERSLEV, SOUTH JUTLAND, DENMARK.

O. N. R. M. Vol. 2. p. 532.

Found in 1822. — Whether a name, a word, a contraction, we cannot say. Only 2 (or 3) letters. Probably the mansname:

LÆ (or GLÆ).

No. 22.

VADSTENA, EAST GOTLAND, SWEDEN.

O. N. R. M. Vol. 2. p. 533. Vol. 3, p. 229.

LUÞÆ TUWÆ.

Of-the-LEDES the-TOG. (Of-the-men the-letter-row. = The Alphabet of the people).

Followed by the first 23 letters of the Old-Northern Runic stave-row:

FUÞÆRCGW;   HNIᵧYOPAS;   TBEMLNGO.

Found in 1774.

No. 23.

OVERHORNBEK, RANDERS, NORTH JUTLAND, DENMARK.

O. N. R. M. Vol. 2, p. 537.

Found in 1848, with Nos. 28 and 30. — Apparently barbarous. My guess in 1867 was:

USSU, ATLITOÆ EÞILLO.

To-USSI, ATHLETE ATHEL (noble).

No. 24.

FYN, DENMARK.

O. N. R. M. Vol. 2, p. 538.   Vol. 3. p. 230.

Found early in the 17th century. — Bugge, Om Run. på Guldbr. p. 199, says the 3rd rune is more like Þ than W, and I agree with him. See the fellow-bracteate No. 55. I now propose:

NÆÞUYÆNG UYÆYLIIL ÆNN HOUÆA.

The-NÆTHUYÆNG UYÆYLIIL ANN (gives-this) to-HOUÆ.

No. 25.

KÖRKÖ (or TJÖRKÖ), CARLSKRONA, SWEDEN.

O. N. R. M. Vol. 2, p. 538.   Vol. 3, p. 230.

ÞUR TE RUNOA! — ÆNWLL, HÆ-CURNE HELDÆA, CUNIMUDIU.

THUR TEE (bless) these-RUNES! — ÆNWLL (= ÆNWULF), the-HIGH-CHOSEN of-the-HELTS (the Elect of the Heroes, the Chosen Leader of the Army), gives-this-to-the-lady-CUNIMUNDIA.

THUR SIGNE dessa-RUNOR! — ÆNWLL, HJELTARNES HÖGT-UTKORADE (Härens utvalde Höfding), gifver-detta-till CUNIMUNDIA.

Found in 1817, together with No. 33. — The dialect here is pure *old* Scandinavian. The name is unknown in Germany, and only occurs here in all Scandinavia. But this rare ANWULF is the name borne by a "Goth" (ANAOLF) who, in 430, at the head of his troops fought against the Roman General Aëtius in Gaul, and was by him defeated and taken prisoner. — Later, a family bearing this name, (EANULF and other spellings), are kinglets in England in the early times, especially the 9th century, and have their seat and power in Somersetshire.

In my Vol. 3, Bracteate No. 75, I have brought together a mass of arguments which, in my opinion, connect this family with the ANWULF (ÆNIWULU) on the Golden Triens No. 75. I there conclude: — "Apparently, in 430 a Swedish-Gothic folk-king called ANWULF fights in the ranks of the Goths in Gaul, but is defeated and made prisoner. Doubtless ransomed or for a time in Roman pay and service, he returns to his country. How long or short *his* life or his *son's*, we cannot say. People *sometimes* lived very long *then* as now. But his son or grandson strikes this beautiful golden Bracteate for CUNIMUNDIA, and sword in hand among bands of other Northmen gains broad lands in England. Here he strikes the golden Triens for the commerce of his people. In time his race are no longer kinglets, but become great chiefs and barons in the English monarchy. Thereafter they disappear. New times, new men. But if this so be, we have here *the first* tie connecting the Bracteates with acknowledged history, and *for the first time* loose objects bearing the Old-Northern runes are brought in contact with our regular annals. I may be so much the more excused in drawing this conclusion, as this is the *only* instance in which I have ventured to give any such loose Old-Northern piece a direct historical application."

No. 26.

SKÅNE. SWEDEN.

O. N. R. M. Vol. 2. p. 539.

Found about 1840, with 2 specimens of No. 19. — Perhaps the mansname:

FUWU (or FUÞU).

No. 27.

TROLLHÄTTA, SWEDEN.

O. N. R. M. Vol. 2. p. 540.

Found in 1844. — May be taken in many ways. Had we a thousand more such monuments. our doubts would be the fewer. I now prefer:

TÆWON ÆÞODU.

TÆWON-made-this for-the-lady-ÆTHODA.

No. 28.

OVERHORNBEK, RANDERS. NORTH JUTLAND, DENMARK.

O. N. R. M. Vol. 2. p. 540.

Found in 1848, with Nos. 23 and 30. — Perhaps barbarous and comparatively late in date. In 1867 my guess was:

SIHUIN ÆND BÆYOUI UUO BÆDE EUWÆDIT.

SIHUIN AND BÆyOUI, SLEW-them BOTH EUWÆTHIT.

No. 29.

CÖRLIN (or CÖSLIN), POMERANIA.

O. N. R. M. Vol. 2, p. 541.

Found in 1839, with the Cörlin (or Cöslin) Golden Ring. See THE GOTHIC MARCH. — Bears only the mansname:

WÆIGÆ (or ÐÆIGÆ).

No. 30.

OVERHORNBEK, RANDERS, NORTH JUTLAND, DENMARK.

O. N. R. M. Vol. 2, p. 542.

Found in 1848, together with Nos. 23 & 28. — Probably as meaningless and comparatively late as No. 28. In 1867 I proposed:

ÆGELÆ BLÆ, BÆSULOE, SYGTRYH.

For-ÆGEL the-BLUE, BASILEUS (king), SYGTRYH (made this).

No. 31.

FYN, DENMARK.

O. N. R. M. Vol. 2, p. 543.

Blind-runes or contractions.   Found in the last half of the 17th century.

No. 32.

ECKERNFÖRDE, SOUTH JUTLAND, DENMARK.

O. N. R. M. Vol. 2, p. 543.

Found in the first half of this year-hundred. — I would now prefer:

TWÆD TIWITÆ.

TWÆD to-TIWIT.

Nos. 33, 34.

33. KÖRKÖ (or TJÖRKÖ), CARLSKRONA, SWEDEN.
34. SKÅNE, SWEDEN.

O. N. R. M. Vol. 2, p. 544.

Both found early in this century; the former in 1817, with No. 25. — Each bears the same mansname:

OTÆ.

Nos. 35—41. b.

SWEDEN; DENMARK; NORWAY.

O. N. R. M. Vol. 2. p. 544—46.

All bear the same name or word (? dat or nom), = to-INGE (mansname), INGA (womansname), or possibly YOUNGSTER, to-BABY.

No. 35. probably found in Sweden, not known when.

ICÆA.

No. 36. Found in Fyn, Denmark, about the middle of the 17th century.

YCÆA.

No. 37. Denmark; found in 1845.

ÝIA.

No. 38. Denmark, unknown when.

ICHIAY.

No. 39.   Maglemose, Vallerslov, Sealand, Denmark.   Found in 1852, in conjunction with Nos. 6 and 55.

ꝅꞓ.ÆA.

No. 40.   Frederiksstad, Smålenenes Amt, Norway.

UGꝄHA.

No. 41.   Sweden, found before 1861.

ꝅꝄꞓ.ÆA.

No. 41, b.   Sogndal, Bergen, Norway, in 1861.   Barbarized.

ꝅGŒA.

See Nos. 83. 84.

No. 42.

SKÅNE, SWEDEN.

O. N. R. M. Vol. 2, p. 547.

Not known when found. — Either an ornament or a bind-rune. If the latter perhaps the mansname

ITO.

Nos. 43—46.

CHIEFLY SWEDEN.

O. N. R. M. Vol. 2, p. 547.   Vol. 3, p. 231.

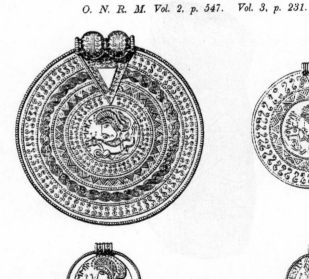

The large Blink to the top left, No. 43, found in Sweden but not known when; No. 44, the top right, found in Gotland in 1843; and the Swedish No. 45, find-tide unknown, all agree in what I now read as the mansname

ELTIL.

No. 46 was found long ago in Denmark, date not markt. It reads, a mansname,

TIL.

See Nos. 85, 86, 87.

No. 47.

SKÅNE, SWEDEN.

O. N. R. M. Vol. 2, p. 548.

Not known when found. — Only the mansname

ELWU.

No. 48.

NORWAY.

O. N. R. M. Vol. 2, p. 549.

Find-tide not known. — Accidentally mis-redd on p. 549. As the staves are reverst, the word must begin from below. The mansname

ÆNOÆNÆ.

Nos. 49, 49 b.

49. VÅSBY. SKÅNE, SWEDEN.
49, b. ESKATORP, HALLAND, SWEDEN.

O. N. R. M. Vol. 2. p. 549, 875.   Vol. 3. p. 231.

Both these pieces have the small errors common with careless die-cutters, but the two texts agree in nearly every particular.   The I in FIHÆDU is hidden by the triangular ornament under the loop.   No. 49 is more correct than 49, b.   The common text, by comparison of both, is:

ᛒᚺLÆÆDU-UIGÆ ALTE-UILÆA FIHÆDU.

HLÆDWIG for-ALTE-UILÆ FAWED (made this).

HLÆDU-WIGÆ means LADE-WIGG, *Pack-horse, Carrying-nag, Sumpter-horse.*   The design in the center is therefore the Goldsmith's Sign or Rebus-play on his own name.   No other Bracteate, with or without runes, bears the above type.   But, as we know, these Blinks are often excessively barbarous.   On some the Helm or Cap, on others the Head, on others the Neck, on others the Animal, almost or entirely disappears.   We may therefore say that the Rebus is "not proven".   But this will not alter the reading, which is so simple and plain and grammatically correct that it remains unshaken.

Find-tide of No. 49 not registered. — No. 49, b. was dug up in 1867.

No. 50.

DENMARK, FINDSTEAD UNKNOWN.

O. N. R. M. Vol. 2, p. 550.

The staves apparently give no meaning, are blind or contractions.   In 1867 I guest at TUU (the God's name) &c.

Nos. 51, 52.

51. BOLBRO, FYN, DENMARK. — 52. VEDBY, FYN, DENMARK.

O. N. R. M. Vol. 2, p. 550.

No. 51 was found in 1852 with No. 56; No. 52 in 1860. Comparing the two, I now propose to read:

OWÆ-ALUT EÆÐLÆUA.

OWÆ-ALUT made (or gave) -this to EÆTHLÆU.

No. 53.

LØGSTØR, NORTH JUTLAND, DENMARK.

O. N. R. M. Vol. 2, p. 551.

Perhaps only barbarous or contractions. Found in 1841. My guess in 1867 (taking the M, E, to be cut in half at the top), the mansname: ETLSTN (= ETHELSTAN).

No. 54.

FYN, DENMARK.

O. N. R. M. Vol. 2, p. 552.

Found in 1848. Only the mansname: LAOKU.

No. 55.

MAGLEMOSE, VALLERSLØV, SEALAND, DENMARK.

O. N. R. M. Vol. 2, p. 552.

Found in 1852, with Nos. 6 and 39. See my remarks on the fellow-bracteate No. 24.
I now explain the simplified ᛗ and the ᚾ with the side-stroke on the right, as caused by the
extremely narrow space, and propose:

SIHMYWNT ÆNN HO(uæ)A.

SIBMYWNT (= SIGMUND) ANN (gives-this) to-HOUÆ.

No. 56.

BOLBRO, FYN, DENMARK.

O. N. R. M. Vol. 2, p. 553.

Found in 1852, with No. 51. Probably barbarous. My guess in 1867 was:

USCEUNIA KOWT HUC ECETIOeA(STU) HILTU UFFTÆIC.

USCEUNIA the-GOTH HEWED-this for-the-most-illustrious HELT (hero) UFFTI(N)G.

No. 57.

SEALAND, DENMARK.

O. N. R. M. Vol. 2. p. 554.   Vol. 3. p. 233.

This costly golden blink was dug up in 1852.   Unique type, a War-Chief spear in hand.   I now agree with Bugge that the 13th rune is C. not L, and read:

HÆ UIU.

HÆ HÆITICÆ.

FÆUÆ. UISÆ! —

GIB UÆLYÆ (TIU)!

Wage thy-battle.
publish thy-war-ban.
O-Fœua our-Wisa (Leader. Captain)! –
Give weal (success) (O God Tiu)!

BATTLE STOUTLY,
BAN THY FOE,
O-FÆUA OUR LEADER! —
GIVE LUCK (O TIU)!

Begynn din kamp, utrop förbannelse öfver fienden, O-Fæua, vår Höfding. —
Gif framgång (O Tiu)!

Should this be so, this is the only Bracteate on which I have found stave-rune verse. — We have an echo of such a Northern Battle-cry in the Hervara Saga. Ch. 18. Bugge's ed., Sec. 92, 93; and in Eyrbyggja Saga, ed. G. Vigfusson, Leipzig 1864. Ch. 44. p. 82. — See the unique example of the Spear-shaft inscribed with the War-ban, to be cast over the border, under KRAGEHUL, Denmark.

No. 58.

HARLINGEN, FRISLAND.

O. N. R. M. Vol. 2. p. 554.

Found before 1846.   Bears the mansname: HAMA.

No. 59:

HESSELAGERGÅRD. FYN. DENMARK.

O. N. R. M. Vol. 2. p. 555. Vol. 3, p. 234.

Not correctly given in Thomsen's Atlas, from which my engraving was made. I therefore re-copy it here from the original, by the kind permission of its owner, the Chamberlain F. Sehested, Broholm, Fyn. The runes may perhaps be divided:

TE NU AD.Æ. OD.

TEE (give) NOW EAD (fortune, happiness) O-OD (= ODIN, WODEN).

But all this is doubtful. The solitary letters may be contractions, and the whole can be variously groupt. — Found in 1856.

No. 60.

ULDERUP, SOUTH JUTLAND. DENMARK.

O. N. R. M. Vol. 2, p. 556.

Found in 1856. May be NIKUI or NUKUI.

No. 61.

FINLAND.

O. N. R. M. Vol. 2, p. 557.

Silver bracteate from 11th or 12th age. Found early in this century.

JULIENI HŪUG ÆMILIU.

JULIENI (= JULIAN) HEWED (struck this) for-the-lady-ÆMILIA.

No. 62.

GÅRDSBY, ÖLAND, SWEDEN.

O. N. R. M. Vol. 2, p. 557.

Find-date not known. Copper blink. Also very late.

IOHN BO.

JOHN HEWED (struck this).

No. 63.

LEKENDE, SEALAND, DENMARK.

O. N. R. M. Vol. 2, p. 558.

Found in 1864. This fine Golden Blink bears only 2 wend-staves — ᴇᴁ —, which, if not a name or a contraction, may mean *AYE. for-AYE, EVER-YOURS.*

No. 64.

SWEDEN.

O. N. R. M. Vol. 2, p. 558.

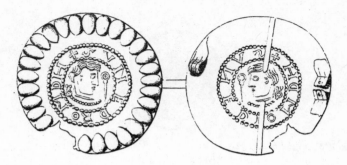

Not known when found. Silver. In Roman letters. If not a contraction (perhaps of Latin words), only the mansname: SUNEDROMDH.

No. 65.

SKÅRKIND PARISH, EAST GOTLAND, SWEDEN.

O. N. R. M. Vol. 2. p. 559.

Found early in this year-hundred. Golden blink. Also Roman staves, and one in Greek. I now read:

TVTO AIVOMIA VRωITO.

TUTO for-the-lady-AIVOMI WROUGHT (made this).

No. 66.

ILAND OF GOTLAND, SWEDEN.

O. N. R. M. Vol. 2. p. 559.

Found in 1837. Middle-age. Silver. Latin staves. Has been mounted on a Chalice or Book &c.

† MAIESTAS: OTI ME FECIT.

Christ-the-Divine-MAJESTY. OTI ME MADE.

No. 67.

SKODBORG MARK, SOUTH JUTLAND, DENMARK.

O. N. R. M. Vol. 2, p. 560.

Found in 1865. Beautiful Golden Blink; nearby lay a golden Brooch of delicate workmanship. All the runes reverst. Begins right, above the Holy Symbol, and runs left.

SÆLÆW IMÆ UNGÆ ÆLÆWINÆ, UNGÆ ÆLÆWINÆ, UNGÆ ÆLÆWIN'.

SEEL (happiness, good luck, success) to-THE YOUNG ÆLÆWINÆ, the-YOUNG ÆLÆWINÆ, the-YOUNG ÆLÆWINÆ!

No. 68.

ØLST, NORTH JUTLAND, DENMARK.

O. N. R. M. Vol. 2, p. 561.

This golden Bracteate was found in 1863.   Reverst staves.

H.EG .ELU.

HEWED ÆLU (= Ælu struck this piece).

No. 69.

DENMARK.

O. N. R. M. Vol. 2, p. 562.

Either a mere mark or a bind-rune. — When found is not known.

No. 70.

WYK. UTRECHT, HOLLAND.

O. N. R. M. Vol. 2, p. 563.   Vol. 3, p. 235.

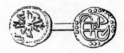

Silver Runic Coin, dug up in 1836, the only one ever found in Holland.   The last date of the other coins lying with it is about 840.   I now agree with Mr. Haigh in taking the first stave to be an inverted L, not a C.

LUL ON ÁUASÀ (or maybe ÁUSA).

LUL ON (of) ÁUASA or ÁUSA (struck this piece).

The ornamental monogram in my opinion gives us the king's name: ECGBERHT. — This suits ECGBERHT titular king of Wessex, but in fact of all England, who died in 836.

No. 71.

BÖRRINGE. VEMMENHÖG HÄRAD, SKÅNE, SWEDEN.

O. N. R. M. Vol. 2, p. 876.

See Nos. 15, 16, 18, 19. Found in 1855. — I now agree with Bugge (Om Rune-indskr. på Guldbr. p. 199) in reading the last word as ÆÆLÆUCÆA. Runes turned round.

TÆNULU ÆÆLÆUCÆA.

TÆNULU (= *DANE-WOLF*) *to-ÆÆLÆUCÆ.*

No. 72.

VISBY KUNGS-LADUGÅRD, GOTLAND, SWEDEN.

O. N. R. M. Vol. 2, p. 877.

Found in 1860. Reverst staves. Bears the mansname: AUTO.

No. 73.

GOTLAND, SWEDEN.

O. N. R. M. Vol. 2, p. 878.

Wend-runes. Found in 1865, probably at Gurfiles, in Ahla Parish. Bears the mans-name: NADÆ.

No. 74.

ENGLAND.

O. N. R. M. Vol. 2, p. 879, LXVIII.

Not known when found. Can only be traced back to king George III, in whose Cabinet it was. Barbaric Golden Solidus. The English provincial runes are apparently only one word, the mansname: SCANOMODU.

No. 75.

ENGLAND.

O. N. R. M. Vol. 3, p. 236.

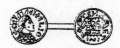

Found at the beginning of this century. Barbarian Golden Triens, in the British Museum. Like No. 74, struck in England. Bears in back-runes on obverse:

ÆNIWULU KU(nung).

ÆNIWULU (= ANWULF) KING.

Has also, in Latin letters, C LIO, which the other copy shows is a contraction for — CORNILIO —, doubtless the name of ANWULF's Chief Fiscal Officer or Head of the Royal Mint. — On reverse we have, in Latin letters, the name of the Moneyer in the genitive (MOT understood): TENAES.

The Leyden Museum possesses a later barbarized copy of this piece, also in gold. When found not known, but before 1870. The obverse omits the runes, but gives the full name:

CORNILIO. — Reverse, also in Latin staves: TENES M. Thus *TEN'S (= DANE'S or DAN'S) MOT (Mothouse or Mint, or Coin, Stamp, Die. — See No. 25.*

No. 76.

DALUM, N. TRONYEM, NORWAY.

O. N. R. M. Vol. 3, p. 245.

Barbarous-runic golden Bracteate. A copy's copy's copy. — Found in 1868.

No. 77.

EASTLEACH TURVILLE, GLOUCESTERSHIRE, ENGLAND.

O. N. R. M. Vol. 3, p. 246.

Found about 1868. English golden Trimessis, of about the 5th century. Bears the common mansname:

BEA(R)TIGO *(= BEARTING, BRIBTING).*

No. 78.

NÆSBJERG, NORTH JUTLAND, DENMARK.

O. N. R. M. Vol. 3, p. 247.

Coarsely cut and difficult to read. Retrograde runes. I venture on the following, taking the small mark after G to be divisional:

TISÆCG HU HÆRÆNGU.

TISÆCG HEWED (cut this) for-the-lady-HÆRÆNGA.

Found in 1870, together with 2 copies from the same die of No. 79, and 3 exemplars from the same stamp of No. 80, besides several other runeless golden Bracteates and some small pieces of golden work, all apparently from the 5th or 6th age.

No. 79.

NÆSBJERG, NORTH JUTLAND, DENMARK.

O. N. R. M. Vol. 3, p. 248.

Found in 1870. See No. 78. Right word as usual. Left word, runes reverst. Apparently we must read:

DÆITUHÆ LILIAÆIWU.

DÆITUHÆ to-the-lady-LILIAÆIWA.

No. 80.

NÆSBJERG, NORTH JUTLAND, DENMARK.

O. N. R. M. Vol. 3, p. 248.

This elegant golden Blenket will always remain doubtful, because the last word (staves reverst) — for want of room — is contracted. The vowels are left out. Usually, in this case, it is the simple vowel I, which is supposed to be included on the foregoing stave. I therefore venture to look on this as a kind of Burial-Medal in memory of a deceast Chieftain, and translate:

NIUWILÆ LDN (= LIDIN).

NIUWILÆ is-LITHEN (dead, is no more).

·As LIDIN properly means *gone,* it is *possible* that it here may signify *departed on some war-expedition.* — A part of the gold-hoard found in 1870. See No. 78.

No. 81.

? MECKLENBURG.

O. N. R. M. Vol. 3. p. 249.

This golden Bracteate bears only one rune, the A, of course the beginning of some word. See NYDAM MOSS, DENMARK, where one of the Arrows has this letter. — Not known when found.

No. 82.

KILLERUP, FYN, DENMARK.

O. N. R. M. Vol. 3, p. 249.

Unhappily a fragment. The runes are

UNDA

but this may be the end of the name, and other words may have followed. The type is rare, the classical motive of the Emperor the Cæsar and Victory. — Part of a gold-hoard, Bracteates and other pieces, found in 1874. Only this one and No. 83 bore runes. It belongs to that class of blinks which illustrates the "Barbaric Gems".

No. 83.

KILLERUP, FYN, DENMARK. ·

O. N. R. M. Vol. 3, p. 255.

Found with No. 82 in 1874.   See No. 84.   Same type as Nos. 35—41, b, which see, and bears substantially the same name (INGE, INGWE), namely: INKI.

No. 84.

HILLERØD, SEALAND, DENMARK.

O. N. R. M. Vol. 3, p. 255.

Found in 1874.   See Nos. 35—41, b, and 83. — Also, as far as I can see, same name as the last, namely, the womans-name (INGA): YÆCA.

Nos. 85—87.

GOTLAND, SWEDEN.

O. N. R. M. Vol. 2, p. 874.   Vol. 3, p. 256.

25*

See Nos. 43, 44, 45. — No. 85, found at Burge in 1859, my 45, b., p. 874, which see. — No. 86 a variation of the above; so nearly identical with No. 45 that it need not be engraved; found at Allmungs in 1873. — No. 87 was found at Djupbrunns in 1872. They all 3, as far as I can see, bear the mansname: ELTIL.

No. 88.

DJUPBRUNNS, HOGRÄNS PARISH, GOTLAND, SWEDEN.

O. N. R. M. Vol. 3, p. 256.

Found with No. 87. Back-runes. Like Nos. 15, 16 bears only the mansname: ÆLU.

No. 89.

UNKNOWN WHERE. — PROBABLY DENMARK.

O. N. R. M. Vol. 3. p. 257.

Observed early in 1876 by Archivary C. F. Herbst among the barbarous Coins in Thomsen's Collection in the Danish Coin-Cabinet. Is a flan of SILVER, struck only on one side, of the usual weight and size of the olden Silver Penny. Museum number 12.186; weight 1.31 grammes. Has been much cut on both sides to see that it was pure metal, and is a good deal worn. Some of the letter-marks are so slight, that they could not be given by the artist. The NO are especially difficult, but there is no doubt that the first word was a mansname. I take the runes to have been:

FÆGANO FÆÆÐÆ.

FÆGANO FAWED (made, struck, this piece).

Apparently a *trial-piece* by a journeyman or beginner in the 7th century, and as such as yet unique. The G (X), A (ᛉ) and (? O, ᛟ) are special O. N. staves, as well as the (Æ) ᚫ.

No. 90.

GETTORF, SOUTH JUTLAND, DENMARK.

O. N. R. M. Vol. 3, p. 258.

Two golden Bracteates were found by a poor person in the Duchy of Slesvig or South Jutland. They past into the hands of a merchant in Kolding, who sold the one here given to the Kiel Museum. It is Runic-Roman-Barbarous, and of course meaningless.

No. 91.

GETTORF, SOUTH JUTLAND, DENMARK.

O. N. R. M. Vol. 3, p. 258.

This is the second Blink, which the owner has hitherto refused to sell or publish or have copied. It is very beautiful, bears a rude Mans-head and the Felefoot, and the following runes:

ᛁᚠᛚᚷᛈᚾ

TÆLINGWU.

To the-lady-TÆLINGWA.

Observe the rune for ING, and see Bracteate No. 78 and the Kovel Spear-head.

No. 92.

LUND, SKÅNE, SWEDEN.

O. N. R. M. Vol. 3, p. 258.

Silver bracteate, found in 1878 in a garden, Lund, Skåne, formerly a Danish folkland. Curious for the masterly intermixture of the Old-Northern, the Old-Roman and the common runic alphabets. Apparently reads:

IAULIGR I SIMI FYIDI IAUÞINI I BIRKOIINUM.

IAULIG (= JOLGEIR) IN SIM (= SEM in N. Jutland) FAWED (struck this) for-IAUÞIN (= EAÞWIN) IN BIRKWIN (= BERGEN, in West Norway).

Type of KNUD V, Magnusson, king of Denmark 1147—1154. SIM is apparently the parish and district now spelt SEM or SEEM near Ribe in North Jutland, Denmark.

No. 93.

WAPNÖ, POSEN, POLAND.

O. N. R. M. Vol. 3, p. 259.

All I know about this Bracteate is, that it is spoken of in passing without further details by Dr. Wimmer, in his letter on the Kovel runic Spear-head. See "Materialien zur Vorgeschichte des Menschen im östlichen Europa", by Kohn and Mehlis, Vol. 2, 8vo, Jena 1879, p. 181. Dr. W. gives the inscription as ᚱᚨᛒᚨᛊ, which will be the mansname: SÆBÆR.

No. 94.

SKIEN, SOLUM PARISH, LOWER THELEMARKEN, S. NORWAY.

O. N. R. M. Vol. 3, p. 260.

In the summer of 1879 *two* copies of this Golden Blink, struck from the same die, were found in a Lady's grave. Several other objects, including a fine silver Brooch, lay nearby. Date apparently the 6th century. Would seem to be, as often, the formula of a nominative and a dative. I take TAÆ (= TAHÆ) to be the common mansname TAA, in England TOE, and the ELWÆO to be a womansname. Thus:

TAÆ ELWÆO.

TAÆ (made-this-for, or, gave-this-to) the-lady-ELWÆ.

No. 95.

ÅGEDAL, BJELLAND, LISTER AND MANDALS AMT, NORWAY.

O. N. R. M. Vol. 3, p. 261.

Found in 1879 in a Lady's grave, containing many rich remains which had escaped the funeral pyre. Date at least as early as No. 94. Inscription apparently barbarous.

THE GOTHIC MARCH.

THANKFULLY INSCRIBED

TO

THE REV. ISAAC TAYLOR, M. A., LL. D.

SETTRINGTON, ENGLAND.

BUZEU, WALLACHIA, ROUMANIA.

? DATE ABOUT A. D. 200—250.

Old-N. R. Mon. Vol. 2. p. 567. Vol. 3. p. 265.

Belongs to the so-called Pétrossa treasure, a golden hoard found in 1838 in old Dacia. Engraved full size. The mound and ruins point out the place as a heathen temple of the Goths, to which this gold-ring was given. — I now divide and translate:

GUTÆ NIO WI HÆILÆG.

Of-the-GOTHS to-the-NEW WIH (temple) HOLY. = *Dedicated to the new-built fane of the Goths.*

KOVEL, VOLHYNIA, RUSSIA.

? DATE ABOUT A. D. 300—400.

Old-N. R. Mon. Vol. 3. p. 266.

Iron Lance-head, the figures and letters filled-in with silver inlay. Full size. Ploughed up in 1858 near Suszyizno, some miles north-east of the hamlet Kovel; now the property of Prof. A. Ssyszkowski, of Warsaw. Bears the owner's name:

TILÆRINGS

a mansname here found for the first time. — Belongs to the early warlike and mercantile wanderings of the Northmen into the Slavic lands, out of which they eventually carved RUSSIA, from RUOTSI, ROTSI, the name given by the Wendish Estonians and wild Fins to the nearest Swedish coast at ROS-LAGEN.

MÜNCHEBERG, MARK-BRANDENBURG, NOW IN GERMANY.

? DATE ABOUT A. D. 300—400.
Old-N. R. Mon. Vol. 2. p. 880.

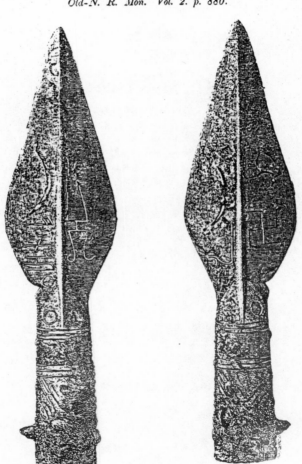

Found in 1865, with other weapons &c. in a grave from the cremation period. The district was Scando-Gothic till about A. D. 300—400, when it was overrun by Wendish (Slavic) tribes. The ornaments and staves inlaid with silver. Full size. — Bears only the mansname:

RÆNINGÆ.

CÖRLIN, POMERANIA, NOW A PART OF GERMANY.

? DATE ABOUT A. D. 400—500.

Old-N. R. Mon. p. 600.

We cannot tell whether the bind-stave above the ÆLU be ÆL or LÆ or yo, or something other; nor whether it is to be taken separately, or with the following word, the mansname:

ÆLU.

Full size. Golden Fingerring, found in 1839 at Cörlin or Cöslin together with a hoard of other golden pieces, including the Bracteate No. 29 and 5 other such which were runeless.

? BOHEMIA.

See the Golden Blink No. 3.

? MECKLENBURG.

See the Golden Bracteate No. 81.

WAPNÖ, POSEN, POLAND.

See the Golden Bracteate No. 93.

WANDERERS.

THE BUZEU RING.

See under THE GOTHIC MARCH.

---

2 NORDENDORF BROOCHES.

See under ENGLAND.

OSTHOFEN BROOCH.

See under ENGLAND.

THE CHARNAY BROOCH.

See under NORWAY.

THE CÖRLIN RING.

See under THE GOTHIC MARCH.

THE BRUNSWICK CASKET.

See under ENGLAND.

THE FREI-LAUBERSHEIM BROOCH.

See under NORWAY.

THE FRANKS CASKET.

See under ENGLAND.

EMS, NASSAU.

? DATE ABOUT A. D. 500—600.

Old-N. R. Mon. Vol. 3, p. 274.

Fragment of a Silver Brooch, found some years ago. Never properly publisht. Dr. M. Rieger thought it had still left on one side ᚢᚹᚫᛞᚫ and on the other ᛗᛁᛞᚫᛞᛝᚷ, the above drawing *not* being correct. — The Pin is doubtless of English origin.

THE WORD-HOARD.

That the reader may the better grasp all the linguistic teachings handed over to us in these precious Scando-Anglic runic remains — the oldest we have of our noble Northern mother-tung in its wide-spread local talks —, I have thought it best to gather together the whole word-stuff in 3 separate groups. For further details see the Word-lists at the end of Vols 2 and 3. In the vocables here given some errors may hereafter be found, for I have repeatedly said that my work is only tentative. We must modestly creep slowly on. Every fresh runic piece helps us to amend, in one direction or another. But still, whatever the shortcomings, I think and hope that in general my readings will be found substantially correct, and consequently that we may use with some confidence at least most of the considerable number of words here before us. A few years back, not even an enthusiast could have dreamed of getting half so many.

All this, however, is on one condition, my being right in my main stand, that the Old-Northern rune-stave ᛦ is a vowel, and this vowel A. An opposing school in Scandinavia has long ago decided (of course at once, and *without appeal,* and in the name of what it calls "High Science"), that this ᛦ is a consonant and this consonant -R, end-R, the falling -R of a word, or of a syllable in a word where it is not a part of the root. — The difference is immense, revolutionizes everything. In fact so serious a discrepancy could only arise in the infancy of this little-studied Old-Northern Rune-lore, when the material was so comparatively slender, and the few monuments gave scarcely any acknowledged formulas. As fresh inscriptions continue to come in, we are better and better able to see our way. Within the last score years or so the number of these pieces has been nearly doubled. So I think we ought now to be able to decide this cardinal question, one way or the other. Let us then take the general outcome of what we this moment have.

But in so doing let us remember, that the only honest and solid Philology is that which is Analagous and Comparative and Comprehensive, everywhere following FACTS. If this be admitted, we must also bear in mind the hundreds of olden overgang Scando-Gothic dialects which have left no written trace behind them, but which have in many ways led up to those which have; — and the endless changes local speech has undergone even in the same landscape; — and the equal right of any and every Runic or Romanlettered piece, stone or metal or wood or parchment, to represent what was then and there spoken, as well as the later skinbooks in a partly fixt and schooled book-tung. But even these latter, as drawn out in Grammars, are largely falsified, scarce older or later forms being usually past over and the

27*

paradigms showing only the "vulgar" forms, while the words are often corrupted and "systematized by the editor" so as to destroy unwelcome peculiarities, sometimes the whole being what is called a "normal text", — that is, wastepaper. [1]

The influence of *time* also, as well as of *place*, must be considered, for time will bring language in one district to the same worn standard as *much earlier* but very *rapid* development in another. And in general 100 years will *largely alter* an "uncultivated" unfixt dialect in its grammar and genders and syntax and word-hoard, and in the meanings of those expressions which are not driven out by others. How much more will this be the case in the lapse of 500 or 1000 or 1500 years? Such epochs materially *re-create* a language. In England, helpt by runes, we can follow the course of our mothertung for nearly 1500 winters. Hence we can see the enormous developments from Old to Early English, and so to Middle and Later and Present English, — more or less in many things 5 speech-systems —, locally modified by scores of shire-talks, for convenience crusht into 3,j the Southern, the Midland and the Northern, the last further influenced by the mighty flood of wiking-settlers in the 9th and 10th centuries. So far therefore from the watchword of Modern Philology, "Unity and Iron Laws", we must largely build on very different TRUTHS, — "Variety and endless Caprice", as *all Nature thro.*

But to return. Assuming Y to be -R; even in the hands of great linguists the system has ended in this: most of these remains are *unreadable*, or only *partly* translatable with the aid of desperate archaisms or unknown constructions, giving meanings to say the least strange and paradoxical; or they are *contractions*; or else they are written in an *unknown tung* invented by the rune-cutter; or else they are *magic*. One must have the Gloves of Thunor to hold fast and doom a Salmon-Lóké school which is helpt by loop-holes like these! — But the doctrine also says that in this olden time — say the first 700 years after Christ — the characteristic nominative-ending of Scandinavia was -R. Some of these epigraphs are much older than Mæso-Gothic, with its exceptionally frequent and favorite -s. This nom. -s, (also common in forn Classical dialects), in Scandinavia as elsewhere eventually passes into -R, and then (Iceland excepted) falls away altogether in the Scandian tungs. But it (and not -R) holds on here and there in the oldest Northern runics, which show 3 nominatives in -s in the sing. and 1 in the plural, and it also survives locally in a score or two pieces bearing Scandinavian or *later* runes, down to the Christian age. The nom. mark was therefore of old still *often* -s, but *never* -R. How then could the *later* -R be the *old* and *primitive* Old-Northern characteristic? As nom. and ac. pl. ending also, this -s is largely vocalized and falls away in most of the *oldest* Scandian runics and parchments; afterwards when this plural consonant revives, the later -R for the older -s in plurals becomes organic in Scandinavia, where, Danish excepted which has no -R in some classes, the common plural mark becomes usually -R. — In the same way, we have in Scandinavia in the oldest runics and vellums such words as IS (our IS, 3 s. pr. and our AS, who or which), and WAS, UAS (our WAS, 3 s. p.). But they also soon get the weaker sound, IR, ER, WAR, VAR, as in some English shires. But this ancient Y *must not be* and therefore *is not* A. What then are we to do with the O. N. runic words

---

[1] See my remarks hereon in the paper "On the Dialect of the First Book printed in Swedish", in Nova Acta Reg. Soc. Sc. Ups. Ser. 3, Vol. 10, part 2, 4to. Upsala 1879.

actually containing it? Nothing is easier. Where it stands *alone*, and is therefore an independent word or else the first letter of a word, it is simply *ignored*. Where it occurs in *the beginning* or *middle* of a word (as in ACEDÆN, AH, ASPING; FAÞUR, INOFASTI, LAING, LAU, TIÞAS), its existence is *denied*, however plainly it may stand; or else all the letters are pronounced *contractions*; should all this be impossible, then the whole is declared to be *magic*, a *"magical formula"*. At the *end* of a word, as for instance in substantives dat. and ac. sing and nom. and ac. pl., it *cannot* be, for this would clash with "Icelandic Grammar"! Yet we naturally expect by sound "Comparative Philology" -A or some such vowel in the oldest Scandian in the like places, for it more or less survived there in *all* the *most antique* Scando-Gothic moles.

But this whole -R system was based on the strange theory, that *one language only* was from the Iron Age downwards spoken over all the Scandian lands; — and that this "Old-Northern" tung was *Icelandic*[1] (the comparatively modern book-dialect whose oldest specimens date from about A. D. 1200 or a little before); — and that therefore the nom. -R ending, and the Infinitive in -A or -Æ or -E, and the Post-article, and the Passive (or Middle) Verb, &c. were necessarily "Old-Northern" as being Icelandic. Hence all dialects not having these peculiarities were unholy and unworthy, and *could not* belong to the Scandian group. Modern Scandinavian doubtless remains such, tho usually it has long since *lost* the nom. -R mark, and in many of its dialects *also* the end-vowel of the Infinitive, — just as *we* have done in England. *Oldest* English (by mixt immigration a mixt and worn dialect-cluster) never had the nom. -R mark and the Passive. It was therefore a *German* speech, tho German at one time often had the -R mark, and nearly developt a Passive in the same way as the later Scandinavians by its use of SIK (SICH), which in Scandia became -SK, -S, and tho large sweeps of German territory early dropt the end-N in the Infinitive, as was done in Scandinavia and North-England.

But the *oldest* runics show that strong nouns had -S as their nom. mark, tho, as in all the other Scando-Gothic tungs (and afterward surprisingly in the Early English and the later Saxon &c.), there was a great tendency to use *weak* forms.[2] Later down the stream

---

[1] I understand that many of the younger and more gifted speechmen in Scandinavia are now abandoning this Icelandic-Old-Northern Fetish. But when I began my battle against it, nearly 30 years ago, I was simply ostracised, execrated and excommunicated. — Nay, Prof. Sophus Bugge, who finds it necessary and useful as an argument to assist his new theory about the modern origin of the Scandinavian-English Mythology, *now* says (Studier over de nordiske Gude- og Heltesagns Oprindelse, I, 1, Christiania 1881, p. 3): "Rundt omkring i Norden raadede, saaledes som vi af Runeindskrifter maa slutte, den ældste Jærnalder og Mellemjærnalderen igjennem, altsaa vistnok til henimod Aar 800, et Sprog, som i Lyd, Former og Ordforraad stod paa et ganske andet Udviklingstrin end de i historisk Tid kjendte nordiske Tungemaal, altsaa ogsaa det Sprog, hvori endog de ældste i Sæmunds Edda optagne mythisk-heroiske Digte er affattede." *We must conclude from the Runic Inscriptions that in the Northern lands, thro the Oldest Iron-age and the Middle Iron-Aye, in other words apparently down to about the year 800, there prevailed a language which in sound and forms and word-material was in a quite other stage of development than the Northern tungs known to us in the historical period, and thus very different from that mole in which even the very oldest mythical-heroic poems in Sæmund's Edda are written.*

[2] With regard to the multitude of local speech-forms — in such immense territories as all the Scandian and Anglic folk-kingdoms during the space of a 1000 years; — of a *much less* land-group during a *much less* period a German dared to say in 1852: "The contrast between the Ohg. and the M. Goth. and Mhg. is immense. In the latter we find simple and transparent relationships in the roots; in the former are crowds of differences. In the one we have but one dialect, or rather no dialect at all but a general orthodox written language; in the Ohg. we meet a mixture of

turns, and a taste sets in for *strong* forms (which by that time show the -s weakened
to -R). — So also in Scandian as in all its sister-dialects. the Infin. must originally have
ended in -AN, tho. as in Old-North-English, this -N rapidly became nasalized and fell away.
Old-Scandian runic Infinitives earlier than A. D. 800 are deplorably rare; we have as yet
only 1, perhaps 2, which already end in -A, -Æ. But I have found *several* examples of
Scandian Infinitives in -AN locally surviving on ancient stones bearing the *later* runes. — It
is also now acknowledged that the primitive Scandian as little had the *Post*-Article as the
Jutland dialects, the English, and all the other eldest Scando-Gothic. The Scandian Passive or
Reflex verb and Post-Article are even more modern than the mighty Wiking outflow to
England in the 9th and 10th centuries. They brought nothing such over with them. for a
very good reason; they were not yet developt in their local talks at home.

On the other hand, the moment we build on Y being A, — these O. N. runic
inscriptions can be redd with reasonable satisfaction, if not always with absolute *certainty,*
for there are of course difficulties and we know little of the manners and dialects of old.
Even some of the things cut in the Scandinavian or *later* runes have not yet been fully
mastered by the best rune-smiths, particularly where the words are not divided by stops.
We find indeed in these oldest pieces no "Icelandic", or any other *one* governmental or
Chancery "written language" over such immense countries under manifold local chiefs, at a
period when no "Denmark" or "Norway" or "Sweden" or "England" existed. We see instead,
here as in every other land all the world over. many nearly allied patois showing the same
general characteristics amid endless minor differences, some being more laggard and conservative
others more go-ahead and revolutionary in admitting phonetic and grammatical changes. In a
word, holding fast A as the value of Y. the Jewels, Weapons, Tools. Grave-stones, bear
words in the usual natural style, scribbles or names or local funeral formulas exactly as
elsewhere, and just as we find them *continued* by *the same* populations on pieces carved with
the *later* runes.

I add two interesting *indirect* proofs[1] that this Y can really only mean A. The first
is, the well-known *fluctuation and interchange* in our dialects, old and new, between A and Æ,
E, the monuments and manuscripts (even in the same line) and the folk-talks swarming therewith. Now also these *oldest* runic pieces (many centuries older than the fornest vellums)

---

dialects, as it would seem in perpetual interweavement. And in like manner with the forms of inflexion."[1] — While as
to the abundance of *weak* forms in the oldest Northern local talks, which mostly afterwards swung over to *strong* forms,
till they at last usually fell away, I will appeal only to *one* authority.[2]

   [1] And here call attention to another, of a *technical* character. In the *later* runic alphabet, besides the *usual*
R (R), as in the *older* futhorc, there is a *second* or so-called *final* -R, A (or, shortened. I). By *the rule*, the former R
is used where that letter belongs to the root, the *second* form only in falling syllables, &c. Accordingly this A or I is
the proper mark for the nom. ending in -R. But *in fact*, the *latter* R is *often*, even on very old stones, used for the
former, sometimes R and A are used almost indiscriminately for each other. Now should the *Old-Northern* Y or A have
really had the power of R, how has it come to pass that R and Y or A have *never* interchanged, so that — thro the
whole O. N. R. period in all the Northern lands — we have *not one* example of a nom. ending in -R?

---

   [1] K. A. Hahn. Althochd. Gram. v. A. Jeitteles. Prag 1866, p. V. — [2] J. Grimm. Von Vertretung männ-
licher durch weiblicher Namensformen. 4to. Berlin 1858.

decidedly show a prevailing tendency to prefer the Æ-sound, especially in Scandinavia[1]. Else we cannot explain the fact, that in them we have often Æ or E where we otherwise *certainly* expect A, and that some of the ristings show no A at all! It is chiefly in the *dat. s. m.* that the A suffers little change. Remembering that the usual A (Y) is also stoopt (ᚪ), as the usual E (M) is also stoopt (ᚹ), let us take examples from each Scandinavian province:

	A.	Æ.	E.	Æ and E together.
Tanum, Sweden	1	5	—	5
Skärkind, „	2	6	—	6
Möjebro, „	2	9	—	9
Björketorp, „	7	24	4	28
Valsfjord. Norway	2	5	1	6
Tune, „	5	15	4	19
Torvik, „	1	4	—	4
Orstad, „	2	6	—	6
Thorsbjerg, Denmark	1	1	—	1
3 Vi Moss pieces, „	2	14	2	16
Gallehus, „	2	5	2	7
Kragebul, „	1	14	4	18
	28	108	17	125

Thus 28 A to 108 Æ, but to 125 Æ and E. — There is not the same *large* predominance of Æ (and E) in England, in whose provincial slightly-modified futhore Y is A. Y eA, yA, and ᚠ is Á, A, (while the exceptional Brough stone, which has no Æ, retains the Scandian ᚪ, ᚫ, for A), the ᚠ remaining Æ.

	Y.	T.	ᚠ.	Á, ᚫ.	A.	Æ.	E.	Æ and E together.
Thames Knife	1	1	1	—	3	1	1	2
Nethii's Casket	—	1	—	—	1	3	1	4
Ruthwell	—	6	24	—	30	24	21	45
Dover	—	1	—	—	1	—	—	—
3 Thornhill stones	—	2	3	—	5	5	22	27
Brough	—	—	—	15	15	—	8	8
Lancaster	—	—	1	—	1	2	1	3
Northumbrian Brooch	—	—	1	—	1	1	3	4
Bewcastle	—	—	11	—	11	2	15	17
Falstone	—	—	1	—	1	8	7	15
Hackness	—	—	1	—	1	1	1	2
Franks Casket	—	—	10	—	10	10	12	22
	1	11	53	15	80	57	92	149

---

[1] This floating dialectic Æ for A in Scandian codices, which the Old-Northern monuments show goes back to the very oldest times, is discust by Rydqvist (Sv. Spr. Lagar 1, 386 and 4, 16, 158) and by Axel Kock (Språkhistoriska Undersökningar om Svensk Akcent, 8vo, Lund 1878, p. 142). They give different explanations, both of them as I think equally unsatisfactory.

The proportion is here only 80 A to 57 Æ (149 Æ and E together). — Old-English *words* are sometimes cut in *Roman* letters, and we all know what the Roman A is; at all events we are sure that it was *not* -R. And we have also one bi-literal stone (Falstone) in England, the English words being carved in Runic staves on the right hand, in Roman on the left. The Runic (ᚨ) Æ is given on this stone by Roman AE, and the Runic ᚠ by Roman A; but the latter vowel only occurs in one word, SAULE, which is not yet found on any O. N. runic piece in Scandinavia. Æðred's Ring is inscribed with *mixt* Runic and Roman letters, among which last is the word AH. Now let us take advantage of all this. — Nothing is *less* doubtful than the common formula of ownership, *N. N. OWES (OWNS, possesses, enjoys) ME*, &c., where we have the 3 s. pr. of the verb AGAN, *to OWN*, in its many local sounds, A, AH, ÆH, O, OH, 12 runic examples. (The ÆH, O, OH — as having no A — I do not use here). Let us now see:

Scandinavia.		*England.*
A, ᛉ.	Orstad, Norway.	AH. ᚠᚺ. Northumbrian Brooch.
AH, ᛉH.	Sigdal, ,,	AH. Æðred's Ring (this word in *Roman* staves).
AH, ᛉH.	,, ,,	The Chatham Brooch (Vol. 2, p. 586) and the
AH, ᛉH.	Thorsbjerg, Denmark.	Sutton Shield (Vol. 1, p. 290) *all* in *Roman* letters, ÆLFGIUI
AH, ᛉᚺ.	Vi Plane, ,,	ME AH, *Ælfgiui me owns*, and ÆDVWEN ME AG.

And let us apply another test, and see how the usual *later* Scandian A, ᛅ, ᚼ, answers to the O. N. ᛉ, ᛣ, in those very few words yet found on these monuments which happen to coincide, A interchanging with Æ, ᚠ, as usual. Let us compare: — DÆGÆ, Einang, Norway; DᛉH, Osthofen, England; Mansname, nom., now in Scandinavia *DAG*, in England *DAY*. — FÆIHIDO, Einang, Norway; FÆÆÞÆ, Bracteate 89; FFUŒÞO, Ruthwell; FᚼᚼÞO, Flemlöse. 3 s. p.; FᛣIÞU, Brough. 3 pl. p. *FAWED*, made, cut, carved. — FᛉÞUR, Vordingborg, Denmark, FᚼÞR, Ösby, Sweden, ac. s. *FATHER*. — HÆILÆG, Buzeu, Wallachia; ᛅILIC, Brough, England, nom. s. f. *HOLY*. — gæHÆLÆIBÆN, Tune, Norway, *LOAF-fellow*, Husband, dat. s. m.; HLᵛFORD, Ruthwell, England, *LOAF-giver*, Lord, ac. s. m. — HÆRIWOLÆFᛣ, Stentofte, Sweden, nom., HᚼRIWULFS, Rāfsal, Sweden, gen. Mansname. — WᛉS, Fonnås, Norway, 3 s. p., WÆS, Ruthwell, England, 1 s. p. *WAS*; WÆS, Tanum, Sweden, 2 s. imperat. *BE!* — STÆINÆ, Tune, Norway, ac. s. m., STᚼIN, Freerslev and Helnæs, Denmark, n. s. m. *STONE*.

Another argument is, taking this vocalic fluctuation in a wider range, and remembering how undoubtedly A, Æ, E, O, U, I, &c. pass into each other often in a way no "laws" can always explain, let us take *two* words, which accidentally and happily occur several times, and see what they show. The first little handful is the word for RUNES, nom. and ac. pl. fem. We have it 5 times ending in ᛉ, ᛣ, = A, RONOA, RUNA, RUNÆA, RUNYA, RUNOA. Let us, as commanded, write RONOR, RUNR, RUNÆR, RUNYR, RUNOR. Well and good. These words can pass, tho not strictly "Icelandic and Grammatical", as respectable specimens of Middle-Scandinavian. They all have the wisht for -R. But we have two other equally undeniable forms, RUNO on the Norse Einang stone (3rd century), and RUNÆ on the Norse Brooch (6th century). What are we to do with these? They are both in the ac. pl., governed by a verb meaning *made wrote, cut.* RUNO FÆIHIDO and WRÆET RUNÆ. We see that the system breaks down. If we may say RUNÆ and RUNO, we may also say RUNA [1]. — Once indeed we really have RNR (carved short for ′RUNAR, to save space); but this is on the invaluable Danish *overgang* Freerslev stone [2], which all admit to be late, not older than the 9th century, thus Middle-Danish in the Wiking period. And as to this ending in -A, -Æ, -O, let us honestly bow to *the fact* of this vocalic ac. pl. ending *surviving* on at least *two score examples* of RUNA, RUNI, RUNO in grave-formulas in the Scandian or *later* runes, — in other words *not yet* having gotten the now incoming ac. pl. mark -R.

The second tiny cluster is the Scandian word for LOW, grave-mound, barrow, in the sing. nom. (? m. or n.), of which I have spoken at length Vol. 2, p. 849 foll. It occurs as nom. thrice, always preceded by the name of the deceast in the genitive singular, and the inscriptions on the 3 grave-blocks are all perfect, no one letter is broken away. The Norse Stenstad stone (3rd century) reads: IGINGON HÆLÆA, *IGING'S LOW*, with the drawl or vowel-richness in HÆLÆA of which we have so many examples on these monuments both in Scandinavia and England in the oldest days. Now *here also* we *may* say HÆLÆR, tho what the meaning of the whole then will be I cannot say. (Prof. S. Bugge writes that we must read HALAR — for, having no A, he makes Æ into A —, and that this is = HALLAR, nom. s. m.. a slab, flattish stone, tho *this particular stone* is nearly *round*, and tho this word-form has never before or since been found in O. N. runic times for a grave-block). Well, let us do so. — But then we have on the Norse Bö stone (3rd century): HNÆBMÆS (or HNÆBDÆS) HLÆIWÆ, *HNÆBMEW'S LOW*, for there surely can be no doubt that the word and the formula is the same; and on the Swedish Skärkind stone (3rd century) we read: SCIDÆ LEUWÆ, *SKITH'S LOW*. also clearly the same word and formula. — Now here again if -Æ and -Æ are correct, surely the ending in -A is equally to be expected. — On the Norse Sigdal stone (5th century) we have again LÆEWE (or possibly LÆIWÆI) in *the ac. s.* for *LOW*.

And generally, with regard to vowel-fluctuations, overgang-forms, dialectic and development differences side by side in the same land and often on the same monument or in the same manuscript, let us take a *very rapid* glance at such things. For instance the Infin. ending, *now*, (where not otherwise or *fallen away altogether* in local dialects), -A in the book-tung of Sweden and Iceland, -E in that of Denmark-Norway, in only 13 lines of the oldest Scandian laws, omitting those of Norway-Iceland, which hold fast -A. The dates are, about: West-Gotland, Elder, 1290, p. 3; Younger, 1350, p. 81; Upland, 1300, p. 11; Södermanland, 1330, p. 25; Skoné (and Runic, which agrees), 1325, p. 3; Björkö, 1345, p. 113; Gotland (26 half-lines), 1350, p. 7; Helsingland, 1350, p. 5; East-Gotland, 1350, p. 3; Westmanland, 1350, p. 4; Småland, 1350—1400, p. 103. Of course the page referred to is that in the last and best editions, by Prof. Schlyter.

---

[1] I believe that the ᛦ = -R school now proposes to get out of this difficulty by taking RUNO, RUNÆ as accus. *sing.* fem. (all the other forms being ac. pl. f. as usual), they translating RUNO, RUNÆ by *runic inscription*. I only answer, that *this* use of the word as *a singular* has *never yet been found* on the *hundreds* of later stones bearing this formula, and that when it was wisht to express *this* meaning on the Scandinavian-runic blocks the term employed was RUNA-RAÞ, or, when both *staves* and *winds* were included, RUNA-RITAR.

[2] This costly Freerslev stone, which see, has *several* such shortenings of words by omission of vowels, for reasons of *space*. Such contractions are rare. Where there is *plenty of room*, it is unreasonable to say the words are contracted, if they otherwise can give a good meaning.

	A.	Æ.	E.	Ô.
West-Gotland, A.	2	13	1	
„ „ B.	21	1		
Upland	1	13		
Södermanland	3	10		
Skåne	—	6	1	
Björkö	2	5		
Gotland	9			
Helsingland	2	10	—	1
East-Gotland	13			
Westmanland	10			
Småland	13	4	(Thus 76 A, 62 Æ, 2 E and 1 Ô.)

The Danish nearly *everywhere* -Æ. But there is a particular formula in some of these Early Laws, and in Norse from 1250—1350. Icelandic (Grágás), 1250 and 1260, and Danish (Jutland, 1290), — the solemn words of Baptism.

West-Gotl., A. i namn faþurs oc sunER oc andÆS helaghA.
(This codex has also fAþir, n. s., fÆþur, ac. s.)

„ „ B. i nampn fathurs oc sons ok thæs hælghA andA.

Södermanland. i namn faþurs oc sons oc þes helghi andA.

Småland. j namn fathurs oc suns oc thes hælghÆ andÆ.

Norse. j nafuE (namfnE, nafnI) fAdur (foðor) oc sunAR oc andA hæilags (andANS hælghA).

Grágås. l nafnE (nafnI) fAUðor (foður) oc sonAR oc andA heilags.

Jutland. i fAthærs nafnÆ (nafn) oc suns oc hin hælghæ (hælegh) andæ (and).

We will add the oldest English, from the Gospels, S. Engl. A, about 1000, S. E. B, ab. 1170: North-Engl. C, ab. 950. N. E. D, ab. 1000.

South-Engl., A. on naman fÆder and sunA and þæs halgAN gastes.

„ „ B. on naman fÆder (fAder) and sunE (sunA) and þas halgEN gastes.

North-Engl., C. in noma fAdorES and sunU and halgES gastes.

„ „ D. in noman fÆder and sunU and þæs halgAN gastes.

The only other *very* old copy is the Frankic, about 850.

in namen fAter inti sunES inti thes heilagEN geistes.

Now we see here that these differences do *not* mark "nationality", they are too intermingled. They are merely the fluctuation of weak and strong forms, the greater or less falling away of the nasal, and a word or two assuming a particular meaning in a particular province at a particular epoch — which is always happening everywhere. Thus GAST has not yet been found in Scandinavia in this sense, and in England OND, AND, is little known and only provincial.

But the most striking words here are FATHER and SON. Let us look at them in gen. and ac. s.

Sanscrit g. s. pItur, ac. pItarAM; g. s. sunOS, ac. sunUM.
M. Goth. „ (? fAdrs. „ ? fAdar); „ sunAUS, „ sunU.
Icelandic „ föður. „ föður; „ sonAR, „ son.

Cædmon (A. D. 680) in his North-English First Song has gen. s. fʌdur, but the South-E. copies give fæder; while the *oldest* English has otherwise g. s. fadores, fædores, fadɛres. fadrɛs. fæder. ac. s. fæder, fʌder: g. s. sunʌs, sunɛs, sunʊ, sunʌ, sunɛ, and in ac. s. sunʌ, sunæ, sunɛ, sunʊ, sono. — The O. Fris. has g. s. fɛder, federɛs, feders, feiders, faders. ac. fɛder. And in the speech-groups called High-German and Saxon the same diversity prevails. Thus Graff gives g. s. fʌter, fʌtir, faterɛs, ac. fʌter, fʌtir, faterʌN; g. s. sunɛs, sunɪs, ac. sunʊ. suno: and M. Heyne for the oldest Saxon g. s. faderʌ, ac. fʌdaer, while Schiller and Lübben in their Lexicon give both VADER and VADERS as gen. from *the same* document, dated 1303. — In the later runes we have simply endless fluctuations in the different cases. As gen. s. FAÐUR, FOÐUR, and 2 examples of FAÐURS: as ac. s. 35 different shapes, among them the valuable FAÐURA, FAÐURI, FAÐURÓ, FAUÐURA, distant echoes of a source whence came the Sanscrit pitarʌM.

I have mentioned the O. E. Gospels. These 4 nearly coeval monuments, translations of one original but in 4 independent local dialects in one land, are a linguistic treasure no other Scando-Gothic kingdom can show. But the mine has never been workt. It awaits more than one "digger". I will only give, as specimens, a couple of the nuggets, for they in a hundred ways explain and defend my O. N. Runic ʌ. At the same time I may remark that in A the infin. ends in -ʌN, in B in -ʌN and -ɛN, in C commonly in -ʌ, otherwise -ɛ, now and then with an -N. D usually -ʌN. otherwise -ʌ. -Æ or -ɛ.

	South-E. A.	South-E. B.	North-E. C.	North-E. D.
A son, n. s.	sunu, suna	sunu, suna, sune	sunu, suna	sunu,suno,suna,sune
g.	sunu, sune, suna	sune, suna, sunas, sunes	sune, sunu, sunes	sune, suna, sunu
d.	suna	sune	sunu, sune	sunu, suno, sunæ
ac.	sunu, sune	sune,sunæ,sunu,suna	sunu, sona	sono, sunu, suno
ac. pl.	suna	sunes	suno, suna, sunu	sunu, sunes
Brother, g. s.	broðor, broður	broðer, broðor	broðres	broþer
ac. pl.	gebroðru, gebroðra	gebroðren, gebroð-ran,&c. gebroðre,&c.	broðera, broðer, broðra, broðero,&c.	gebroðer, broeþre, broðræ, broþer,&c.
Name, ac. s.	naman	name	noma	noma
Twain, two.	twegen	twegen	tuoege	twegen
Dove, ac. s.	culfran	culfran	culfre	*(columba)*
Hands, d. pl.	on handum	on hande	in hondum	hondum
Kingdoms, ac. pl.	ricu	riche, rice	ricas, ricu	rice
Devil, n. s.	sceocca	succa	wiðerworde	wiþerwearde
Pinnacle, d. s.	heahnesse	heahnysse	horn-sceaðe	heh-storre
Down, adv.	nyþer	niðer	ufa hidune	niþer
Betrayed.	belæwed	belæwed	gesáld	afongen
Shadow, d. s.	scade	scede	scuia	scade *vel* scua
Saw, 3 s. p.	geseh	geseah	gesæh	sáe, gesæh, gesægh
Shoes, ac. pl.	gescy	gescy	gesceoe	scoaś
Hand, d. s.	handa	hande	hond	honda
Us two, d.	unc	unc	(ús, usig)	unc

	South-E. A.	South-E. B.	North-E. C.	North-E. D.
Fan, n. s.	fann	fann	(ventilabrum)	windiu-scoful
Threshing-floor. ac.s.	þyrscel-flore	þyrscel-flore	bere-tun	bære-flor
Grasshoppers, n. pl.	gærstapan	gærstapen	(locustæ)	græshoppa
Adders. g. pl.	næddrena	næddrena	ætterna	nedrana
Prophet, ac. s.	witegan	witegan, witega	witgo, witga, witge	witgu
Star, n. s.	se steorra	se steorre	stearra, gen.stearres	þe steorra
ac.	steorran	steorran, steorie	sterra, stearra	steorran, steorra
Child, ac.	cild	chyld	cnæht	cneht
Eyes, n. ac. pl.	eagena, eagan	eagan, eagen	egna, egan	ego
Tide, time.	tid, fem.	fem.	masc. fem.	fem. neut.

Add, n. and ac. pl. n. *Seeds,* SEDA; *Works,* WERCA; *Words,* WORDA; *Lands,* LONDO (as well as LOND and LAND and ÆCERAS); gen. pl. *Trees,* TREUNA; *Wives,* WIFEN; ac. s. f. and n. *Meed,* MEDEN and MEDE, MEARDA, MEARDE, MEARD, Mæso-Gothic MIZDON; d. s. f. *Wife's mother,* SWEGRAN, M. G. SWAIHRON; *Hand,* ac. s. f. HANDA, HANDÆ, Mæso-Gothic HANDU; and hundreds of other such things.

One valuable feature in these *Northern* Gospels is the wonderful number of 1 s. pres. in -UM, -OM and (the -M nasalized) -O, &c., as compared with the very few in the S. Engl. moles, — *one* only being left in modern English, — I A-M, AM — while in Scandinavia *not* one is left, now that EC EM has died out in Iceland, where it lived long side by side with EC ER, which last has killed it. The only example of this 1 s. pr. in O. N. runes is the IH BIM (I BE, = I AM) of the Norse Fonnås Brooch, left in German in ICH BIN, in Fris. BIN, and prov. Fris. SAN, Saxon BIN and SIN. As a proof, in this direction as in others, how little *theory* is able a priori to fix the course of *facts,* I will mention that in the 2nd vol. of Th. Wright's valuable "Vocabularies" is, Vol. 2, p. 98—124, a glost list from the 8th century, taken from No. 144 in Corpus Christi College, Cambridge, and apparently written in Canterbury. In this Latin-English Gloss, — all by the same man with the same pen and ink on the same parchment, we have 1 example of verbs in the 1 s. pr. indic. in the oldest ending -UM. 7 in -U, 9 in -O, 1 in -A, and 2 in -E. If now only a leaf containing the -UM or the -E were left, what would a critic say as to the speech-forms and age of this codex? — In Sweden, where the IAK ÆM is extinct,. some districts still keep up the olden 2 s. in two forms, EST (our ART and the Icel. ERT) and ES (as in Sanscr. ASI and M. Goth. and still English IS), and the 1 plur. ERUM, E'M, the popular Æ, E, ER, the ĀRO of the book-dialect, ARE in England.

No division of words into time-periods is quite satisfactory. For convenience, I have groupt those here from the earliest to A. D. 400, from 401 to 800, and from 801 downwards. But I have also given *the whole* results from the beginning to 800, adding tabulated endings where needful. England, being a colony, of course comes in *after* 400. And the Bracteates &c. are thrown together in the 401—800 epoch, tho some belong to England, either struck there r by artists using the O. English futhorc. — I will now hazard a few very short and cursory remarks, merely to open the subject.

NOUNS to 400. Nom. s. masc. ending in -S. of which I have spoken above, 3 examples (-AS, -ES, -INGS); in -A and -EA, 4 ex.; in -O and -U, 5; in -E and -I, 3, besides -INGE, -INGI, -ONG, -UNG. — Nom. s. fem. in -EA and -IA, 2 ex., besides -INGOA and -INGE. — Nom. s. neut. n -EA, 1; in -E, 2. — Gen. s. m. in -ES and -IS, 2, but also 3 in *weak* terminations, -E, -INGON and -INGEN. — Gen. s. f. in -U, 1. — Dat. s. m. in -A, -EA and -IA, 11 examples; in -E, 1; in -EN, 1. — Dat. s. n. in -I, 1. — Ac. s. m. in -E, 4. — Ac. s. n. in -E, 1. — Nom. pl. m. in -ES, 1. — Gen. pl. n. in -E, 1. — Ac. pl. f. in -O, 1.

Now these *facts* speak for themselves. They *cannot* be *all* "misredd" by myself or "miscut" by the writers. And the Tables from 401 to 800 show *the same general features.* And in this latter period, where *English* pieces come in, the English endings are substantially *the same* as those in the Scandian mother-country.

ADJECTIVES, 1 to 800. The Gotho-Scandian forms already agree — from the slurring of the -N — with the O. North-English, which here as elsewhere is the key to the rapid leveling Scandian development, as compared with the English Midland and especially with the Southern English.

PRONOUNS. 1—800. Several costly archaic forms, the O. Scandian and the O. Engl. throwing light on each other.

VERBS, 1—800. I have spoken of the 1 s. pr. indic. — Exceptionally interesting here is the 3 s. pres., which unhappily but naturally occurs so very seldom in the oldest runics. The usual Scando-Gothic ending is, as we all weet, -D (-TH, -T. -D. &c.), which goes back to the earliest known Aryan times. In modern English it is still formally -TH, but actually and conversationally and commonly and in the book-language this -TH is lispt into -S. More than 1000 years ago this -S had become the usual N. E. mark of the 3 s. pr., which it still is, but in this dialect it had *then as now* (in North-English) mostly crept-in also as the mark of the *plural* present. In Shakespear's day it was by a very narrow chance that this North-country -S in s. and pl. did not gain admittance into the accepted book-dialect. In olden and modern Scandinavian the 3 s. pr. ends in -R, not -TH. How is this? Again the O. N. E. helps us. We see that as in N. England the -TH was lispt into -S, so in Scandinavia with its quickly growing distaste for -S it was further softened into -R. In modern Danish this -R (like the -S in N. English) has even become the common form also in the *plural*, and this evolution is silently spreading into Sweden and elsewhere. In fact we have examples of it as old as *the Middle Age* both in Iceland and Sweden. Such things *begin* much earlier than we sometimes suspect.

I have said that we have no *very* old Scandian 3 s. pr., none in the Old-Northern runes. But there is *one* comparative exception, tho not very old, for I cannot give it a higher date than the 9th century. But as bearing one of the O. N. runes it is *overgang* and *conservative.* The famous Picts house at Maeshowe, in the Orkneys, was for some 3 year-hundreds the resort of Scandinavian wikings, and its slab-built walls are covered with their scribbles, many of them quite short in the regular John Bull style, merely *the name,* or *N. N. cut this, N. N. carved these runes,* others a little longer and ending *N. N. wrote this,* &c. One of the oldest of these ristings reads:

ÞORNᴙ SᴁRᴅ. HᴁLHI RᴁISTO.

Both these short sentences seem risted by the same man, who in the first has used the later
ᛰ and in the latter the older ᛉ for O, perhaps merely to show that he was acquainted with
both. But whether all inscribed by one person or no. the words are so simple that probably
few will dispute the translation:

a-THORN SORETH. HᴁLHI RISTED (cut this).

Should we take the first words *figuratively*, as was common in the warlike wiking age, of
course the meaning will be: *a-war-THORN (= JAVELIN or DART or SPEAR) WOUNDETH*. But
however this may be, the whole is most orthodox middle-Scandinavian. We have the familiar
nom. ᴙ-mark of that time. and the everyday Scandian mansname HELGE, and the olden 3 s. p.
-O, that verbal ending so common in the earliest days. — But then we have the 3 s. pr. SᴁRᴅ.
ending not in -ᴙ as we had expected, nor even in -S, but in the still forner -ᴅ, -TH. Now
what is this -ᴅ? Is it English, pickt up in Northumbria, or is it a *first* example of *the oldest
Scandinavian 3 s. pr.*, brought over from some "slow" backwood dialect far away in the
Scandian home? Northumbrian, however, in the 9th and 10th century had already long ago
generally adopted the sibilant -S; while the -ᴙ in ÞORNᴙ and the name HᴁLHI are not
Northumbrianisms. The *likelihood* is therefore nearly a *certainty*, that the ᴅ in SᴁRᴅ is oldest
Scandinavian. If so, it is excessively costly. Should the reader say no, no harm is done.

I have spoken of the 3 s. p. in -O, &c. But as to the 3 *plural* past. We have
one most ancient Scandian instance of this 3 pl. p. ending in -ᴜN, the DᴁLIDᴜN of the
Norwegian Tune block (3rd century). The other oldest O. N. runic examples are N. English
(date 680), and are in -ᴜN, -ON and -ᴜ, the -N early tending to fall away in N. England, which
it soon did entirely in all the N. English and Scandinavian vernaculars. Now a whole mountain
has been made out of this molehill, this precious but unfortunate DᴁLIDᴜN. Tho this final -N
is *in common* to *all* the known antique Scando-Gothic tungs, and lived-on in South-England
("Book-language" England) to the 14th and 15th centuries, and is *at this moment* the fixt
form in the usual Frisic and Dutch and Saxon and German — an immense slice of Scando-
Gothic Europe —. we are called upon to believe by my learned opponents that this end-
nasal *could not* possibly, *even once*, be kept up *locally* in a venerable dialect like that inscribed
on the fine Tune monolith. which all its critics agree cannot be much *later* than *the 3rd year-
hundred* after Christ!

But let us turn the argument round. In England by the 14th century the -N in this
3 pl. p. was usually gone, only the -E (in the -EN) being left. About the same time Scandian
writings had also come to the same stage. -ᴁ. -A, -E, the Swedish still mostly keeping its
older -O, -ᴜ. By the 15th century the -E in England has almost perisht, and has never
been heard or seen since in English. This final slur was reacht in Scandinavia a couple of
centuries later, and at this moment all the living local Scandian talks (Icelandic excepted,
which has always held fast its. -ᴜ), as well as the Dansk-Norsk book-language, have entirely
dropt the vowel. The Swedish book-tung still insists on its useful and expressive -O in strong
verbs, but numbers of careless and uneducated Swedes have given it up. Thus the
Scandinavians and English have practically come to the same result in the same way, only
the Scandians made great haste as to the -N. while they were more backward and slow in
casting off the remaining vowel. — What, then, should we say, supposing that England had

no really old parchments to help us, if, on some person modestly and quietly showing that he had found this 3 pl. p. in -N on an antique runic piece in England, he was met by the "infallible" protest — that such an instance was "absurdly impossible"?

PREPOSITIONS and ADVERBS. 1—800. Call for no remark. Again we see how the -N is usually nasalized (I for IN, O for ON) in N. England and Scandia, tho instances occur in much *later* Scandian remains of both IN and ON, while in Midland and Book-English it continues to this day.

As far as I can see, there is only one conclusion from the whole. With the facts staring us in the face, we must admit that *manifold* dialects were in continual growth and change thro the Northern lands, tho in *the oldest* time all agreed in their bolder features. But local developments and fluctuations of population and settlement went on unceasingly (as they do still) both on the Scandian main and in the English colony; disparities multiplied, and in time the great Scandian and Anglic branches show differences wide indeed. The Scandian creation of its Post-article and its Passive was itself a revolution, equaled only by the large Romance elements which became so much more interwoven with the English than with the Scandinavian. — But in Scandinavia itself, as in England, how greatly do not the "languages" and "dialects" differ! At this moment the *written* languages of Scandinavia, however near, cannot be generally redd out of the country, and *translations* from Danish-Norwegian to Swedish and the reverse go on *daily*. The *spoken* dialects are very many in each Scandian land, and folk in the one district can often not understand the natives of another, — just as a Londoner is helpless face to face with a poor Cumberland "statesman", books in the broad North-English almost unreadable by a common Englishman. But the Scandian talks in general (specially the Danish) greatly liken the English (especially the North-English), and a farm-laborer (from Jutland for instance) can after a couple of days be hob and nob with the peasantry in Northern England and Southern Scotland — the olden North-English march. — Now in the Old-Northern Runic age all these folkships could get on well together, while they were also very closely allied in speech and blood with the Frisic and Saxon clans (some of which took part in the settlement of England), the Old-High-German showing greater differences[1]. Only *one* of all these Scando-Gothic offshoots has *real* organic variations of weight, pointing to peculiar development by intermixture &c. — the Mæso-Gothic. This talk stands considerably apart from the rest — has become a kind of Gothic "Icelandic" — from its excessive sibilation, its peculiar or archaic forms, and its Middle Verb, and it probably differed in some of these things from those *other* Gothic clans whose talks we have LOST and of which we consequently know nothing. But even as we have it — a regulated schooled Chancery book-dialect — Mæso-Gothic, like every other tung, has its curious abnormities and

---

[1] This is *now* acknowledged by Prof. S. Bugge (in his new work on the Northern Mythology, I, p. 28): "Dets nordiske Særpræg er paa dette Trin saalidet udfoldet, at man med Grund kan betegne Sproget som kun en germansk Dialekt." *Its [the Scandinavian tung's] Northern characteristics are in this stage [down to the end of the 8th century] so little developt, that we may well call the language a Teutonic [= Scando-Gothic] dialect.*

exceptions and absurd contradictions within itself, — and is no more worthy of being made a tyrant-fetish than Icelandic or Sanscrit.

I need not add that the words in these lists which may wear the same general outward shape may actually mask several independent roots, — that the *meanings* of *some* words we shall perhaps never know, — that the same *ending* may be borne by words of *different* genders, — that the *date* of these runic pieces has only been fixt approximately, and so on. We know very little of all such things as yet. How should we? Few and far between are the lights which glimmer over the clan-lands of our forefathers 1000 years before and after Christ. We may learn a little more in time, if we work hard and theorise less. But whatever we can now master as to this Old-Northern language, we have learned FROM THE MONUMENTS.[1] These therefore we must respect at all hazards, whatever *systems* may have to give way, and even tho the upshot should be that much of our boasted "Modern Philology" — with its "iron laws" and "straight lines" and "regular" police-ruled developments — is only a *House built upon the Sand!*

NOUNS AND NAMES. To A. D. 400.

SWEDEN.

Masc. Nom. Ænæhæ; Fino; Hæislæ; Hæi-tinæ; Hæring (but *Hæringæ* if we divide *Hæringæ gileugæ*); Hæuc; Siaæluh. — *Gen.* Sciþæ: Þræwingæn. — *Dat.* Fræwæærædæa; Oþua.

Fem. Nom. Ginia. Sæligæstia.

Neut. Nom. Leuwæ. — *Acc.* Leugæ.

NORWAY.

Masc. Nom. Ælu; Dægæ; Godægæs; Hao; Ingost; Læmæ (? Lædæ); Lia; Wiwiln. — *Gen.* Hnæbmæs; Igingon (? fem.). — *Dat.* Aþæa; gæHælæibæn; Hægustældia; Mirilæa; Sæg(a); Þewæa; Wæringæa; Woduride². — *Acc.* Stæinæ. — *Nom. pl.* Ærbingæs.

Fem. Nom. Ærbingæ; Dohtr; Ecwiwæa; Noþuingoa. — *Ac. pl.* Runo.

Neut. Nom. Hælæa; Hlæiwæ.

DENMARK.

Masc. Nom. Æædægæs(li); Æisg; Echlew; Erilæa; Gisliong; Hæringæ; Hæriso; Hleung; Lææsæuwingæ; Leþro (? Luþro); Luæ; Tæling; Tiþas; Tunba; Þe; Wili; Wiis(a). — *Gen.* Æs-ugis. — *Dat.* Holtingæa; Owlþuþewæa; Wiyu-bigi(? æ). — *Acc.* Hægælæ; Hornæ; (or also ac. pl. neut.) Smuhæ.

Fem. Nom. Niwæng-mæria. — *Gen.* Riigu.

Neut. *Ac. pl.* Hornæ; (or also ac. s. m.). — *Gen. pl.* Ælæ; Læ-orb(æ).

---

[1] Thus here. They show us 3 examples of -ʀ as sing. nominative-mark *older* than the assumed date 801 after Christ. But ALL these 3 (the two Danish, ꜰᴜɴᴘʀ, Frederiksberg, ʀʜᴜᴄʟꜰʀ, Helnæs; and ʀʜᴏᴌʟᴛʀ, Vatn, Norway) date from the last half of the 8th century, somewhere about 800. The other, yet older, nominatives have ALL either *no* consonantal mark or that consonant is -s.

THE GOTHIC MARCH.

Masc. Nom. Ælu; Ræningæ; Tilærings. — *Gen. pl.* Gutæ.
Neut. *Dat.* Wi.

NOMINAL ENDINGS.

SWEDEN.

Masc. Nom. -æ[3]; -ing(? æ); -o; -[2]. — *Gen.* -æ; -ingæn. — *Dat.* -a; -æa.
Fem. Nom. -ia[2].
Neut. Nom. -æ. — *Acc.* -æ.

NORWAY.

Masc. Nom. -a; -æ[2]; -æs; -o; -u; -[2]. — *Gen.* -æs; -ingon. — *Dat.* -a (?); -æa[4]; -æn; -e[2]; -ia. — *Acc.* -æ. — *Nom. pl.* -æs.
Fem. Nom. -æa: -ingæ; -ingoa; -. — *Ac. pl.* -o.
Neut. Nom. -æ; -æa.

DENMARK.

Masc. Nom. -a (? [2]); -æ[1] (? [2]); -æa; -as; -e; -i (? [2]); -ing; -ingæ[2]; -o[2]; -ong; -ung; -[2]. — *Gen.* -is. — *Dat.* -æa[2]. — *Acc.* -æ[3].
Fem. Nom. -ia. — *Gen.* -u.
Neut. *Ac. pl.* -æ (?) — *Gen. pl.* -æ.

THE GOTHIC MARCH.

Masc. Nom. -æ; -ings; -u. — *Gen. pl.* -æ.
Neut. *Dat.* -i.

OLD-NORTHERN.

Masc. Nom. -a (? [3]); -æ[3]; -æa; -æs; -as; -e; -i (? [2]); -ing[2]; -ingæ[2]; -ings; -o[4]; -ong; -u; -ung; -[6]. — *Gen.* -æ; -æs; -ingæn; -ingon; -is. — *Dat.* -a (? [1]); -æa[7]; -æn; -e; -ia. — *Acc.* -æ[4]. — *Nom. pl.* -æs. — *Gen. pl.* -æ.
Fem. Nom. -æa; -ia[3]; -ingæ; -ingoa. — *Gen.* -u. — *Ac. pl.* -o.
Neut. Nom. -æ[2]; -æa. — *Dat.* -i. — *Acc.* -æ. — *Gen. pl.* -æ.

ADJECTIVES & PARTICIPLES. To A. D. 400.

NORWAY.

Dat. s. m. WITÆI (defin.).

DENMARK.

Dat. s. m. ÆGÆSTIA (sup. def.). UGÆ (defin.).

THE GOTHIC MARCH.

Nom. s. f. HÆILÆG. — *Dat. s. n.* NIO (defin.).

OLD-NORTHERN.

Nom. s. f. -. — *Dat. s. m. def.* -æ; -æi. — *Dat. s. m. sup. def.* -æstia. — *Dat. s. n. def.* -o.

PRONOUNS. To A. D. 400.

NORWAY.

Nom. pl. neut.   Ia.

DENMARK.

Nom. s.   Ec.

VERBS. To A. D. 400.

SWEDEN.

2 s. imperat.   Wæs! — *3 s. pr. subj.* Ægi.

NORWAY.

3 s. p.   Fæihido; Woræhto — *3 pl. p.* Dælidun. — *Inf.* (Set)a.

DENMARK.

1 s. pr. Hæite. — *3 s. pr.* Ah²; O. — *3 s. p.* Tæwido. — *2 s. imperat.* Gæ²; He. — ? *Inf.* Niyæ.

OLD-NORTHERN.

1 s. pr. -e. — *3 s. pr.* -. — *3 s. p.* -o³. — *3 pl. p.* -un. — *2 s. imperat.* -³. — *Inf.* -a; æ (?).

PREPOSITIONS. To A. D. 400.

NORWAY.

Æfter.

DENMARK.

Gægin.

ADVERBS. To A. D. 400.

SWEDEN.

A; Ai; Hær.

NOUNS AND NAMES. From 401 to 800.

SWEDEN.

Masc. Nom.   Æbæ²; Ælu; Erilæa; Gæfing; Hæidar-runo; Hæriwolæfa; Hæþuwolæfa; Haufþuûkû; Iit; Mirîlæ; Mwsyouingi; Sæaþ; Þorlæf; Uþær; Uanæbæræh. — *Gen.* Hœges. — *Dat.* ? Æawelæ; Bæruta (? fem.); Hyþuwulæfa; Hyriwulæfæ; Læa; Syoænæa. — *Acc.* Fælæ; Ibaæ; Ruma; Stænæ. — *Gen. pl.* Hælhæda; Helæhedduæ.

Fem. Nom.   Æheker; Hyeruwulæfia; Olþa. — *Dat.* Ælu; Unboæu. — *Acc.* Æræ²; Mucnu; Ro; Ûkisi. — *Nom. pl.* Ginæ-runæa; Runoa. — *Ac. pl.* Gino-ronoa; Runoa; Runya.

Neut. Nom.   Æanb. — *Dat.* Tuma. — *Nom. pl.* Hidear-rungno.

NORWAY.

Masc. Nom.   Aceþæn; Ælwa; Asping; Boso; Laing; Mirilæ; Rhoæltr; ? Sæmæng; Særælũ; Þurmuþ; Ŭnnbo; Uþ; ? Wættæt. — *Gen.* Mænis. — *Dat.* Hiligæa; Icwæsuna; Iddæn; Iuþingæa; Wærua. — *Gen. pl.* Dæþyonæ; Hældæo.

Fem. Nom.   Dælia. — *Gen.* Goiþu; (O)þc(u). — *Acc.* Ciægo; Ræw, Roaæ, Roae. — *Acc. pl.* Runæ.

Neut. Nom.   Iod; Lau. — *Acc.* Læewe.

DENMARK.

Masc. Nom.   Æni; Æuair; Nura-kuþi; Rhuulfr; Ruulfasts; Stæin; Trũbu; Tu; Þiwbyo-funþr. — *Gen.* Hurnburæ; Suiþiks. — *Dat.* ? Isingþæa. — *Acc.* Æþisl; Bruþur-sunu; Faþur; Kuþumut; Stain.

Fem. Nom.   Uþæict. — *Acc.* Þrui.

ENGLAND.

Masc. Nom.   Ægili; Ælcfrith; Æleubwini; Alla; Alwin; Æðred; Baeda; Beagnoþ; Cadmon; Krist[2]; Cuhl; Cũnũng; Kung; Dægmund; Dah; Dom; Eadbierht; Eadred; Eanred; Els; Eomær; Eomaer; Eþelberht; Fisc-flodu; Gisl; Gyoslheard; God[2]; Gonrat; Gudrid; Hwætred; Ikkalacgc; Isah; Lonæwore; Oeki; Olwfwolþu; Osbiol; Oscil; Ræhæbul; Reumwalus; Romwalus; Wodæn; Wop; Woþgar; Wulfhere. — *Gen.* Alhs; Kũninges; Ecgfriþu; Heafanæs; Hronæs. — *Dat.* Æli; Breodera; Buciaehom; Dering(æ); Ecbi; Eomæ; Erha; Eþelwini; Hroethberhtæ; Roetberhtæ; . . . . rhtae; Mungpælyo; Oþlæ; Raira; Sighyor; (tru)mberehct. — *Acc.* Alcfriþu; Berchtvini; Cũnibalþ; Kũning; Cũningc; Cuþbœre(hting); Dœp-stan; Fergenberig; Galga; Greut; Hlafard; Houh; Laiciam; Onswini; Oswiung; Sigi. — *Nom. pl.* gibroþæra; Men. — *Gen. pl.* Myrcna. — *Dat. pl.* Strelum. — *Ac. pl.* Men.

Fem. Nom.   Claæo; Kũneswiþa; Kũnnburug; Hilddi(g)ũþ; Hildiþrũþ; Igilsuiþ; Wũlif. — *Gen.* Cearungia; Cimokoms; Coinu; Gæliea; Ultyo. — *Dat.* Berhtsuiþe; Birlínio; Eateyonne; Rodi; Romæcæstri; Sowhula; Saule[3]; Winiwonæyo. — *Acc.* Aclihck. — *Dat. pl.* Sorgum.

Neut. Nom.   *Gen.* Dæbs; Licæs; Rices. — *Dat.* Beornæ; Bergi; Blodœ; Gear. — *Acc.* Becun[4]; Brok; Cuombil-bio; Lic-bæcun; Sig-becn. — *Dat. pl.* Heafdum. — *Ac. pl.* Ban.

THE GOTHIC MARCH.

Masc. Nom.   Ælu.

BRACTEATES, &c.   A. D. 401—800.

Masc. Nom.   Alu[4]; Æniwulu; Ænwll; Ænoænæ; Auto; Beartigo; Cornilio; Cũn(ung); Ku(nung); Dæituhæ; Ecmu; Eltil[7]; Elwu; Fæwæ; Foslæu; Fuwu; Gææcallu; Gal; Glæ; Hama; Hhlææðu-uigæ[2]; Huthu; Ichiay; Inki; Ito;

Laoku; Lul; Naþæ; Næþuyæng; Niuwilæ; Otæ²; Oti; Owæ-alut; Sæbær; Sihmywnt; Sunedromdh; Taæ; Tallwe; Tænulu; Tæwon; Til; Tisæcg; Tvto; Twæd; Þasco (or Þusco); Þur; Wæigæ; Uyæyliil; Uodn. — *Gen.* Tenaes; Tenes. — *Dat.* Æælæucæa; Ælæwinæ²; Ælewin; Alte-uilæa²; Æohaæææ; Aþ; Aulilyoæ; Eæþlæua; Houæa; Læucæa; Læwuloucæa; Tiwitæ. — *Acc.* Uelyæ. — *Gen. pl.* Heldæa.

Fem. Nom. Voc. Icæa, Yæca, Ycæa², Ykcæa, Yia, Ygœa, Ugha; Sælæw, Sælu. — *Dat.* Aivomia; Æþodu; Auasa; Cunimudiu; Elwæo; Glyoæu-giauyou; Hærængu; Liliaæiwu. — *Ac. pl.* Hæiticæ; Runoa.

Neut. Nom. *Acc.* Uia.

NOMINAL ENDINGS.

SWEDEN.

Masc. -a²; -æ⁸; -æa; -ing; -ingi; -o; -u; -ü; -⁵. — *Gen.* -es. — *Dat.* -a³; -æ²; -æa. — *Acc.* -a; -æ²; -aæ. — *Gen. pl.* -a; -uæ.

Fem. -a; -ia. — *Dat.* -æu; -u. — *Acc.* -æ²; -i; -o; -u. — *Nom. pl.* -æa; -oa. — *Ac. pl.* -ya; -oa².

Neut. -. — *Dat.* -a. — *Nom. pl.* -o.

NORWAY.

Masc. -a; -æ; -æng; -ing; -o; -r; -u; -⁴. — *Gen.* -is. — *Dat.* -a²; -æa; -æn; -ingæa; -. — *Gen. pl.* -æo; -yonæ.

Fem. -ia. — *Gen.* -u². — *Acc.* -aæ; -ae; -o; -. — *Ac. pl.* -æ.

Neut. -². — *Acc.* -e.

DENMARK.

Masc. -i²; -r²; -s; -³. — *Gen.* -æ; -inks. — *Dat.* -æa? — *Acc.* -u; -⁴.

Fem. -. — *Acc.* -i.

BRACTEATES.

Masc. -a; æ-¹¹; -e; -i; -o⁴; -on; -u¹³; -¹². — *Gen.* -aes; -es. — *Dat.* -a; -æ³; -æœ; -æa⁶; -yoœ; -². — *Acc.* -yæ. — *Gen. pl.* -æa.

Fem. Icæa, Yæca, Ycæa², Ykcæa, Yia, Ygœa, Ugha; -u; -. — *Dat.* -a; -æo; -ia; -iu; -u²; -you. — *Ac. pl.* -incæ; -oa.

Neut. *Acc.* -u.

SCANDINAVIAN OLD-NORTHERN.

Masc. -a⁴; -æ¹³; -æa; -e; -i³; -ingi, -ing², -æng; -o⁶; -on; -r³; -s; -u¹⁵; -ü; -²⁴. — *Gen.* -æ; -aes, -es²; -inks; -is. — *Dat.* -a⁶; -æ⁵; -æœ; -æa (? 9); -æn; -ingæa; -yoœ; -³. — *Acc.* -a; -æ²; -aæ; -u; -yæ; -⁴. — *Gen pl.* -a; -æa; -æo; -uæ; -yonæ.

Fem. -a; -ia²; Icæa, Yæca, Ycæa², Ykcæa, Yia, Ygœa. Ugha; -u; -. — *Dat.* -a; -æo; -æu; -ia; -iu; -u (? 5); -you. — *Acc.* -aæ²; -ae; -æ; -i; -o²; -u; -. — *Nom. pl.* -æa; -oa. — *Ac. pl.* -æ; -incæ; -oa³; -ya.

Neut. -³. — *Dat.* -a. — *Acc.* -e; -u. — *Nom. pl.* -o.

Masc.   -a[2]; -e[2]; -i[3]; -u[2]; -ung; -g; -us (Lat.): -[33]. — *Gen.* -æs[2]; -es; -s; -u. — *Dat.*
-a[3]; -æ[5]; -i[4]; -yo; -[5]. — *Acc.* -i[3]; -u[2]; -ing, -ingc, -ung; -[7]. — *Nom. pl.* -a; -. —
Gen. pl. -na. — *Dat. pl.* -um. — *Ac. pl.* -.

Fem.   -a; -o; -[4]. — *Gen.* -ia; -iea; -s; -u; -yo. — *Dat.* -a; -æyo; -e[5]; -i ; -io;
-yonne. — *Acc.* -. — *Dat. pl.* -um.

Neut.   *Gen.* -æs; -es; -s. — *Dat.* -æ[2]; -. — *Acc.* -[5]. — *Dat. pl.* -um. — *Ac. pl.* -.

ADJECTIVES AND PARTICIPLES. A. D. 401—800.

Nom. s. masc. Iilæ (defin.); Mæ (defin.); Sbæ (defin.). — *Dat. s. neut.* Niu (defin.).

Nom. s. masc.   *Nom. s. fem.* Inglsk.

Nom. s. masc. Almeyottig; Aluwaldo (def.); Gasric; Grorn; Modig. — *Nom. s. fem.*
Ailic; giᴅrœfed; biᴄoten; bistemid; Timþ; giwundad. — *Nom. s. neut.*
Đun. — *Dat. s. masc.* Lanum. — *Dat. s. neut.* Fruman (defin.). — *Acc.*
s. m. Iukc; Lim-wœrigne; Riicnæ. — *Acc. s. neut.* Al. — *Nom. pl. masc.*
Æþþilæ; Fusæ; Giuþeasu; Twœgen. — *Acc. pl. masc.* Ale. — *Acc. pl.*
neut. Ba.

Nom. s. masc. Hæ-curne (defin.); ? Liþin. — *Dat. s. masc.* Sehs-cunæ (defin.); Tille
(defin.); Ungæ[3] (defin.).

PRONOUNS. From A. D. 401—800.

Nom. sing. Ec. — *Nom. s. masc.* Sæ. — *Acc. sing.* Mic. — *Nom. pl. fem.* Sæa; Usa. —
Gen. pl. masc. Deræ. — *Acc. pl. fem.* Đyiya.

Nom. s. fem. Hu. — *Acc. s. fem.* Yoiæ. — *Acc. s. neut.* Đætæa. — *Nom. pl. neut.* Ia.

Acc. s. masc. Sin. — *Acc. s. fem.* Điæu.

Nom. sing. Ic[7], Ik, Ih. — *Nom. s. masc.* He[2]. — *Gen. s. m.* His[3]. — *Gen. s. neut.* Đæes. —
Dat. s. masc. Him. — *Dat. s. fem.* Đer[2], Daer, Đær. — *Acc. sing.* Mic[2], Mik,
Mec[4], Meh, Mæ. — *Acc. s. masc.* Hinæ[2]; Đœ, The. — *Acc. s. neut.* Đis; Đæt. —
Dual acc. Ungcet. — *Nom. pl. masc.* Hiæ[2]. — *Dat. pl.* Us. — *Acc. pl.* Us. —
Acc. pl. masc. Hiæ.

Dat. s. masc. Imæ; Đam.

VERBS.　From A. D. 401 to 800.

SWEDEN.

1 s. pr. Hæte'c. — *3 s. pr.* Æh, O. — *3 pl. pr.* Hæbo; Mælæ². — *3 s. p.* Dæude; Hiuk: Oæg; (ræis)ti; Sæte; Wæryit, Wæritæ, Riuti; Wortæ. — *3 pl. p.* (I)ugo (or (W)ugo). — *Imperat.* 2 *s.* Gæa.

NORWAY.

3 s. pr. A, Ah², O, Oh. — *3 s. p.* Fyþæi; Was; Wræitæ, Wræet. — *Imperat.* 2 *s.* Ah².

DENMARK.

3 s. p. Kærþi; Faþi; Sati. — *3 pl. p.* Truknaþu.

ENGLAND.

1 s. pr. Bim; Yce. — *3 s. pr.* Ah², Oh; Coecas; Drygyþ; Recs; Sbærædh. — *3 pl. pr.* Fegtaþ. — *1 s. p.* Darstæ, Darste; biHeald; Hnag; aHof; Wæs. — *3 s. p.* Beckcto; Fœdde; Fauœþo, Fuþe; onGeredæ; aGrof; Het; aHof; aRærde; Ysetae, Sete, Settæ, Settae, Sœttœ; giswom; Walde; Warþ; Wæs; Wolk; Worhte; Urit. — *3 pl. p.* Kwomu; Faiþu; biHealdun; aLegdun; Setton; bismæredu; gistoddun. — *2 s. imperat.* geBid! giBid! Wisæ! — *2 pl. imperat.* giBidæþ, geBidaed, geBidæd, giBiddad, geBiddaþ, geBiddæþ! — *3 s. pr. subj.* Helipæ; Iwi; Lice; usmæ — *Inf.* Buga; Hælda; Hiewan; gistiga.

BRACTEATES, &c.

3 s. pr. Ænn². — *3 s. p.* Fihædu; Hæg; Hu; Vrœito. — *2 s. imperat.* Gib! Hæ²! Te²!

PREPOSITIONS.　From A. D. 401 to 800.

SWEDEN.

Yfæta; Æt, Et; I (or Uti); I; Mut; Uti (or I).

NORWAY.

? Æt; Ute.

DENMARK.

Aft, Æft.

ENGLAND.

Aft, After, Æfte. Æftar, Æfter², Æftær², Aeftaer², beAftær; Ift; Æt, At; Foræ, Fore, Für; In², I⁴; Miþ³; Of; On⁴, O; Ti, Tyo.

BRACTEATES.

To.·

ADVERBS.　From A. D. 401 to 800.

SWEDEN.

Æ, Æiu; Geu, Geuw; Hæeræ, Heræ; Ni; Nu.

NORWAY.

Ao; Hær(œ).

ENGLAND.

Aici; And, End; Ean; Fearran; Ætᴄadre; Her; Hweþræ; Ni²; Eac; Sare; Đer², Đær.

BRACTEATES.

Nu.

NOUNS AND NAMES. From 801 to —.

SWEDEN.

Masc. Nom. Enruk; Halstun; Iiæuri; Inofasti; Ruti; Samsi. — *Gen.* Æsmuts; Hariwulfs. — *Dat.* Roaul. — *Acc.* Faþr; Sigi; Stun; Sul; Tæen. — *Nom. pl.* Stainar.
Fem. Nom. Kearstin. — *Gen.* Unu. — *Dat.* Mariu.
Neut. Nom. Riusii.

NORWAY.

Masc. Nom. Aluer; Bonte; Oþinkar; Prestr; Toue; Đormuþ; Đorrsonr; Đort. — *Dat.* Ænsægui.
Fem. Nom. Ossk. — *Dat.* Sikktale. — *Acc.* Auik; Kloko.

DENMARK.

Masc Nom. A(Rfik)I; Æslaikir: Olufr; Skær; Siuarþ; Stæin; Tyw; Unitr. — *Gen.* Kunuælts; Ruhalts; Sikwulfs; Sunar; Tadis; Đular. — *Acc.* Stain. — *Dat. pl.* Sal-haukum.
Fem. Nom. Sol; Đoræ. — *Gen.* Afai; Inkur. — *Ac. pl.* Ær-runar.

ENGLAND.

Masc. Nom. Emundr; Hælhi; (Hl)ydwyg; Myredah; Onlaf; Rikarth; Tidfirþ; Đornr. — *Gen.* Eadvlfes. — *Dat.* Osberchtae.
Fem. Nom. *Dat.* Merthe; Sav(le).
Neut. Nom. *Dat.* Æsboa.

BRACTEATES, &c.

Masc. Nom. Iauligr; Iohn; Iulieni. — *Dat.* Iauþini; Simi.
Fem. Nom. *Dat.* Æmiliu. — *Dat. pl.* Birkoiinum.

ADJECTIVES AND PARTICIPLES. From 801 to —.

SWEDEN.

Dat. s. fem. Uena (defin.).

ENGLAND.

Masc. s. nom. Ȝernr; Siuilfurn.

PRONOUNS. From 801 to —.

SWEDEN.

Dat. s. Dik. — *Acc. s. m.* Sin; Đansi; Đoniæ.

NORWAY.

Acc. s. f. Đissa. — *Nom. pl. f.* Siæ.

DENMARK.

Gen. s. f. Sinær. — *Ac. pl. f.* Þisi.

ENGLAND.

Nom. s. Þis. — *Nom. s. m.* He. — *Dat. s. f.* This. — *Acc. s.* Meh², Me.

VERBS. From 800 to —.

SWEDEN.

3 s. ·p. Æa; Korþe, Karþi; Risti; Wraiti.

NORWAY.

3 s. pr. Oh. — *3 s. p.* G (? = Garþe); Styŏpte. — *3 pl. p.* Leto. — *Inf.* Styŏpa.

DENMARK.

3 s. pr. Huiler. — *3 s. p.* Raisti; Uk. — *2 s. imper.* Al!

ENGLAND.

3 s. pr. O; Is; Særþ. — *3 s. p.* Brokte; Feg(de); Ræisto; Sete; IWrokte.

BRACTEATES.

3 s. p. Fyidi; Ho, Hûng.

PREPOSITIONS. From 801 to —.

SWEDEN.	NORWAY.	DENMARK.	ENGLAND.	BRACTEATES.
Yuir.	I; Aa.	O.	O, On³; To.	I; On.

ADVERBS. From 801 to —.

NORWAY.	DENMARK.	ENGLAND.
Ok, Uk.	Afta; Hæræ; In; Iwika.	Þær.

FRESH FINDS,

TOO LATE FOR ROOM IN THEIR PROPER PLACE.

———

KROGSTAD, UPLAND, SWEDEN.

? DATE ABOUT A. D. 400—500.

See page 14 in this volume. Old-N. R. Mon. Vol. 3. p. 452.

Here repeated. from drawings kindly forwarded by the Swedish Rune-smith Adjunct
K. A. Hagson of Linköping. showing the stone *as it now stands*. There never have been any
dots on the figure. and therefore the idea of chain-mail falls away. Adjunct Hagson thinks
the bild that of a man praying ro the Gods. Helpt by this ingenious hint, I now suggest
that the deceast was *a Christian*. the attitude of prayer reminding us of similar figures
(ORANTES) in the Catacombs and elsewhere in the oldest West. Isolated Christian families
were found in the otherwise heathen North hundreds of years before the historical Missions.

VISBY, GOTLAND, SWEDEN.

? DATE ABOUT A. D. 1250—1300.

Old-N. R. Mon. Vol. 3, p. 404.

Golden Finger-ring, found by workmen digging near Visby in 1880. Is now in the Husaby Museum, Småland, Sweden. Here given full size. More than a dozen such, more or less of the same type, and all or nearly all met with in Gotland, are in the National Museum, Stockholm. The retrograde runes spell the name of the owner:

INOFASTI.

STRAND, RYFYLKE, STAVANGER, NORWAY.

? DATE ABOUT A. D. 200—300.

Old-N. R. Mon. Vol. 3, p. 453.

Found as building-stone in the roof of an outhouse, in the autumn of 1882. Had been lifted from a grave-mound near the farm-house. Another such rune-stone, with a short risting, had stood on another how nearby, but has disappeared. Taken out and sent to Christiania in July 1883. Coarse-grained gray granite, about 7 feet 7 above ground, 9 inches thick, greatest breadth nearly 21 inches. From the beginning, surface rough and weathered; runes not elegantly cut. Part of the tips of the staves in the right line has suffered from weathering, and one letter here (the L) is doubtful, as the top is gone. In general, the characters can be fairly made out. All wend-runes, redd from right to left (from below upward). I propose (right line, middle, left):

HÆDU(L)ÆICÆA. ECAI ÆGSI STÆDÆA. HÆÆIWIDO MÆGUM IN INO.

To-HÆDU(L)ÆICÆ. AYE the-AWE of-the-STEADS (coasts, = ever bravely harrying the foemen's harbors). HOWED (buried in his grave-mound) with-his-MAUGS (kinsfolk) HIM INO (= Ino laid him in his barrow, to rest with his kindred).

TORVIK, HARDANGER, NORWAY.

? DATE ABOUT A. D. 200—300.

Old-N. R. Mon. Vol. 3. p. 405.

Now in the Bergen Museum.   Engraved ¹/₁₅ of the size.   Granite.   Found in the spring of 1880 in a ruined grave-mound which contained a stone-kist built up of slabs.   One of the long side-stones (the only one of granite) had been taken from a far older barrow, and had been slightly cut that it might fit in.   But it bore rune-words in minne of the

dead man on whose grave it had stood, and, when used as building-material and a small part cut away, at least the arm of one letter disappeared. As the grave-chamber and its contents date from about the 6th century, and a long time must have elapst before the olden tomb would be thus desecrated, and as the runes and word-forms point back to very ancient times, we cannot well fix it later than about the 3rd yearhundred. This is the *first* Old-Northern *heathen* stone found as *building-gear* in a still later *heathen* tumulus. The angle above the Æ and before the w, I take to be a dividing mark. As we have here the *short* type which may stand for either ᛗ (D) or ᛘ (M), we are not sure whether the name was LÆMÆ or LÆDÆ. Should anything more have followed, it was most likely the usual *WROTE* or *WROTE these RUNES.* What stands on the block is:

LÆMÆ (or LÆDÆ) WÆRINGÆA.

LÆMÆ (or LÆDÆ) to-WÆRING.

TORVIK, HARDANGER, NORWAY.

? DATE ABOUT A. D. 200—300.

Old-N. R. Mon. Vol. 3. p. 457.

A second stone, clay-slate, belonging to a long side of the same grave-kist in this
heathen tumulus. Measures 8 feet 10 inches in length by 2 feet 2 in breadth, with a

thickness of from $2^{1}/_{3}$ inches to $3^{1}/_{8}$. The runes rubbed-in, like those on the Einang block; they were first seen in June 1883 by the Norse Oldlorist A. Lorange, Keeper of the Bergen Museum, where this slab now is. A very faint beginning-mark (|||, as on the Forsa Ring and the Valsfjord Rock) stands *before* the first letter (Þ). The inscription is quite complete, the name of the sleeper below:

ÞIEÞRODWENC.

This is equal to ÞIEÞROD*ING* or *SON*, and is found here for the first time. Several of the staves have ornamental -feet.

SÆBÖ, HOPREKSTAD, SOGNEFJORD, NORWAY.

? DATE ABOUT A. D. 750—800.

Old-N. R. Mon. Vol. 3. p. 407.

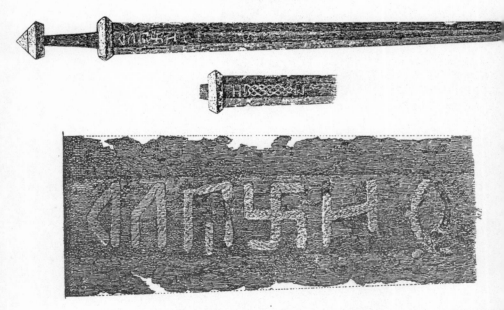

One of a class of Iron Wiking-swords; found 1825 in Norway, studied and identified in 1881 by the Norwegian antiquary A. Lorange, Keeper of the Bergen Museum. Engraved $^{1}/_{5}$th, but the runes full size. Many of these blades are damascened, and not a few have inscriptions on the one side and trade-marks or ornaments on the other, the letters or marks being first cut-in with a chisel, and then bits of STEEL WIRE hammered in. These ristings are in the older staves, or in Roman or mixt Roman and Runic letters. This sword has not only the Old-Northern runes, but has also the Thor-mark, ⚒, with its *phonetic or sounded* value THUR, like as ✝ or ✗ is often used with its phonetic value CHRIST. — The form of the M is a costly variant. The whole lettering, in reverst runes, reads from right to left. The words are, quite clearly:

OH ÞURMUÞ.

O WNS (possesses-me) THURMUTH.

RÖMES-FELL, S. TRONYEM, NORWAY.

? DATE ABOUT A. D. 800—900.

Old-N. R. Mon. Vol. 3, p. 411.

In 1880 two fine Walrus-teeth were found in a deep rock-cleft. They are now in the Tronyem Museum. The one bears, in the usual runes,

KÆTIL A   *KÆTIL OWNS-me.*

The other, here given ⅓rd of the size, has the Old-Northern o and the archaic K, and is therefore transitional. The letters, given separately full bigness, are merely the name of the lady

OSSK

whose property it was. The valuable teeth may therefore have belonged to husband and wife, or to brother and sister, and are from the time when the Norwegian landholder Ohthere told king Alfred of England how he got similar teeth by Walrus-fishing in the Northern seas.

EIDSBERG, SMÅLENENE, NORWAY.

? DATE ABOUT A. D. 1100—1200.

Old-N. R. Mon. Vol. 3. p. 412.

In the summer of 1880, during the repairs of Eidsberg Church, a granite slab was found bearing the name of the builder, in later runes but also having *one* Old-Northern letter (ᚷ). It is here given ¹/₁₆th of the original. Four other runish slabs of brick also turned up, connected with later alterations. The name, chiefly used in Denmark in olden days, is here seen for the first time in Norway.

OÞINKAR G(arþi).

OTHINKAR G(ared, made, built this).

SEALAND, DENMARK.

? DATE ABOUT A. D. 1200—1300.

Old-N. R. Mon. Vol. 3. p. 458.

Copper. Engraved full size. Found in June 1879 by a man digging, sold by him
o a dealer, from whom I bought it for a trifle in August 1883. Is now in the Husaby
Museum, Småland, Sweden. Has a modern look, but the O. N. runes are absolutely genuine.
give it as I find it. looking upon the piece as a stamp or punch, for striking impressions
with a hammer on soft lead or wax or terra-sigillata flans or blanks. Such things were
immensely used all thro the middle ages. Only 2 reverst letters, whose impression would
ive — perhaps the beginning of a name:

HU.

CHESSELL DOWN, ILE OF WIGHT, ENGLAND.

? DATE ABOUT A D. 500—600.

Old-N. R. Mon. Vol. 3. p. 459.

The above drawing is half the bigness. Iron Sword, now in the British Museum. Found about the middle of this century in an Old English grave. But the runes were first seen in 1882 by Aug. W. Franks. Esq., the Director. Present length of blade from the guard, 2 feet 6¹/₂ inches; from the guard to the tip of the pommel 6¹/₂ inches. The runes are on the inner side of the silver scabbard-mount, and were only seen lately when the piece was cleaned. Hence their perfect preservation, tho so slightly cut-in. They have been hidden for some 1300 winters! I give them and the mount here full size:

? ÆCO SŒRI!

? ᚪWE (terror, death and destruction) to-the-SERE (brynie. armor, weapons, of the foe)!

In this case the owner had cut this spell. singing therewith some chaunt of super-natural power, to overcome the easier his unsuspecting enemy. All such witchcraft and amulet-bearing &c. was strictly forbidden. Whatever the staves mean, this is the only such *secret* rune-risting yet found.

CHESTER-LE-STREET, N. DURHAM, ENGLAND.

? DATE ABOUT A. D. 700—800.

Old-N. R. Mon. Vol. 3, p. 461.

Found in June 1883, in repairing the Chancel of the once Collegiate Church. Closish-grained sandstone, 2 feet 11 high by 8 inches broad below, 7 above. The lowest uncarved 5 inches went into the socket of the grave-cross, of which this square pillar is all that is left. The back has knot-winds almost identical with those below the horseman on the front. All the writing seen here is the dead man's name,

EADMUND.

Only the ᛗ and ᚾ are O. Northern runes, the other staves being Roman.

FRONT.

RIGHT SIDE PATTERN.

LEFT SIDE.

SELSEY, SUSSEX, ENGLAND.

? DATE ABOUT A. D. 700—800.

Old-N. R. Mon. Vol. 3, p. 463.

Two bits of a golden finger-ring, now in the British Museum. They were pickt up a few years ago, along with 280 small British golden Coins and other objects, down to the middle age. Such things are thrown on the coast there from time to time.

These ring-morsels are so much injured and the runes so faint from long friction, that I will not attempt any engraving. But my decipherment of the staves was approved by Mr. Franks and by Mr. C. H. Read, of the British Museum. The first fragment seems to bear ᛒᚱᚢᚦᚱᛣ (BRUÐRN), the second ᚠᛏ ᛗᛁ (ON EL). The ᚢ in BRUÐR is not quite perfect. The distances between ON and E and L are from the shape of the ring, here slightly raised and past over. The N is *the beginning* of a lost mansname — let us say NICLAS. The whole will then be:

BRUÐR Niclas ON EL . . . . .

BROTHER Niclas ON (of) EL . . . . .

THORNHILL, YORKSHIRE, ENGLAND.

? DATE ABOUT A. D. 700—800.

Old-N. R. Mon. Vol. 3. p. 414.

FRONT.   SIDE.   BACK.

Found at the close of 1881 in the Tower of Thornhill Church, up in the bell-chamber. Now taken out and carefully preserved in the holy house. Is 21 inches long, 12¹⁄₂ broad below to 10³⁄₄ above, thickness 7¹⁄₂ inches at bottom to 7 at top. Part of the tapering shaft of a sandstone grave-cross, raised by a Lady to a Lady. The relationship or friendship — then known locally to all — is not mentioned. Gives the earliest instance in England of ARÆRDE, and the only runic example yet found in England of BERG for *BARROW, grave-mound.* Only 3 other such runic instances are known in the Scandinavian mother-land. The womans-name IGILSUITH has never before turned up in England. Observe the bind-runes. — As we see, the grave-words are 4 lines of stave-rime verse:

† IGILSUID AR.ERDE   *IGILSUITH A-REARED (raised)*
    ÆFTER BERHTSUIDE   *AFTER (in minne of) BERHTSUITH*
    BECUN AT BERGI.   *this-BEACON (pillar-stone) AT (on, close to)*
    geBIDDAÐ ÐÆR SAULE.   *the-BARROW (how. tumulus).*
                                BID-ye (pray-ye) for-THE SOUL.

DEARHAM, NEAR MARYPORT, CUMBERLAND, ENGLAND.

? DATE ABOUT A. D. 850—950.

Old-N. R. Mon. Vol. 3, p. 420. 447.

Taken out of the Church during its restoration in 1882, and the end-inscriptions found, by the Rev. W S. Calverley, whom I have to thank for all details and materials. A later personal examination has convinced me of their entire correctness. This sarcophagus, of yellowish sandstone, once stood alongside a wall, where the further side and ends would not be seen. Length, 4 feet by 3 inches and a quarter; least width 13 inches, greatest 15, depth 6. Is the second sarcophagus slab bearing runes known to me in England. Dover (p. 140 above) being the first.

The principal scene, Man fallen and Man redeemed, is clear. It is shown in a masterly way, which I have never seen before. What strikes us is, that Adam and Eve are *draped*, a conventional handling. It is not the sin in Paradise; it is the Man-kind, the Human Race, for whom Christ died. And so the Serpent, his revenge and punishment, shown on the same plane by doubling his form, as so often in olden art, pagan and Christian. — We must wait for fresh finds, before we can speak with certainty on the other symbols.

At the bottom is the name of the deceast, probably an ecclesiastic, in early Roman letters.

ADAM.

Above, a corner of the stone is broken away. Originally the runes doubtless were:

(krist S)U(L) GI-NLÆRA.

May-Christ his-SOUL NÆRE (save, bless)!

First time this common O. Engl. and Scando-Gothic word NÆRA(N) has been found IN RUNES in a prayer for the dead. We have otherwise HELP, LETE, SEE, &c. The -A in gi-NLÆRA. 3 s. pr. subj., is an antique ending. The + in the bind for ÆR is also a rarity in England

---

BRACTEATES.

Nos. 90, 91. Old-N. R. Mon. Vol. 3. p. 463. 4. — The seller said, *in Kiel*, these pieces were found at GELTORF, not GETTORF. It is immaterial. Both villages are in the Danish province of Slesvig or South Jutland. — No 91 has lately been bought by the Kiel Museum, and its learned Keeper, Prof Handelmann, has kindly favored me with an Electrotype, here drawn and Chemityped by Prof. *MAGNUS PETERSEN.*

SPARLÖSA, WEST-GOTLAND, SWEDEN.

? DATE ABOUT A. D. 700—800.

Old-N. R. Mon. Vol. 3, p.

From materials kindly furnisht by Adjunkt Karl Torin, Skara, W. Gotland. The base of this granite boulder is largely broken away, but it still measures about 5 feet 4 inches in height and 2 feet in breadth. It lies flat on its side in the outer wall of Sparlösa Church, in Wiste Härad (Hundred). The runes by far the largest yet known, the longest measuring nearly 2 feet! They are not divided into words. The stone has been split centuries ago, but no great damage has been done. A narrow unwritten border has been used, *a couple of centuries later*, for a *fresh* inscription. The barbarous head and part-bust of THU(NO)R, with the decoration of his Holy HAMMER-MARKS, are equal to the rune-formula on some Scandian heathen stones, "ÞUR UIHI", = *may-THUR WIH (bless-these-runes-and-this-tomb)!*

As I suppose, the oldest risting clearly says:

AEGGIULS KAEF UGU, AEIRIKIS SUNCE, KN-FAELIIKI.

AEGGIULS (= sword-EDGE-WOLF, = SWORD-WOLF) GAVE-this-minne to-UG, AEIRIKS-SON,
his-GUN-FELLOW (war-mate, brother-in-arms).

The later memorial is simply:

KISLI KARÐI IFTIR KUNAR. BRUÐ(R).

KISLI GARED (wrote this) AFTER KUNAR, his-BROTHER.

The name AEGGIULS is another Old-Northern (overgang) example of the ancient nominative-ending in -s, which afterwards became -R and then fell away.

THE GOTHIC MARCH.

TORCELLO, VENEZIA, ITALY.

? DATE ABOUT A. D. 300—400.

Old-N. R. Mon. Vol. 3, p.

Found by Dr. INGVALD UNDSET, the Norse Old-lorist, Oct. 1883, in the small local Museum at Torcello, an iland in the Lagunes, about 2 hours' row from Venice. The Founder and Keeper of this forn-hall, Consul the Cavaliere *Nicolo Battaglini*, came across it last February in a farmer's house, where it had been as long as the family remembered; fitted with a wooden handle, it had done duty as a Poker! It is of Bronze, 16½ inches long, the incised lines filled with circlets and stars stampt boldly in. To judge from its patina, it has been dug from a boggy soil. For the drawings (each side 1—3rd, runes apart full size) we have to thank the Danish Architectural Designer J. T. HANSEN. See the similar Spear-heads pp. 204, 205, especially the latter, of which this one is almost a counterpart, only much richer and larger.

This WANDERER, doubtless originally from THE GOTHIC MARCH, may have been war-plunder or what not, and is another proof how things change hands and may accidentally turn up. The small ring is a beginning-mark, as on the Müncheberg piece. Should my transliteration be right, the reverst runes give

TENINGÆ

the name of the owner, or of the officer by or before whom it was carried in battle, and which means DAN'S or DANE'S SON. The reader will please to remark the single-armed T and the straight-armed F. The peculiar and elegant workmanship of the runes and symbols has not, I believe, been seen before. — This precious old-lave reacht me at the very last moment. Just therefore it stands where it does.

BRACTEATE.

No. 96.

ÅSUM, SKÅNE, SWEDEN.

Old-N. R. Mon. Vol. 3. p. 464.

Found by a man ploughing, Nov. 27, 1882. Here given full size. Is the largest golden blink yet known. Weighs 100.3 grammes. The loop is broken away. Bears 13 wend-runes, not divided into words. Reversing the letters, I read:

SNEIC ÆCÆA FÆHI(do or fæhide).

SNEIC (= SNEING = SNOWSON) to- or for-ÆCÆ (= AGE, ÅGE, OVE) FAWED (made this).

There was no room to finish the verb. The I comes under the animal's snout, and is therefore much *shorter* than usual, and the following -DO or -DE (or whatever the ending was) is therefore *understood*. This exceptionally splendid 6th century Old-Danish Jewel is now in the Stockholm Forn-hall.

BETTERINGS.

Page 8. — *For* Vanga *read* Vånga.

P. 27, l. 9. — *Read* BELÆHEDDUÆ.

P. 156. ALNMOUTH. — Plate 117 of the late Dr. John Stuart's noble "Sculpture Stones of Scotland", folio, Vol. 2, which reacht me after the publication of my Vol. 2, gives *all the 4 sides* of these Cross-fragments, tho not quite correctly. We can thus examine also *the back* of the large piece, which shows the Crucifixion This is carved in the oldest way the Sun and Moon above, the 2 Thieves under the arms of the Rood. and below them the Centurion and the reacher up of the sponge with vinegar, with costly interlaced work as the base of the Cross. Add hereto the very antique character of the Roman letters. — I therefore now think that Mr. Haigh's *first date* (about A. D. 705) is undoubtedly the correct one. The EADULF here commemorated is thus the king who usurpt the crown at the death of king ALDFRID, but was shortly after defeated and slain. See Vol. 1, p. 462.

P. 159. — A French savant. Mons. L. L. H. Combertigues-Varennes, a learned student of Runic and other Calendars, has just (Jan. 1882) favored me with a valuable Ms treatise on this curious Calendar. We will hope that he will make it public. Meantime he has kindly permitted me to say, that his paper closes as follows: "En résumé. ce calendrier non terminé par son auteur. donne, pour la portion que Worm nous en a conservée (quoique avec de grandes fautes d'exécution), les Signes des fêtes, le Cycle Solaire et le Cycle Lunaire c. a. d. qu'il appartient à la classe que Worm nomme Calendriers parfaits. L'année y commence avec le 14 Octobre et le nombre d'or du 1er Janvier est 3. Il offre, en outre, comme ren seignements complémentaires, un Cycle Solaire complet, un Cycle Lunaire défectueux e quelques monogrammes ou dessins sans importance. — Ce qui constitue l'interét capital offer par ce calendrier, c'est qu'il est probable que la Série de son cycle lunaire (correspondant comme toujours, à un alphabet) runique. est tout-à-fait inédite."

In this memoir the learned author identifies the festivals, among them those o S. Edmund (England), S. Thorlak (Iceland) and S. Knut, Duke and Martyr (Denmark), thu making the Calendar a century *more modern* than the date I had assigned to it.

P. 168. Bracteate No. 6. — I now prefer to take SEHS-CUNÆ in the meaning SAX-KEEN, *sword-bold, falchion-daring*. So, if I am right in my rendering of the Tjursåker stone we have SAKSE-TÜNDR = *Sax-lord, Sword-Captain*, as an epithet of and kenning for (W)ODEN.

P. 234. — The reader will please to add and tabulate for himself the grammatica forms and endings given in THE FRESH RUNIC FINDS. They are of the same general characte and abundantly strengthen my argument.

HAND-LIST

OF ALL THE OLD-NORTHERN WORDS

IN THE THREE FOLIO VOLUMES.

A, Æ, see under Agan, Æiu, On.

A, *Bracteate 81; Nydam Arrow.* Doubtless first letter of a Name beginning with A. Aa, under On. — Æa, u. Hiewan.

ÆANB, *Lindholm.* ? Voc. ? Neut. s. ? Snake.

ÆBÆ, *Björketorp; Stentofte.* Mansname, nom. See SBÆ and Word-lists.

Æcæa, under OEKI.

ACEDÆN, *Belland.* Mansuame, nom. The broken .... ÆN of the Tomstad stone was probably a part of the same name.

ÆCO, *Chessell Down.* ? Nom. s. f. ? AWE, terror, death. — ÆGSI, *Strand.* ? Dat. s. m. The-AWE, fear, fright. — ÆGÆSTIA, *Gallehus.* Dat. s. m. def. superl. To-the-AWEST, most awful, most dread or venerable.

ACLIHCK, *Brough.* ? Place-name. ? dat. s. f. See ECBI.

Æædægæsli, u. Aþæ.

ADAM, *Dearham.* Mansname, nom. (In Roman letters).

AFAI, *Freerslev.* Gen. s. f. Grandmother.

AFT, *Bewcastle; Helnæs;* ÆFT, *Vordingborg;* AFTA, *Freerslev;* ÆFTAR, *Collingham;* ÆFTÆR, *Falstone;* AEFTAER, *Falstone;* ÆFTE, *Thornhill;* ÆFTER, *Thornhill; Tune;* AEFTER. *Dewsbury; Wycliffe; Yarm;* YFÆTA, *Istaby;* IFT, *Brough;* B(eAFTÆr), *Crowle.* AFTER, BE-AFTER. in memory of. Prep. gov. dat. and ac., and adverb.

[AGAN]. — To OWE, OWN, possess, have, enjoy. — A, *Orstad;* AH, *Æthred's Ring; Northumbrian Brooch; Sigdal,* (perhaps imperat.), *Thorsbjerg;* Vi Plane; ÆH, *Upsala;* O, *Björketorp; Förde; Hackness;* Vi Plane; OH, *Osthofen; Sæbö.* 3 s. pres. OWNS. — AH, *Sigdal.* ? 2 s. super. (perhaps 3 s. pr. ind). — ÆGI, *Skå-äng.* 3 s. pr. subj. Let-him-keep, may-he-enjoy. Ægæstia, u. Æco. — Ægi, u. Agan.

ÆGILI. *Franks Casket.* Mansname, nom. — IGILSUID, *Thornhill.* Womans-name, nom.

Agrof, under Grof. — Ægsi, u. Æco. — Ah, Æh, u. Agan. — Æheker, u. Inge. —
aHof, u. Hof. — Ai, Æi, Aici, u. Æiu. — Ailic, u. Hæilæg.

ÆISG, *Thorsbjerg.* Mansname, nom.

ÆIU, *Stentofte;* A, *Tanum;* Æ, *Lindholm;* AI, *Skå-äng;* AO, *Sigdal;* EÆ, *Bracteate 63;* ECAI
Strand. EVER, AYE, always. — IWKA (= IWIKA), *Freerslev.* For ever, for aye. — AICI, *Brough*
Aye-not, never. — ÆLEUBWINI, *Nordendorf.* Mansname, nom. — EOMÆR, EOMAER, *Falstone*
Mansname, nom. — EMUNDR. *Hackness.* Mansname, nom. — AIVOMIA, *Bracteate 65.* Womans
name, dat.

ÆIWU, see LILIAÆIWU.

AL, *Jyderup.* ELE-thou, help-thou. 2 s. imper.

AL = ALL. — AL, *Ruthwell.* Ac. s. n. — ALE, *Ruthwell.* Ac. pl. m. — ALMEYOTTIC
Ruthwell. ALMIGHTY. Adj. n. s. m. — ALUWALDO. *Whitby.* ALL-WALD, ALL-WIELDING, almighty
Nom. s. m. def. — ALWIN, *Brough.* ALL-WINE, the friend of all, all-loving. Nom. s. m.

ÆLÆ, *Kragehul.* Of storms. Gen. pl. n.
Ælæwinæ, u. Ælu.

ÆLC, ALH. — ALHS, *Brough.* Mansname, gen. — ÆLCFRITH, *Northumbrian Brooch*
nom.; ALCFRIÐU, *Bewcastle,* ac. Mansname.

Alhs, under Ælc. — Æli, Alla, u. Ælu.

ALTEUILÆA, *Bracteates 49, 49 b.* Mansname, nom.

Æltr, Alts, u. Wald. — Alu, u. Al.

ÆLU, *Bracteates 15, 16, 18, 68, 88; Cörlin; Elgesem;* ALLA, *Yarm.* Mansname, nom. —
ÆLI, *Northumbrian Casket.* Mansname, dat. — ÆLU, *Lindholm.* Perhaps dat. of womansnam
ÆLA. — ÆLUA, *Förde.* Mansname, nom. — ELWÆO, *Bracteate 94.* Probably womansname in dat. —
ELWU, *Bracteate 47.* Mansname, nom. — ELTIL, *Bracteates 43, 44, 45, 85, 86, 87.* Mansname
dat. — ÆLÆWINÆ, *Bracteate 67.* Mansname, dat.

ÆÆLUCÆA, *Bracteate 71.* Mansname, dat.

ALUER, *Holmen.* Mansname, nom.

ALUT, see OWÆALUT.

Aluwaldo. Alwin, u. Al.

ÆMILIU, *Bracteate 61.* Womansname, dat.

AN. — EAN, *Bewcastle.* AN, ONCE, formerly, late. — ? ÆNI, *Veile.* Mansname, nom. —
ÆNÆHÆ, *Möjebro.* Mansname, nom. — ÆNOÆNÆ, *Bracteate 48.* Mansname, nom. — EANREI
Æthred's Ring. Mansname, nom. — ÆNWLL, *Bracteate 25;* ÆNIWULU, *Bracteate 75.* Mans
name, nom.

..... ÆN, see under Aceþæn.

AND, *Bridekirk; Franks Casket; END, Franks Casket.* AND, also.

Æng, u. Inge. — Æniwulu, u. An. — Ann, u. Unna. — Ænoænæ, u. An.

ANS. — ÆNSÆGUI, *Gjevedal.* Mansname, dat. — OSBERCHTAE, *Thornhill.* Mansnam
dat. — ÆSBOA, *Hackness.* Placename, dat. s. m., ASBO or ASBU or ASBY. — OSBIOL, *Broug*
Mansname, nom. — OSCIL, *Brough.* Mansname, nom. — ÆSLAIKIR, *Freerslev.* Mansname, nom. —
ÆSMUTS, *Sölvesborg.* Mansname, gen. — ÆSUGIS, *Kragehul.* ANS-UGG'S = (W)ODEN'S. Gen. —
ONSWINI, *Collingham.* Mansname, ac. — OSWIUNG, *Bewcastle.* Mansname, ac. = OSWI-SON.

Ænwll, u. An. — Ao, u. Æiu.

ÆOAHÆÆ, *Bracteate 6.* ? Dat. s. m. ? To the horseman.

.... (AP)Æ, *Crowle.* Mansname. dat. or ac.

ÆRÆ, *Björketorp, Stentofte.* Ac. s. f. ARE, ORE. lustre, fame. honor. — ERILÆAS, *Lindholm.* Adj. nom. s. ARELESS. ORELESS, unfamed, honorless. — ÆR-RNR, *Freerslev.* Ac. pl. f. ARE-RUNES, honor-staves, respectful epitaph.

A-rærde, u. Raisa.

ÆRBINGÆS, *Tune.* Nom. pl. m.; ÆRBINGÆ, *Tune.* Nom. s. f. (ARVING), heir; heiress. — ARFIKI, *Freerslev.* Heir, son. Nom. s.

Arth, u. Heard.

ÆRÜRIUFLT, *Amulet Rings.* See text.

Æs, u. Ans.

ASPING, *Fonnås.* Mansname, nom. = ASP-SON.

ÆT, *Björketorp, Ruthwell; (? Seude); AT, Thornhill; ET, Varnum.* AT, in, on, near. Prep. gov. dat. and ac. See æt-GADRE.

ADÆ, *Bracteate 59.* Ac. s. m. EAD, fortune, bliss, treasure. — AUTO, *Bracteate 72;* OTÆ, *Bracteates 33, 34;* OTI, *Bracteate 66.* Mansname, nom. — ADÆA, *Einang.* Mansname, dat. — ODUA, *Vånga.* Apparently mansname in dat. See SÆAD. — EADBIERHT, *Bingley.* Mansname, nom. — ÆÆDÆGÆS(LI), *Vi Moss Buckle.* Mansname, nom. — ÆDISL, *Vordingborg.* Same mansname in ac. — (O)DC(U), *Freilaubersheim.* Womansname, dat. — E·ÆDLÆUA, *Bracteates 51, 52.* Mansname, dat. — ÆDODU, *Bracteate 27.* Womansname, dat. — ÆDRED, *Æthred's Ring;* EADRED, *Thornhill.* Mansname, nom. — eADVLFES. *Alnmouth.* Mansname, gen. — EDELBERHT, *Thornhill.* Mansname, nom. — EDELWINI, *Thornhill.* Mansname. dat. — ODLÆ, *Franks Casket.* Dat. s. m. OTHAL, ADAL, home, country, patrimony. — ÆÐÐILÆ, *Ruthwell.* Nom. pl. m. ADEL-ones, nobles.

... ÆÆU ... (or ... NÆU ...), *Kragehul.* See text.

ÆUAIR, *Helnæs.* Mansname, nom.

AULILYOÆ, *Bracteate 8.* Mansname, dat.

ÁUASA (or ÁUSA), *Bracteate 70.* Placename, dat. or ac. ? m.

Auto, under Aþæ.

ÆAWELÆ, *Björketorp.* Probably placename in d. or ac.

AUIK, *Holmen.* Steadname in d. or ac.

BA, *Ruthwell.* Ac. BOTH.

BA, see TUNBA.

BAEDA, *Wycliffe.* Mansname, nom.

BALD, see CÜNIBALD.

BAN, *Franks Casket.* Ac. pl. n. BONES.

Bæræh, under Berig.

BÆRUTA, *Björketorp.* (If not steadname, then) BARRAT, BARRATRY, battle. Dat. s. ? m.

Be, under Bi.

BEAGNOD, *Thames Blade.* Mansname, nom.

Beartigo, u. Berhtæ.

BECKCTO, *Brough.* 3 s. p. BIGGED. built up, raised.

BECUN, *Dewsbury; Falstone; Thornhill; Wycliffe.* Ac. s. n. BEACON, pillar, gravestone. See LIC-BÆCUN, SIG-BECN.

BEORNAE. *Dewsbury.* Dat. s. n. BARN, BAIRN, child, son.

BERÆ, *Kragehul.* See text.

Berg, u. Berig.

BERHTÆ. — See EADBIERHT, ECGBERHT, HROETHBERHTÆ, ... RHTAE, ROETBERHTÆ. — BEARTIGO, *Bracteate 77.* Mansname, (BARTING, BRIGHTING), nom. See CUÞBŒRE(Hting). — BERHTSUIÞE, *Thornhill.* Womans-name. (? Dat.). — BERCHTVINI, *Wycliffe.* Mansname, ac.

BERIG (= BERG, hill). — See FERGEN-BERIG, UANÆ-BÆRÆH. — BERGI, *Thornhill.* Dat. s. n. *The BARROW,* grave-mound, tumulus. — BIRKOIINUM, *Bracteate 92.* Dat. pl. BERGEN, in West Norway.

BI, BE. See beAFTÆ(r), biGOTEN, biHEALD, biHEALDUN, biSMÆRÆDU, biSTEMID.

Bi, under Bua.

geBID, *Bewcastle;* giBID, *Bingley.* 2 s. imperat. BID-thou, pray-thou. — geBIDAED, *Falstone;* geBIDÆD, *Falstone;* giBIDÆD, *Lancaster;* geBIDDAÞ, *Thornhill;* geBIDDÆÞ, *Irton;* giBIDDAD, *Dewsbury.* 2 pl. imperat. BID-ye, BEDE-ye, pray-ye.

Bierht, u. Berhtæ.

BIGI, see WIHUBIGI(æ).

BIM, *Fonnås.* 1 sing. pres. I BE, I am.

Bio, under Bua. — Biol, u. Bul.

BIRLNIO (= BIRLINIO), *Nordendorf.* Womansname, dat.

BLODÆ, *Ruthwell.* BLOOD, dat. s. n.

Bo, Boa, Boæn, u. Bua. — Bœre(hting), u. Berhtæ. — Bonte, u. Bua.

BOSO, *Freilaubersheim.* Mansname, nom.

BRUÞR, *Selsey.* Nom. s. BROTHER. — BRÆODERA, *Yarm.* Dat. s. BROTHER. — giBROÞÆRA, *Franks Casket.* N. pl. BROTHERS. — BRUÞUR-SUNU, *Helnæs.* Ac. s. BROTHER-SON, nephew.

BROK, *Brough.* Ac. s. n. BROKE, sorrow, death.

BROKTE, *Bridekirk.* 3 s. p. BROUGHT.

BUA, *Thames fitting.* Inf. To BOO, BO, bide, dwell. — See ÆSBOA, UNNBO, UNBOÆU. — BONTE, *Holmen.* Nom. s.; B(Uætæ), *Varnum.* Ac. s. BONDE, husband. — See CUOMBILBIO, ECBI.

BUCIAEHOM, *Brough.* Placename, ? dat. s. m.

(B)UG(A), *Ruthwell.* Inf. To BOW, bend.

BUL, see OSBIOL, RÆHÆBUL. — BURÆ, see HURNBURÆ. — BURG, see KUNNBURCG.

K....., u. CUMBEL.

CADMON, *Ruthwell.* Mansname, nom.

CALLU, see GÆÆCALLU. — KAR, see GAR.

Kærþi, Karþi, u. G.

CÆSTRI. see ROMÆCÆSTRI.

CEARUNGIA, *Brough.* Gen. s. f. CARING'S, sorrow's.

Kearstin, u. Krist.

KER, see ÆHEKER, and GAR.

CIÆGO, *Charnay.* Ac. s. f. (KEENG), brooch, fibula.

CIL, see OSCIL.

CĪMOKOMS, *Brough.* Womansname, gen.

CLÆO. *Cleobury.* ? f. Nom. s. A CLAW (pointer, sundial-gnomon).

KLOKO. *Holmen.* Ac. s. f. CLOCK, bell.

COECAS, *Brough.* 3 s. pr. QUETCHES, shall move, shall afflict.

COINŪ, *Brough.* QUENE, wife, gen. s.

KOMS, see CĪMOKOMS.

CORNILIO, *Bracteate 75.* Mansname, nom.

Korþe, under G.

KRIST, *Brough; Ruthwell;* KRISTTUS. *Bewcastle.* Nom. CHRIST. — KEARSTIN, *Mörbylånga.* Womansname (CHRISTINA), nom.

Ku, under Cūnūng.

CUHL, *Brough.* Mansname, nom.

CUMBEL. — K....., *Mörbylånga.* Ac. s. or pl. neut. CUMBEL, gravemark. — CUOMBIL-BIO, *Brough.* CUMBEL-BOO, grave-kist. Ac. s. n.

CUN, see SEHS-CUNÆ.

CUN, CUD. — CUNIBALD, *Lancaster.* Mansname, ac. — CUDBŒRE(Hting), *Lancaster.* Mansname, ac. = CUTHBERTSON. — KŪNNBURUG. *Bewcastle.* Womansname, nom. — CUNIMUDIU, *Bracteate 25.* Womansname, dat. — KUÞUMUT, *Helnæs.* Mansname, ac. = GUDMUND. — GONRAT, *Osthofen;* GUDRID, *Northumbrian Brooch.* Mansname, nom. — KŪNESWIÞA. *Bewcastle.* Womansname, nom. — KUNUÆLTS, *Snoldelev.* Mansname, gen.

CŪNŪNG, *Bingley;* KŪNG, *Bewcastle;* CUN, *Bracteate 75;* nom. — KŪNINGES, *Bewcastle,* gen. — KŪNING, *Bewcastle;* CŪNINGC, *Ruthwell;* CUN(ŪNC). *Leeds;* CU...., *Collingham.* Accus. KING. CŪN(niæs), *Whitby.* Gen. s. n. KIN. family.

Cuombil, u. Cumbel.

CURNE, see HÆCURNE.

Cuþbœre(hting), u. Cun. — Kuþi, u. God. — Kuþumut, u. Cun.

KWOMU, *Ruthwell.* 3 pl. p. CAME.

DÆBS, *Thames fitting.* Gen. s. n. The DEEP, sea, ocean.

Daer, under Þe.

DÆGÆ, *Einang;* DAH, *Osthofen.* Mansname, nom. See GODÆGÆS. — DÆGMUND, *Gilton Sword.* Mansname, voc. — DÆITUHÆ, *Bracteate 79.* Mansname, nom.

DÆLIDUN, *Tune.* 3 pl. p. DEALED, shared, took part in.

DÆRING(e), *Thornhill.* Mansname, dat.

DARSTÆ, DARSTE, *Ruthwell.* 1 s. p. DURST, dared.

DÆÞYONÆ. *Freilaubersheim.* Gen. pl. Of the DÆTHE clan or family.

DÆUDE, *Björketorp.* 3 s. p. DIED, fell.

Der, under Þe.

DIK, *Ingelstad.* Dat. s. To-THEE.

DOHTR, *Tune.* Nom. s. DAUGHTER.

DOM. *Franks Casket.* Nom. s. m. DOOM, Court, Judgment. DOMGISL may possibly be the artist's name.

DŒP-STAN. *Bingley.* Ac. s. m. DIP-STONE, Font.

DRYGYÞ, *Franks Casket.* 3 s. pr. DREETH, suffers; or, does, performs.

geDRŒFED, *Ruthwell.* Pp. DROVED, harrowed, grieved.

DROMDH, see SUNEDROMDH.

E, Eæ, under Æiu.

EAC, *Bewcastle;* EC, *Brough;* OK, *Holmen;* UK, *Holmen.* EKE, and. — YCE, *Gilton Sword.*

1 s. pr. I EKE, EIK, increase, add to.

EAN, u. AN.

EATEYONNE, *Thornhill.* Womansname (? EATEYA), dat.

Eæþlæua, u. Aþæ.

Ec, u. Eac and Ic. '— Ecai, u. Æiu.

ECBI, *Brough.* Placename, ? dat. s. m.   See ACLIHCK.

ECG, ECH, EC. — ECGBERHT, *Bracteate 70.* Mansname, nom. — ECGFRIDU, *Bewcastle.* Mansname, gen. — ECHLEW, *Gallehus.* Mansname, nom. — ECMU, *Bracteate 5.* Mansname, nom. — ECWIWÆA, *Tune.* Womansname, nom.

EL . . . ., *Selsey.*

ELS, *Nordendorf.*   Mansname, nom.

Eltil, Elwu. u. Ælu. — End, u. And.

ENRUK, *Mörbylånga.*   Mansname, HENRIK, HENRY, nom.

EOMÆ, EOMAE, *Falstone.* Dat. s. m. EME, uncle.

Eomær, under Æiu.

ERHA, *Thames fitting.* Dat. s. m. ARG, wave-rush, trough of the sea.

ERILÆA, *Kragehul; Lindholm.* Mansname, nom.

Et, under Æt.

F, *Konghell.* Probably for FUR or FORÆ, FOR, over.   See FORÆ.

FÆHI (no room for more), *Bracteate 96;* FÆIHIDO, *Einang;* FÆÆDÆ, *Bracteate 89;* FAADO, *Flemlöse;* FADI, *Helnæs;* FAUŒDO, *Ruthwell;* FEG(de). *Alnmouth;* FIHÆDU, *Bracteates 49, 49 b;* FYIDI, *Bracteate 92;* FYDÆI, *Charnay;* FUÞE, *Osthofen.* 3 s. p. — FAIDU, *Brough.* 3 pl. p. — FAWED, FAYED, made, carved, stampt, wrote, built up, raised.

FÆLÆ, *Björketorp.* Ac. s. m. FELE, multitude, much, many.

FASTS, see RUULFASTS. — FASTI, see INOFASTI.

Faþi, u. Fæihido.

FADUR, *Vordingborg;* FADR, *Ösby.* Ac. s. FATHER.

FÆUÆ, *Bracteate 57.* Mansname, voc.

FEARRAN, *Ruthwell.* Adv. FAR-FROM.

Feg(de), under Fæihido.

FEGTAÐ, *Franks Casket.* 3 pl. pr. FIGHT.

FERGEN-BERIG, *Franks Casket.* Ac. s. m. Steadname in Northumbria.

FH, *Konghell.* Probably = FUR HARI, for the army.

Fihædu, Fyidi, u. Fæihido.

FINO, *Berga.* Mansname, nom.

Firth, under Frith.

FISC-FLODU, *Franks Casket.* Nom. s. m. FISH-FLOOD, sea, ocean.

Fyþæi, u. Fæihido.

FLODU, see FISC-FLODU.

FŒDDE, *Franks Casket.* 3 s. p. FED. nourisht.

FORÆ, *Irton, Lancaster;* FORE, *Ruthwell;* FÛR, *Bingley.* FOR (dat.); FORE. before (ac.). See F.

FOSLÆU, *Bracteate 14.* Mansname, nom.

FRÆWÆRÆDÆA, *Möjebro.* Mansname, dat.

FRID, see ÆLCFRITH, ALCFRIDU, ECGFRIDU, TIDFIRD.

FRUMAN, *Bewcastle.* Abl. s. n. def. In the FRUM, first.

FUNDR, see DIWBYO-FUNDR.

Fûr, under Foræ.

FUSÆ, *Ruthwell.* N. pl. m. FUSSY, eager, hurrying.

Fuþe, under Fæihido. .

FUWU, *Bracteate 26.* Mansname, nom.

G (= GARDI), *Eidsberg;* KÆRDI, *Vordingborg;* KARDI, *Ingelstad;* KORDE. *Mörbylånga.* 3 s. p. GARED, made, set up, built up, raised (the grave, grave-stone). — ONGEREDÆ, *Ruthwell.* 3 s. p. A-GARED, prepared.

GÆ, *Kragehul;* GÆA, *Lindholm.* 2 s. imperat. GO! — GÆGIN, *Kragehul.* Prep. GAIN, AGAIN, against.

GÆÆCALLU, *Bracteate 19.* Mansname, nom.

ætGADRE, *Ruthwell.* AT(-to)GETHER.

GÆFING, *Stentofte.* Nom. = GÆF'S-SON; or = of the Gæf family.

Gægin, u. Gæ. — Gæhælæibæn. u. Hælæibæn.

GAL, *Bracteate 7.* Mansname, nom.

GALGU, *Ruthwell.* Ac. s. m. GALLOW(s), rood, cross.

GÆLIEA, *Northumbrian Casket.* ? Gen. s. f. Of GAUL, in GALLIA.

GAR. see ÆHEKER, IAULIGR, ODINKAR, WODGAR.

Gæsli, under Gisli.

GASRIC, *Franks Casket.* Nom. s. m. GAS-RICH, gambol-rich, playful, tossing.

GÆSTIA, see SÆLIGÆSTIA.

GEAR, *Bewcastle.* Abl. s. n. YEAR.

Gebid, &c. u. geBID. — On-geredæ, u. G.

ȝERNR, *Bridekirk.* Nom. s. m. YERN, GIRN, willing, glad.

GESSUS, *Bewcastle.* Nom. JESUS.

GEU, *Björketorp;* GEUW, *Stentofte.* Adv. YO, YAY, YEA, truly, indeed.

Giauyou, under Gib.

GIB, *Bracteate 57.* 2 s. imperat. GIVE, lend, send! — GIAUYOU, see GLYOÆU-GIAUYOU.

Gibid, u. Bid. — Gibroþæra, u. Bruþr. — Gileu, u. Hlæiwæ. — Gileugæ, u. Hlæiwæ and Licgan.

GINÆ-RUNÆA, *Björketorp.* Nom. pl. f.; GINO-RONOA, *Stentofte.* Ac. pl. f. GIN- (= begin, origin, essence, power) RUNES, Mighty Letters.

GINIA, *Möjebro.* Womansname, nom.

Giniæra, u. Niæra. — Gino, u. Ginæ.

GYOSLHEARD, *Dover.* Mansname, nom.

GISL, *Franks Casket.* Nom. s. m. Hostage. See ÆDÆGÆSLI, ÆDISL, DOM. — GISLIONG-WILI, *Vi Plane.* Mansname, nom.

GIUÞEASU, *Franks Casket.* Nom. pl. The JEWS.

GLÆ, *Bracteate 21.* Mansname, nom. — GLYOÆU-GIAUYOU, *Bracteate 7.* Womansname, dat.

GLÆSTÆPONTOL, see *Amulet Rings.*

GOD, *Ruthwell;' Whitby.* Nom. The Lord GOD. — KUÞI, *Helnœs.* Nom. s. m. GUTHI, (hereditary) Priest-and-Judge. — GOIÞU, *Freilaubersheim.* Gen. s. f. Priestess. See HILDDIGUÞ.

GODÆGÆS, *Valsfjord.* Mansname (GOODDAY), nom. Goiþu, u. God. — Gonrat, u. Kuni.

biGOTEN, *Ruthwell.* Pp. n. s. f. BE-YOTEN, besprinkled, bathed.

GREUT, *Franks Casket.* Ac. s. m. GRIT, gravel, sand, shingles, coast.

aGROF. *Æthred's Ring.* 3 s. p. A-GROOF, A-GRAVED, engraved, cut. made.

GRORN, *Franks Casket.* Pp. GRUSEN, crusht, dasht in pieces, killed.

GUTÆ, *Buzeu.* Gen. pl. Of the GOTHS.

GUÞ, see HILDDIGUÞ and GOD.

Gudrd, under Kun.

H, *Konghell.* Probably for HARI, dat. s. m., the HÆR, HERE, army, fleet. See HÆRISO. Hæ, under Hao.

HÆBO, *Stentofte.* 3 pl. pr. They HAVE, shall have.

HÆDULÆICÆA. *Strand.* Dat. s. Mansname. To-HÆDULÆICÆ. — HÆÞUWOLÆFA, *Stentofte.* nom.: HÆFUWOLÆFÆ, *Gommor,* HYÞUWULÆFA, *Istaby,* dat. — Mansname.

Hæere, u. Heræ. — Hæg, u. Hieawan.

HÆGÆLÆ, *Kragehul.* Probably ac. Mansname.

HÆGUSTÆLDIA, *Valsfjord.* Dat. s. m. To the HAGUSTALD, chief. lord, captain. Hæi-tinæ. under Hao.

HÆIDAR, masc. (HADOR), brightness, honor, fame. — HÆIDAR-RUNO. *Björketorp.* Nom. s. (HADOR-RUNA). that honor's friend. — HIDEAR-RUNGNO, *Stentofte.* Nom. pl. neut. (HADOR-REGEN), those honor's lords.

HÆILÆG, *Buzeu.* ? Nom. s. f.: AILIC, *Brough.* Nom. s. f.; HELG . . ., *Bakewell.* HOLY. sacred: dedicated. — HÆLHI, *Maeshowe.* nom.; HILIGÆA, *Orstad,* dat. — Mansname (HELGI, HELGE).

HÆISLÆ, *Möjebro.* Mansname, nom.

Hæite, Hæiticæ. u. Hætec. — Hæi-tinæ, u. Hao. — Hælæa, u. Hlæiwæ. — Hæræiwido, u. Hœges.

gœHÆLÆIBÆN, *Tune.* Dat. s. m. LOAF-fellow, com-panion. mate, husband. — HLAFARD, *Ruthwell.* Ac. s. m. LORD.

Hældæa. Hældæo. Hælbæda, u. Heldæa. — Hælhi, u. Hæilæg.

HALSTUN, *Ösby.* Mansname, nom.

HAMA. *Bracteate 58.* Mansname, nom.

HAO. — HÆ, *Bracteate 57:* HE, *Kragehul.* 2 s. imperat. HIGH. lift up, raise. carry on, wage, cause, make, let. — HAO, *Einang.* Mansname, nom. — HÆ-CURNE, *Bracteate 25.* Nom. s. m. def. The HIGH-CHOSEN. — HEO-SINNA, *Bewcastle.* Dat. s. f. The HIGH-SIN. or HIGH-SINFUL. — HÆI-TINÆ. *Tanum.* Nom. s. m. HIGH-TINE, high token, grave-pillar. — HÆUC, *Vânga.* Mansname. nom. — See HŒGES.

Hær. Hæeræ, Hæræ, under Heræ.

HÆRING.E. *Vi Moss:* HÆRING, *Skå-äng.* Mansname, nom. (But HÆRINGÆ, if we divide HÆRINGÆ GILEUGÆ). — HÆRENGU. *Bracteate 78.* Womansname, dat.

HÆRISO, *Himlingöie.* (? Mans)-name, nom. — HÆRIWOLÆFA, *Stentofte,* nom.; HARIWULFS, *Röfsal,* gen.; HYRIWULÆFÆ, *Istaby,* dat. — Mansname. — See WULFHERE and H.

HÆTEC (= HÆTE EC), *Lindholm;* HÆITE, *Kragehul;* 1 s. pr. I HIGHT, bid, command. — HET. *Bingley.* 3 s. p. HOTE, ordered, let. — HÆITICÆ, *Bracteate 57.* Ac. pl. f. HETINGS, imprecations, threats, *the war-ban.*

Hæþuwolæfa, &c., under Hædulæicæa. — Hæuc, u. Hao. — Haufþuükü, u. Heafdum. HÆURI, *Hoga.* Mansname, nom.

HE, *Bridekirk: Franks Casket; Ruthwell.* Nom. s. m. HE. — HIS, *Ruthwell: Yarm.* Gen. Of him, HIS. — HIM, *Ruthwell.* Dat. To HIM. — HINÆ, *Ruthwell.* Ac. HIM. — HLE, *Ruthwell.* N. pl. m.; HI.E, *Franks Casket.* Ac. pl. m. They; them. — See IS. He. under Hao.

HEAFDUM, *Ruthwell.* Dat. pl. n. HEAD(S), temples, head. — HAUFÞUÜKÜ, *Konghell.* Nom. s. m. (As if HEADING), Headman, Leader, Commander. Chief.

HEAFUNÆS, *Ruthwell.* Gen. s. m. HEAVEN'S.

biHEALD, *Ruthwell.* 1 s. p.; biHEALDUN, *Ruthwell.* 3 pl. p. BEHELD.

HEARD, see GYOSLHEARD, RIKARTH.

HELDÆA. *Bracteate 25;* HÆLHÆDA, *Björketorp:* HÆLDÆO, *Sigdal;* HELÆHDDUÆ, *Stentofte.* Gen. pl. m. Of HELTS, kemps, heroes.

Helg . . ., under Hæilæg.

HELIPÆ, *Whitby.* 3 s. pr. subj. May-HELP.

Heo-sinna. under Hao.

HERÆ. *Stentofte:* HÆR, ? *Skå-äng:* HÆR(Æ), *Orstad: Thisted;* HER. *Franks Casket;* HÆERÆ, *Björketorp.* HERE. in this place.

Here, u. Hæriso. — Het, u. Hætec. — Hiæ, u. He. — Hidear, u. Hæidar.

HYERUWULÆFIA. *Istaby.* Womansname, nom.

HIEWAN, *Bingley.* Inf. To HEW, carve, cut; stamp, strike. — ÆA, *Hoga;* HÆG, *Bracteate 68;* HIUK. *West Thorp;* HO, *Bracteate 62;* HU, *Bracteate 78;* HÜUG, *Bracteate 61;* UK, *Freerslev.* 3 s. p. HEWED, made, inscribed.

HILDDIGÜD, *Hartlepool.* Womansname, nom. — HILDIÞRÜÞ, *Hartlepool.* Womansname, nom. Hiligæa, u. Hæilæg. — Him, Hine, u. He. — Hyriwulæfæ, u. Hæriso. — His, u. He. — Hyþuwulæfa, u. Hædulæicæa. — Hiuk, u. Hiewan.

HHLÆÆDU-UIGÆ, *Bracteates 49. 49 b.* Mansname, nom.

Hlafard, under Hælæibæn.

HLEIWÆ, *Bö;* HÆLÆA, *Stenstad:* LAU, *West Tanem;* LEUWÆ, *Skärkind.* Nom. s. m. or n. — LÆEWE (or LÆIWÆI), *Sigdal.* Ac. s. — LOW (LOWE, LOE, LAW), grave-mound, barrow, tumulus. The LEUGÆ of the Skå-äng stone is probably the same word; and we might possibly divide: HÆRINGÆ giLEUGÆ AI, or HÆRINGÆ giLEU gæAI. Fresh finds may help us. See Vol. 2. p. 890.

HLEUNG. *Vi Plane.* Mansname, nom., = HLESON, (LEESON, LEASON).

HLVÞWYG, *Alnmouth.* Mansname, nom.

HNÆBMÆS (or HNÆBDÆS), *Bö.* Mansname, gen.

Hnag, under Niyæ. — Ho, u. Hiewan.

aHOF, *Ruthwell*, 1 s. p.; *Franks Casket*, 3 s. p.   A-HOVE, lifted up, raised.

HŒGES, *Stentofte.* Gen. s. m.; HOUH, *Brough.* Ac. s. m. HOW, grave-mound, tumulus.
See SAL-HAUKUM. — HÆÆIWIDO, *Strand.* 3 pl. p. HOWED, set in the grave-how, buried. —
See HAO.

HOLTINGÆA, *Gallehus.* Dat. s. m. HOLT-INGE, Wood-god (= FREA, FROE, FREY).

HOM, see BUCIAEHOM.

HORNÆ, *Gallehus.* Ac. pl. neut. These-HORNS. (Perhaps ac. s. masc. This-HORN). —
HURNBURÆ, *Kallerup.* Mansname, gen.

HOUÆA, *Bracteate 24 (? and 55).* Mansname, dat.
Houh, u. Hœges. — Hroetberhtæ, u. Hroþor.

HRONÆS, *Franks Casket.* Gen. s. m. Of the HRONE (whale).

HROÐOR. — HROETBERHTÆ, ROETBERHTÆ, *Falstone.* Mansname, dat. — RHOÆL(T)R, *Vatn,*
nom.; RUHALTS, *Snoldelev,* gen. Mansname, = HRODWALD, ROALD. — RHUULFR, *Helnœs,* nom.;
ROAUL, *Hoga,* dat. Mansname, = HRODWULF, ROLF. — RUULFASTS, *Voldtofte,* nom. Mansname,
= HRODWULF-FASTS.

HU. *Fonnås.* (HO), *she.* — *Sealand.* Probably the beginning of a Mansname.
Hu, under Hiewan. — Hurnburæ, u. Hornæ. — Hûug, u. Hiewan.

HUTHU, *Bracteate 4.* Mansname, nom.

HW, *Bårse, Vordingborg.* Probably H ... (a name beginning with H) and WRAIT, wrote.

HWÆTRED, *Bewcastle.* Mansname, nom.

HWEÐRÆ, *Ruthwell.* Adv. WHETHER-or-no, yet, lo!

HUILER, *Thisted.* 3 s. pr. WHILES, rests, reposes.

I, under In. — Ia, u. Is. — Yia. u. Inge.

IAM, see LAICIAM.

IAULIGR, *Bracteate 92.* Mansname, nom.

Iauþini, under Aþ.

IC, *Ruthwell;* IK, *Gilton;* IH, *Fonnås;* EC, *Kragehul, Lindholm.* The pronoun I. — MIK,
Gilton; MIC. *Osthofen;* MC, *Etelhem;* MEC, *Æthred's Ring, Northumbrian Brooch;* MEH, *Alnmouth;*
ME, *Bridekirk;* MÆ, *Ruthwell,* ME. — UNGCET, *Ruthwell.* Acc. dual. US-TWO. — US, *Bingley,*
dat. pl.: Whitby, ac. pl. US. — USA, *Björketorp.* Nom. pl. fem. OUR.

Icæa, Ycæa, Ykcæa, u. Inge. — Yce, u. Eac. — Ichiay, Ikr, Ikkalacgc, Icwæsuna,
u. Inge.

IDDÆN, *Charnay.* Mansname, dat.
Yfæta, Ift, u. AFT. — Ygœa, Ihœæ, u. Inge. — Igilsuiþ, under Ægili.

IGINGON, *Stenstad.* Man's (? Woman's) name, gen. = IGING'S.

IGLEUGÆ (if we divide HÆRINGÆ IGLEUGÆ), *Skå-äng.* Nom. sing. def., *the* GLEG, bright,
prudent, wise.

Ih, u. Ic. — Ihae, u. Inge.

ILÆURI, *Hoga.* Mansname, nom.

ILLÆ, *Lindholm.* Nom. s m. defin. The ILL, fierce, destructive to his foes.
Imæ, under Is.

IN, *Franks Casket, Northumbrian Casket;* I, *Björketorp, Bracteate 92, Brough. Holmen,*
Thames Fitting, Varnum. IN.

ɪɴ, *Freerslev.* Adv. (ɪɴ, ᴇɴ, ᴀɴ), *but.*

In, under Is.

ɪɴɢᴇ, ɪɴɢᴡᴇ, (and ᴡɪɴɢs, &c.). — ᴜɴɢᴀ, *Bracteate 67.* Dat. s. m. def. The ʏᴏᴜɴɢ. — ᴊᴋᴄ, *Brough.* Ac. s. m. or n. ʏᴏᴜɴɢ. renewed. — ʏᴀᴄᴀ. *Bracteate 84;* ɪᴄᴀᴀ. *Bracteate 35;* ᴄᴀᴀ, *Bracteates 36, 39;* ʏᴋᴄᴀᴀ. *Bracteate 41;* ʏɢᴏᴀ, *Bracteate 41, b;* ʏɪᴀ, *Bracteate 37;* Womansname, nom. — ɪᴋʀ (= ɪɴᴋᴜʀ). *Freerslev.* Womansname, gen. — ɪɴᴋɪ, *Bracteate 83;* ᴄʜɪᴀʏ, *Bracteate 38,* nom.; ɪʜᴀᴀ, *Varnum,* dat. Mansname. — See ᴀᴀʟᴀᴜᴄᴀᴀ, ᴀʀʙɪɴɢᴀ, ᴀʀʙɪɴɢᴀs, ɪsᴘɪɴɢ, ʙᴇᴀʀᴛɪɢᴏ, ᴅᴀʀɪɴɢ(e), ᴇʟᴀᴜɪɴɢs, ɢᴀғɪɴɢ, ɢɪsʟɪᴏɴɢ, ʜᴀᴜғᴅᴜᴏᴋᴜ, ʜᴀɪᴛɪᴄᴀ, ʜᴇʀɪɴɢ, ʜᴀʀɪɴɢᴀ, ᴋᴀᴜᴄ, ʜʟᴇᴜɴɢ, ɪɢɪɴɢᴏɴ, ʜᴏʟᴛɪɴɢᴀᴀ, ? ɪsɪɴɢᴅᴀᴀ. ɪᴜᴅɪɴɢᴀᴀ, ʟᴀɪɴɢ, ʟᴀᴀsᴀᴜᴡɪɴɢᴀ, ʟᴀᴜᴄᴀᴀ, ᴀᴇᴡᴜʟᴏᴜᴄᴀᴀ, ᴍᴡsʏᴏᴜɪɴɢɪ, ɴᴀᴅᴜʏᴀɴɢ, ? ɴɪᴡᴀɴɢ, ɴᴏᴅᴜɪɴɢᴏᴀ, ᴏsᴡɪᴜɴɢ, (ᴏ)ᴅᴄ(ᴜ), ʀᴀɴɪɴɢᴀ, sᴀᴍᴀɴɢ, ɴᴇɪᴄ, sᴜɪᴅɪᴋs, ᴛᴀʟɪɴɢ, ᴛɪsᴀᴄɢ, ᴅɪᴇᴅʀᴏᴅᴡᴇɴᴄ, ᴅʀᴀᴡɪɴɢᴇɴ, ᴡᴀʀɪɴɢᴀᴀ. — ɪɴɢᴏᴀ, fem. See ɴᴏᴅᴜɪɴɢᴏᴀ, ᴀᴇʟɪɴɢᴡᴜ. — ᴀʜᴇᴄᴇʀ (= ɪɴɢᴇᴋᴇʀ), *Varnum.* Womansname, nom. — ɪᴋᴋᴀʟᴀᴄɢᴄ, *Brough.* Mansname, nom. — ɪɴɢᴏsᴛ, *Tune.* Mansname, nom. — ɪᴄᴡᴀsᴜɴᴀ, *Reidstad.* Mansname, dat.

ɪɴɢʟsᴋ, *Fonnås.* Nom. s. fem. ᴇɴɢʟɪsʜ. an Englishwoman.

ɪɴᴏ, *Strand,* n. Mansname. — ɪɴᴏғᴀsᴛɪ, *Visby,* nom. Mansname.

ɪᴏᴅ, *Freilaubersheim.* Nom. s. neut. A ʏᴏᴜᴛʜ, child, son, daughter.

ɪᴏʜɴ, *Bracteate 62.* Mansname, nom.

Yoiæ, u. Is.

ɪs. — ɪᴍᴀ, *Bracteate 67.* Dat. s. masc. To the. — ɪɴ, *Strand.* Ac. s. m. Him. — ʏᴏʟᴀ, *Charnay.* Ac. s. f. The. this. — ɪᴀ, *Tune,* (ʜɪᴀ), they, nom. pl. — See ʜᴇ.

Is, under Wæs.

ɪsᴀʜ, *St. Andrews.* Mansname, nom.

Ysetae, u. (Set)a.

? ɪsɪɴɢᴅᴀᴀ. *Veile.* Mansname, dat.

Isl, under Gisl.

ɪɪᴛ, *West Thorp;* ɪᴛᴏ, *Bracteate 42.* Mansname, nom.

Ito, u. Iit. — Iukc. u. Inge. — (I)ugo, u. Oæg.

ɪᴜʟɪᴇɴɪ, *Bracteate 61.* Mansname, nom.

ʏᴜɪʀ, *Osby.* ᴏᴠᴇʀ, in memory of. Prep. gov. acc.

ɪᴜᴅɪɴɢᴀᴀ, *Reidstad.* Mansname, dat.

ɪᴡɪ, *Cleobury.* ᴇʏᴇ. give eye to, show, point out: 3 s. pr. subj.

Iwka, u. Æiu. — iWrokte, u. Woræhto.

K, under C.

ʟ, *Nydam Arrow.* A contraction, (beginning of a name).

-ʟᴀ, -ʟᴀ, see ᴍɪʀɪʟᴀ, ɴɪᴜᴡɪʟᴀ.

Læ, under Læwu.

ʟᴀᴀ, *Varnum.* Dat. or ac. s. Placename.

ʟᴀ-ᴏʀʙ(ᴀ), *Vi Plane.* Acc. s. or gen. pl. ʟᴇᴀ-staff, sithe-shaft.

ʟᴀᴄɢᴄ, see ɪᴋᴋᴀʟᴀᴄɢᴄ.

ʟᴀᴅᴀ (perhaps ʟᴀᴍᴀ), *Torvik.* Mansname, nom.

Læewe, under Hlæiwæ.

ʟᴀғ, see ᴏʟᴜғʀ. ᴏɴʟᴀғ, ᴅʀʟᴀғ.

ʟᴀɪᴄ, see ᴀsʟᴀɪᴋɪʀ. ʜᴀᴅᴜʟᴀɪᴄᴀᴀ.

34

Laiciam, under Licæs.

LAING, *Fonnâs.* Nom. = LA-ING, = LA's-child.

LÆMÆ (perhaps LÆDÆ), *Torvik.* Mansname, nom.

LANUM, *Ruthwell.* Dat. s. m. (LEAN), worn, death-weary.

Laoku, under Læucæa.

LÆÆSÆUWINGÆ, *Vi Moss Buckle.* Mansname, nom.

Lau, u. Hlæiwæ. — Læu, u. Læwu.

LEUCÆA, *Bracteate 18.* Dat.; LAOKU, *Bracteate 54.* Nom. Mansname. See ÆÆLÆUCÆA, LÆWULOUCÆA.

Læuwæ, under Hlæiwæ.

LÆWU. — LÆ, *Bracteate 21.* Mansname, nom. — LÆWULOUCÆA, *Bracteate 19.* Mansname, dat. — See EÆDLÆUA, ECHLEW, FOSLÆU.

aLegdun, under Lice.

LETO, *Holmen.* 3 pl. p. LET, caused, ordered.

LEDRO (perhaps LUDRO), *Dalby.* ? Woman's (? Man's) name, nom.

LEUBWINI, see ÆLEUBWINI.

Leugæ, u. Lice. — Leuwæ, u. Hlæiwæ. — Lew, u. Læwu.

LIA, *Tune.* Mansname, nom.

LICÆS. *Ruthwell.* Gen. s. neut. Of a LICH, LIK, corpse. — LIC-BÆCUN, *Crowle.* Ac. s. n. LIK-BEACON, corpse-pillar, grave-stone. — LAICIAM, *Brough.* Ac. s. m. LICH-HOME, fleshy-cover, body, soul-robe.

LICE, *Bewcastle.* 3 s. pr. subj. Let-him-LIE, sleep, rest. — aLEGDUN, *Ruthwell.* 3 pl. p. A-LAID, laid down. — LEUGÆ, *Skâ-äng.* ? Ac. s. n. LEY, couch, bed, grave. See u. HLÆIWÆ. But also see IGLEUGÆ.

LIHCK, see ACLIHCK.

LILIAÆIWU, *Bracteate 79.* Womansname, dat.

LIM-WŒRIGNE, *Ruthwell.* Ac. s. m. LIMB-WEARY.

LIN, see BIRLINIO.

LONÆWORE, *Nordendorf.* Mansname, nom.

Loucæa, under Læucæa.

LDN, *Bracteate 80.* Perhaps a contraction of LIDIN, p. part. nom. s. LITHEN, gone; deceast.

LUÆ, *Nydam.* Mansname, nom.

Lufr, under Læf.

LUL, *Bracteate 70.* Mansname, nom.

LUDÆ, *Bracteate 22.* Gen. pl. m. LEDES, men, people.

Luþro, under Leþro.

M (? = MARKADE), *Sigdal.* 3 s. p. MARKT, carved, inscribed. — M (= MOT), *Bracteate 75.* N. s. f. (or neut.). MOT, stamp, die, mint, coin, minthouse.

MÆ, see HNÆBMÆS, and under Ik, Magan.

[MAGAN]. — MÆ, *Stentofte.* Nom. s. m. MO, great, mighty. — alMEYOTTIG, u. AL. — MUCNU, *Stentofte.* Ac. s. f. A MUCKLE, MICKLE, multitude.

MÆGI, *Franks Casket.* Latin. N. pl. m. MAGI, Wise Men.

MÆGUM, *Strand.* Dat. pl. With his MAUGS, kinsfolk.

MÆLÆ, *Björketorp, Stentofte.* 3 pl. pr. MELE, MELL, say, tell.

MÆNIS, *West Tanem.* Mansname, gen.

MÆR, see EOMÆR. — MÆRIA, see NIWÆNG-MÆRIA.

MARIU, *Ingelstad.* Womansname (MARIA, MARY), dat.

Mc, Mec, Meh, u. Ic. — Men, u. Mon.

MERGE, *Gilton.* Adv. MERRILY. — MERTHE, *Bridekirk.* Dat. s. f. MIRTH. beauty.

MIA, see AIVOMIA. — Mic, Mik, u. Ic.

...(M)INGH(O).., *Bakewell.* See text.

MYRCNA, *Bewcastle.* Gen. pl. Of-the-MERCIANS, of Mercia.

MYREDAH, *Alnmouth.* Mansname, nom.

MIRILÆ, *Sigdal,* nom. or voc.; MiRiLÆ, *Etelhem.* nom. — MIRILÆA, *Væblungsnæs,* dat. Mansname.

MID, *Ruthwell.* Prep. (MITH), WITH.

MODIG, *Ruthwell.* Nom. s. m. MOODY, bold.

MODU, see MUD.

MON, see CADMON. — MEN, *Ruthwell.* Ac. pl. MEN.

Mrlæ, u. Mirilæ. — MU, see ECMU. — Mucnu, u. Magan.

MUND, MUNDR, see ÆSMUTS, KUDUMUT, DÆGMUND, EMUNDR, SIHMYWNT. — MUNDIA, see CUNIMUDIU.

MUNGPÆLYO, *Northumbrian Casket.* Placename, probably dat. s. Now MONTPELLIER.

MWSYOUINGI, *Krogstad.* Mansname, nom.

MUT, *Lindholm.* Prep. Against.

Muts, u. Mund. — MUD, see SCANOMODU, DURMUD.

N...., *Selsey,* rest of the word gone.

NADÆ, *Bracteate 73.* Mansname, nom. — NÆDUYÆNG, *Bracteate 24.* Mansname, nom.

...NÆU... (or ...ÆÆU...), *Kragehul.* See text.

unNEG, *Franks Casket.* Prep. gov. dat. UN-NIGH, far from.

NEDII, *Northumbrian Casket.* Mansname, nom.

NI, *Lindholm, Ruthwell.* Adv. (NE), NAY, NO, NOT.

giNIÆRA, *Dearham.* NÆRE, save, bless, 3 s. pr. subj.

NIT, NID, see UNITR.

NIU, *Stentofte;* NIO, *Buzeu.* Dat. s. n. defin. The-NEW, fresh. — NIUWILÆ, *Bracteate 80.* Mansname, nom.

NIYÆ, *Kragehul.* Prob. inf. To (NEEG), bow, bend, fall. — HNAG, *Ruthwell.* 1 s. p. I inclined.

NIWÆNG-MÆRIA, *Thorsbjerg Sword.* Womansname, nom.

NOD, see BEAGNOD. — NODUINGOA, *Tune.* Womansname, nom.

NU, *Björketorp, Bracteate 59.* Adv. NOW.

NURA, *Helnæs.* Of the NUR clan or land.

O, under Agan, On.

OÆG, *Björketorp.* 3 s. p.; (I)UGO. or perhaps (W)UGO, *Stentofte.* 3 pl. p. (WOOG), slew, hunted, routed.

OC. *Brough.* Adv. (AC, OC), but, but indeed.

Ok, u. Eac. — Od, u. Wod. — ODU, see ÆDODU.

34*

OEKI, *Brough.* Mansname, nom. — ÆCÆA, *Bracteate 96.* Mansname, dat., To-ÆCÆ.

OF, *Ruthwell.* Prep. OF, out of, from.

Oh, u. Agan. — OIINUM, see BIRKOIINUM, and u. WINI.

OLDA, *Upsala.* Name, probably fem., nom.

Olufr, Olwf, u. Onlaf.

ON, *Bracteate 70; Franks Casket; Hackness; Ruthwell; Selsey;* AA, *Holmen;* O, *Brough;*
Snoldelev. Prep. gov. d. and ac. ON, upon, in, at. See AGROF, AHOF, ALEGDUN, USMÆ.

ONLAF, *Leeds,* ac. s.; OLUFR, *Maglekilde,* n. s. Mansname. — OLWFWOLDU, *Bewcastle.*
Mansname, nom.

(On)gerede, u. Kærþi. — Ons, u. Ans.

ORB(Æ). see LÆ-ORB(Æ).

Os, u. Ans. — Otæ, Oti, (O)þc(u), Oþlæ, Oþua, u. Aþæ.

OWI, *England.* Mansname, nom. — OWÆ-ALUT, *Bracteates 51, 52.* Mansname, nom.

Owlþu, under Wulþu.

PRESTR, *Holmen.* Nom. s. m. PRIEST.

PRO, *Yarm.* Latin. For.

R, R ..., under Runæ.

RÆD, see ÆÐRED, EADRED, EANRED, FRÆWÆRÆDÆA, HWÆTRED, ÐIEÐRODWENC.

Ræw, u. Roaæ.

RAHÆBUL, *Sandwich.* Mansname, nom.

RAIRA, *Brough.* ? Dat. s. m. (HRYRE), ruin, death.

RAISA. — ... TI, *Varnum;* RAISTI, *Freerslev;* RISTI, *Osby.* 3 s. p. RAISED, placed. —
A-RÆRDE, *Thornhill.* 3 s. p. A-REARED, ARAISED, lifted up, set up (the stone).

Ræisto, u. Rista.

RANINGÆ, *Müncheberg.* Mansname, nom.

RECS, *Brough.* 3 s. pr. REACHES, brings again.

Red, under Ræd.

REUMWALUS, *Franks Casket.* Nom. The Roman king REMUS.

Rhoæltr, Rhuulfr, u. Hroþor.

RICES, *Bewcastle.* Gen. s. n. RIKE, REEK. kingdom. — RIICNÆ, *Ruthwell.* Ac. s. m. RICH,
mighty, strong. See ÆIRIKIS, GASRIC. — RIKARTH, *Bridekirk.* Nom. RICHARD, mansname.

RIDE, see WODURIDE.

RIIGU, *Vi Plane.* Womansname, gen.

RINGS, see TILÆRINGS.

RISTA. — RÆISTO, *Maeshowe;* 3 s. p. RISTED, carved, cut (runes).

Risti, u. Raisa.

RIUSII, *Sölvesborg.* Nom. s. n. (HRUSE), RASSE, RAISE, cairn, stone-heapt grave.

Riuti, u. Writan. — Rur, u. Runæ.

ROAÆ, ROAE, *Sigdal;* RO. *Björketorp;* RÆW, *Orstad.* Ac. s. f. ROO, rest, repose.

Roaul, u. Hroþor. — Rod, see Ræd.

RODI (or RODÆ), *Ruthwell.* Dat. s. f. ROOD, cross.

Roetberhtæ, u. Hroþor.

ROMÆCÆSTRI, *Franks Casket.* Dat. s. f. (ROME-CASTER, ROME-CHESTER), Rome-city, Rome.

ROMWALUS, *Franks Casket.* Nom. The Roman king ROMULUS.
Ronoa, under Runæ.

RUNÆ, *Freilaubersheim;* RUNYA, *Istaby;* RUNO, *Einang;* RUNOA, *Bracteate 25, Varnum;*
R . . . ., *Tune;* R, *Sigdal.* Ac. pl. f. RUNES, runic letters. See ÆR-RNR, GINÆ-RUNÆA, GINO-RONOA.
RUTI, *Sölvesborg.* Mansname, nom.
Ruhalts, Ruulfasts, u. Hroþor.
RUMA. *Stentofte.* Ac. s. m. (ROME, REME), lustre, praise, glory.
RUNGNO, see HIDEAR-RUNGNO.
RUNO, *Björketorp.* Nom. s. m. (RUNA, ROWNER), fellow-talker, comrade, friend. See
HÆIDAR-RUNO.
SÆ, *Lindholm.* Nom. s. m. — SÆA, *Stentofte;* SLÆ, *Gjevedal.* Nom. pl. f. (SA), the,
these, yon.
SÆAD. *Björketorp.* Mansname, nom.
SĀC = SACERDOTI, *Yarm.* Latin. Bishop.
Sæg(a), under Sigi.
SÆLEW, *Bracteate 67;* SÆLU, *Bracteate 20.* Nom. s. f. SEEL, joy, luck, success.
SALHAUKUM. *Snoldelev.* Dat. pl. m. The SAL-HOWS, now SALLOW, in Snoldelev parish,
Sealand, Denmark. See HŒGES.
SÆLIGÆSTIA. *Berga.* Womansname, nom.
Sælu, under Sælæw.
? SÆMÆNG, *Seude.* Mansname, nom. or ac.
SAMSI, *Ingelstad.* Mansname, nom.
SÆRÆLU. *Orstad.* Mansname, nom.
SÆRD, *Maeshowe.* 3 s. pr. SORETH, wounds. — SORGUM, *Ruthwell.* Dat. pl. f. SORROWS. —
SARE, *Ruthwell.* Adv. SORE, sorely.
Sæte, Sati, under (Set)a.
SAULE, *Bingley; Dewsbury; Falstone; Thornhill;* SAU . ., *Alnmouth;* SOWHULA, *Bewcastle.*
Dat. s. f. SOUL, ond. spirit.
SBÆ, *Björketorp.* (ÆBÆ SBÆ). Nom. s. m. defin. The SPAE, wise, counselor.
SBERÆDH, *Thames fitting.* 3 s. pr. SPEIRETH, asks, requests.
SCANOMODU, *Bracteate 74.* Mansname, nom.
SKÆR, *Sœding.* Mansname, nom.
SCIDÆ, *Skärkind.* Mansname, gen. Of-SKITH.
Skwlfs, under Sigi.
SEHS-CUNÆ, *Bracteate 6.* Dat. s. m. def. To the SAX-KEEN, sword-bold.
(SET)A, *Tune,* infin.; ÏSETAE, *Yarm;* SÆTE, *Gommor;* SATI, *Helnœs;* SETE, *Thornhill;*
SETTAE, *Falstone;* SETTE, *Thornhill;* SŒTTŒ, *Falstone;* 3 s. p. — SETTON, *Bewcastle;* 3 pl. p. To SET,
set up, raise, place.
Siæ, under Sæ.
SIAÆLUH, *Kinneved.* Apparently mansname, nom.
SIKKTALE, *Holmen.* Dat. s. f. Place-name. SIGDAL in Aggershus, Norway.
SIGI, *Gilton.* Ac. s. m. SIGE, victory. — *Osby.* Mansname, acc. — SÆG(A), *Fröhaug.*
Mansname, or (dat.) for-SIGE, for-victory. — SIGBECN, *Bewcastle.* Ac. s. n. SIGE-BEACON, victory-

pillar. funeral cross.   See BECUN. — SIHMYWNT, *Bracteate 55.* Mansname, dat. — SIGHYOR, *Northumbrian Casket.* Dat. s. m. To the SIGORA, Lord, Captain. — SIKKTALE, *Holmen.* Dat. s. f. SIGDAL, in Aggershus, Norway. — SIUARD, *Maglekilde.* Mansname, nom. — SKWLFS (= SIKWULFS), *Freerslev.* Mansname, gen.

  SIGNUM, *Yarm.* Latin. Ac. s. n. This SIGN, pillar, grave-cross.

  SIMI, *Bracteate 92.* Dat. s. ? SEM in N. Jutland, near Ribe.

  SIN, *Helnæs, Osby.* Ac. s. m. (SIN), his. — SINÆR, *Freerslev.* Gen. s. f. (SINRE), his.

  SINNA, see HEO-SINNA.

  SYOÆINÆA, *Krogstad.* SWAIN, mansname, dat.

  (SI)DC(U), *Freilaubersheim.* Perhaps to be redd (O)DC(U). which see.

  Siuarþ, under Sigi.

  SIUILFUR(N), *Coquet Iland.* Nom. s. SILVERN, of silver.

  Skwlfs, under Sigi.

  USMÆ, *Whitby.* 3 s. pr. subj. May- he- (ON-SMEE), look on, watch over, bless!

  bisMÆRÆDU, *Ruthwell.* 3 pl. p. (BE-SMEARED), mockt, insulted.

  SMUHÆ, *Kragehul.* Ac. s. m. (SMOOGER), thro-flier, darter thro, penetrater.

  SNEIC, *Bracteate 96.* Mansname, nom., = SNEINC, = SNEING, *SNOW-SON.*

  SOL. *Thisted.* Nom. s. f. (SOL), sun, darling.

  Son(r), u. Sun. — Sorgum, u. Særþ.

  SŒRI, *Chessell Down.* ? Dat. s. n. ? To the SERE, armor, weapons (of the foe).

  Sowhula, under Saule.

  STÆDÆA, *Strand.* Gen. pl. of-the-STEADS, road-STEADS, harbors, coasts.

  STAIN, *STONE,* masc. — STAIN, *Freerslev;* STÆIN, *Kallerup, Snoldelev.* Nom. s.; STAIN, *Helnæs;* STÆINÆ, *Tune;* STÆ(N)Æ, *Gommer.* Ac. s. — STAINAR, *Røfsal.* Nom. pl. — (STAN), *Truro.* Absolute, as mansname. — STUN, *Osby.* Mansname, acc. See DŒP-STAN, HALSTUN.

  STÆLDIA, see HÆGUSTÆLDIA.

  Stan, Stænæ, u. Stain.

  bisTEMID, *Ruthwell.* P. p. (BE-STEAMED), bedabbled.

  gisTIGA, *Ruthwell.* Inf. To (STEEG), step, mount.

  STYÖPA, *Holmen.* Inf.; — STYÖPTE, *Holmen.* 3 s. p. To (STEEP), yote, cast, found.

  gisTODDUN, *Ruthwell.* 3 pl. p. STOOD.

  STRELUM, *Ruthwell.* Dat. pl. m. With STRELES, missiles, darts.

  Stun, under Stain.

  SUL, *Ingelstad.* Ac. s. m. (or pl. n.). SILL, ground-frame, timber-frame.

  SUN. — SUNAR, *Snoldelev.* Gen. s. — SUNŒ, *Sparlösa.* Dat. s. SON. See BRUÞURSUNU, ICWÆSUNA, ÞORRSON(R).

  SUNEDROMDH, *Bracteate 64.* Mansname, nom.

  SWI(K), *Franks Casket.* Ac. s. n. (SWIKE), treachery.

  SWID, SWIDA. See BERHTSUIDE, KUNESWIDA, IGILSUID. — SUIDKS, *Kallerup.* Mansname, gen. (SWID-INGS), = SWITHE-SON.

  gisWOM, *Franks Casket.* 3 s. p. SWAM.

  TAÆ, *Bracteate 94.* Mansname, nom.

  TADIS, *Thisted.* Mansname, gen.

Tæen. under Tinæ.

TAL, see SIKKTALE.

TALLWE. *Bracteate 9.* Mansname. nom. — TÆLING, *Vi Plane.* Mansname, nom. = TELL's-son. — TÆLINGWU. *Gettorf.* Womansname, dat. = TELL's-daughter. See TIL.

TAN. — TENAES, TENES, *Bracteate 75.* Mansname, gen. — TÆNULU, *Bracteate 71.* Mansname, nom.

TÆWIDO, *Gallehus.* 3 s. p. (TAWED), shaped, made.

TÆWON, *Bracteate 27.* Mansname, nom.

TE. *Bracteates 25. 59.* 3 s. pr. subj. May he (TEE), give, grant. show, bless, guard. Tenaes, Tenes, under Tan.

TI, *Ruthwell:* TYO, *Thames fitting;* TO, *Bracteate 8; Bridekirk.* Prep. TO.

.... ti, under Raisa.

Tidfirþ, u. Tiþas.

TIL. *Bracteate 46.* Mansname, nom. — TILÆRINGS, *Kovel.* Mansname, nom. — TILLE, *Bracteate 8.* Dat. s. m. defin. To the (TILL), good, excellent. See ELTIL. — See TALLWE.

TIMID, *Brough.* P. p. n. s. f. TEEMED, brought forth, begotten, born.

TINÆ. — TÆEN, *Hoga.* Ac. s. m. TINE, grave-pillar, funeral stone. See HÆI-TINÆ.

Tyo, under Ti and Þewæ. — Tisæcg, u. Tu.

TITUS, *Franks Casket.* Nom. The Roman Emperor.

TIDAS. *Vi Plane.* Mansname. nom. — TIDFIRÐ, *Monk Wearmouth.* Mansname, nom.

Tyw. under Tu.

TIWITÆ. *Bracteate 32.* Mansname, dat.

TOUE. *Holmen.* Mansname, nom.

TRCBU, *Vordingborg.* Mansname, nom.

TRUKNADU. *Helnæs.* 3 pl. p. DROWNED, were drowned.

(tru)MBEREBCT. *Yarm.* Mansname, dat.

TU. *Glostrup;* TYW, *Jyderup.* Apparently the God of TUE'sday. — TISÆCG, *Bracteate 78.* Mansname, nom.

TUHÆ, see DÆITUHÆ.

TUMA. *Stentofte.* Dat. s. n. (TUME. TOME, TOOM), open space or time, chamber, free time, leisure, rest.

TUNBA, *Balkemark.* Mansname, nom.

TVTO, *Bracteate 65.* Mansname, nom.

TUWÆ, *Bracteate 22.* Nom. s. ? f. A (TOG), row, line, here a series of letters, *an alphabet.*

TWED. *Bracteate 32.* Mansname, nom.

TWŒGEN. *Franks Casket.* Nom. pl. m. TWAIN, two.

Ð (? a name beginning with Ð), *Sigdal.*

ÐA, *Ruthwell.* Adv. THO. THEN, then-when, when.

Ðæa, u. Ðewæ. — Ðæes, u. Ðe.

ÐÆICT. see UÐÆICT.

ÐÆLIA. *Bratsberg.* Womansname, nom.

Ðam, u. Ðe. — ÐÆN, see ACEÐÆN. — Ðansi, Ðær, u. Ðe. — Ðær, u. Ðe.

ÞASCO (or ÞUSCO), *Bracteate 3.* Mansname, nom.

Þæt, Þætæa, under Þe.

ÞE. — ÞIS, *Coquet Iland.* Nom. s. m. THIS. — ÞÆES, *Bewcastle.* Gen. s. n. Of THIS. — ÞAM, *Bracteate 9.* Dat. s. m. To THE. — ÞAER, *Dewsbury;* ÞER, *Bridekirk, Falstone;* ÞÆR, *Thornhill;* dat. s. f. For THE. — ÞANSI, *Ösby;* ÞŒ, THE, *Falstone;* ÞŌNIÆ, *Hoga.* Ac. s. m. — ÞIÆU, *Vordingborg;* ÞISSA, *Holmen.* Ac. s. f. THE, THIS. — ÞÆT, *Ruthwell;* ÞÆTÆA, *Sigdal;* ÞIS, *Bewcastle.* Ac. s. n. THAT, THIS. — ÞERÆ, *Stentofte.* Gen. pl. THEIR. — ÞYITA, *Istaby;* ÞISI, *Freerslev.* Ac. pl. f. (THEY, THO), THESE. — ÞÆR, *Franks Casket;* ÞER, *Ruthwell.* Adv. THERE. . . . ÞES(? i), *Bårse.* Probably THIS or THESE, ac. s. or pl. of ÞE.

ÞEWÆ. — ÞE,. *Vi Plane.* Nom. s. m. A THEOW, thrall, slave, servant. — ÞEWÆA, *Valsfjord.* Mansname, dat. See ISING-ÞÆA, OWLÞU-ÞEWÆA. As fem. see ULTYO.

Þiæu, Þyiya, Þisi, Þissa, under Þe.

ÞIEÞRODWENC, *Torvik.* N. s. mansname, equal to ÞEODRADING or ÞEODRADSON.

ÞIWBYO-FUNÞR, *Frederiksberg.* Nom. s. m. THIEF-FIND, finding out the thief.

Þöniæ, u. Þe. — Þoræ, Þorrson(r), u. Þur.

ÞORNR, *Maeshowe.* Nom. s. m. THORN; (or javelin, dart).

Þorr-son(r), Þort, under Þur.

ÞRÆWINGÆN, *Tanum.* Mansname, gen.

Þrlæf, u. Þur.

ÞRUI, *Vordingborg;* Þ. . . ., *Alnmouth.* Ac. s. f. THRUCH, THROH, stone-kist, stone-coffin, grave.

ÞUL(R), a (THYLE), Speaker, Chanter, Priest. — ÞULAR, *Snoldelev.* Gen. sing.

ÞUR. — ÞORÆ, *Thisted.* Womansname, nom. — ÞRLÆF, *Gommor.* Mansname, nom. — ÞURMUÞ, *Sæbö.* Mansname, nom. — ÞORRSON(R), *Holmen.* Mansname, nom. — ÞORT, *Holmen.* Mansname, nom.

Uk, under Eak, Hiewan.

ŪKISI, *Upsala.* Ac. s. f. AXE.

Ugæ. u. Ugis.

UGIS, *Kragehul.* Gen. s. UGG'S (= WODEN'S, ODIN'S). See ÆS-UGIS. — UGU, *Sparlösa.* Ac. s. Mansname. — UGÆ, *Kragehul.* Ac. s. m. defin. The (OUG), fierce.

ŪLTYO, *Fonnås.* Womansname, gen. . . . . UMÆ, *Kragehul.* See text.

UNNBO, *Reidstad.* Mansname, nom. — UNBOÆU, *West Thorp.* Womansname, dat.

UNÞA, *Bracteate 82.* As this piece is broken, we do not know whether more letters belonged to this word.

Ung, Ungæ, u. Inge. — Ungcet, u. Ik.

UNITR. *Freerslev.* Mansname, nom.

UNNA(N). To (UN), give, grant. — ÆNN, *Bracteates 24, 25.* 3 s. pr. (UNS), gives. Un-Neg, under Neg.

UNU. *Mörbylånga.* Womansname, gen. UNA'S (daughter).

URIURIÞON, *Amulet Rings.* See text.

Us, Usa, u. Ik — U-Smæ, u. Smæ.

UT (or UTI), *Björketorp;* UTE, *Sigdal.* OUT, out in.

ᚢᚦ, *Charnay.* Mansname, nom. — ᚢᚦᚫᚱ. *Björketorp.* Mansname. nom.

ᚢᚦᚫᛁᚳᛏ, *Sealand.* Nom. s. f. Unluck. disfavor. a bad throw.

Uþær, under Uþ. — ᚢᚨ, see ᚫᛚᚢᚨ.

ᚹᚫᛁᚷᚫ. *Bracteate 29.* Mansname, nom.

ᚹᚪᛚᛞ. See ᚪᛚᚢᚹᚪᛚᛞᛟ, ᚲᚢᛝᚷᚫᛚᛏᛋ, ᛟᛚᚹᚠᚹᛟᛚᛞᚢ. ᚱᚺᛟᚫᛚ(ᛏ)ᚱ.

ᚹᚪᛚᛞᛖ. *Ruthwell.* 3 s. p. ᚹᛟᚢᛚᛞ.

ᚢᚫᛚᚣᚫ, *Bracteate 57.* Ac. s. m. ᚹᛠᛚ. success. victory. See ᚫᚪᚹᛖᛚᚫ.

Uælts, Waludo, under Wald.

ᚢᚪᚾᚫᛒᚫᚱᚫᚺ, *Varnum.* Mansname. acc.

Wæryit, Wæritæ, under Writan.

ᚹᚪᚱᛞ. *Franks Casket.* 3 s. p. ᚹᚪᚱᚦ. ᚹᛟᚱᚦ, became, was. — ᚹᚪᚱᛞ, see ᛋᛁᚢᚪᚱᛞ.

ᚹᚫᚱᚢᚨ, *Tomstad.* Mansname, dat. See ᚪᛚᚢᛖᚱ. — ᚹᚫᚱᛁᛝᚷᚫᚪ, *Torvik.* Mansname, dat.

ᚹᚫᛋ. — ᛁᛋ. *Coquet Iland.* 3 s. pr. ᛁᛋ. — ᚹᚫᛋ. *Ruthwell;* ᚹᚪᛋ, *Fonnás.* 1 and 3 s. p. ᚹᚪᛋ. — ᚹᚫᛋ, *Tanum.* 2 s. imperat. Be-thou! Stand-thou!

? ᚹᚫᛏᛏᚫᛏ (? ᚹᚫᛏᛏᚫ ᚫᛏ), *Seude.* Mansname. nom.

Wele, u. Uælyæ.

ᚢᛖᚾᚨ, *Ingelstad.* Dat. s. f. (ᚹᛖᚾᛖ), fair.

ᚹᛖᚾᚳ, see ᛁᚾᚷᛖ. — Uer, u. Wærua. See Aluer.

ᚹᛁ. *Buzeu.* Dat. s. n. (ᚹᛁᚺ), temple. fane.

ᚢᚣᚫᚣᛚᛁᛁᛚ. *Bracteate 24.* Mansname. nom. — ᚢᛁᚲ, see ᚪᚢᛁᚲ.

ᚢᛁᚷᚫ, see ᚺᛚᚢᛞᚹᚣᚷ, ᚺᚺᛚᚫᚫᛞᚢᛁᚷᚫ. — ᚢᛁᚲ, *Bracteate 57.* Ac. s. n. (ᚹᛁᚷᚷ). battle, war. — ᚹᛁᚣᚢ-ᛒᛁᚷᛁ(ᚫ), *Kragehul.* Dat. s. m. In his ᚹᛁᚷ-ᛒᛁᚾᚷ, war-bed, camp.

ᚹᛁᛚᛁ, see ᚷᛁᛋᛚᛁᛟᛝᚷᚹᛁᛚᛁ. — Win, u. Wini. — Wings, u. Inge.

ᚹᛁᚾᛁ, friend. See ᚫᛚᚫᚹᛁᚾᚫ. ᚪᛚᚹᛁᚾ. ᚫᛚᛖᚢᛒᚹᛁᚾᛁ, ᛒᛖᚱᚳᚺᛏᚹᛁᚾᛁ, ᛖᛞᛖᛚᚹᛁᚾᛁ, ᛁᚪᚢᛞᛁᚾᛁ. — ᚹᛁᚾᛁᚹᛟᚾᚫᚹᚣᛟ. *Nordendorf.* Womansname, dat.

ᚹᛁᚾᛁ, pleasant mead. See ᛒᛁᚱᚲᛟᚻᚾᚢᛗ.

ᚹᛁᚺᛋ(ᚨ). *Vallöby.* Mansname, nom. — ᚢᛁᛋᚫ, *Bracteate 57.* Nom. s. (ᚹᛁᛋᚨ), leader, captain. — ᚹᛁᛋᚫ, *Gilton.* 2 s. imperat. (ᚹᛖᛁᛋᛖ. ᚹᛁᛋᛖ, ᚹᛁᛋᛋ) lead out, show, draw, brandish.

ᚹᛁᛏᚫ, see ᛏᛁᚹᛁᛏᚫ.

ᚹᛁᛏᚫᛁ, *Tune.* Dat. s. m. defin. The (ᚹᛁᛏᛏᚣ), wise, mighty, illustrious.

Uiu, Wiyu, u. Uigæ. — ᚹᛁᚹᚫᚪ, see ᛖᚳᚹᛁᚹᚫᚪ.

ᚹᛁᚹᛁᛚᚾ, *Voeblungsnoes.* Mansname. nom.

ᚹᛟᛞ. — ᚹᛟᛞᚫᚾ, *Nordendorf;* ᛟᛞ, *Bracteate 59.* Mansname, nom., and name of the God of ᚹᛖᛞᛖᚾᛋ-day; ᚹᛟᛞᛖᚾ. ᛟᛞᛁᚾ. — ᛟᛞᛁᚾᚲᚪᚱ, *Eidsberg;* ᚹᛟᛞᚷᚪᚱ, *Bewcastle.* Mansname, nom. — ᚹᛟᛞᚢᚱᛁᛞᛖ. *Tune.* Mansname. dat.

ᚹᛟᛚᚲ, *Brough.* 3 s. p. ᚹᚪᛚᚲᛏ, went.

Wolþu. u. Wald. — ᚢᛟᛗᛁᚪ, see ᚪᛁᚢᛟᛗᛁᚪ. — ᚹᛟᚾᚫᚹᚣᛟ. see ᚹᛁᚾᛁᚹᛟᚾᚫᚹᚣᛟ.

ᚹᛟᛈ, *Brough.* Nom. s. m. ᚹᚺᛟᛟᛈ, cry. ᚹᛖᛖᛈᛁᚾᚷ, tears.

ᚹᛟᚱᚫᚺᛏᛟ, *Tune;* ᚹᛟᚱᚺ(ᛏ)ᛖ, *Northumbrian Brooch;* ᚢᚱᚹᛁᛏᛟ, *Bracteate 65;* ᛁᚹᚱᛟᚲᛏᛖ. *Bridekirk;* ᚹᛟᚱᛏᚫ, *Etelhem;* ᚹᛟ . . . . ., *Alnmouth.* 3 s. p. ᚹᚱᛟᚢᚷᚺᛏ. ᚹᛟᚱᚲᛏ. made. carved.

ᚹᛟᚱᛖ, see ᛚᛟᚾᚫᚹᛟᚱᛖ. — ᚹᚩᛖᚱᛁᚷ. see ᛚᛁᚾᚹᚩᛖᚱᛁᚷᚾᛖ.

ᚹᚱᛁᛏᚪᚾ. — ᚱᛁᚢᛏᛁ, *Stentofte;* ᚹᚫᚱᚣᛁᛏ. *Istaby:* ᚹᚫᚱᛁᛏᚫ, *Varnum:* ᚹᚱᚫᛖᛏ. *Freilaubersheim;* ᚹᚱᚫᛁᛏᚫ, *Reidstad;* ᚢᚱᛁᛏ, *Northumbrian Casket:* ᚹᛏᛁ (= ᚹᚱᚪᛁᛏᛁ). *Sölvesborg.* 3 s. p. ᚹᚱᛟᛏᛖ. cut, inscribed (the runes).

iWrokte. Wrtæ. Vrœito, u. Woræhto. — Wti, u. Writan. — (W)ugo, u. Oæg.

WULF, nom. s. m.   See ÆGGIULS, ÆNIWULU, ÆNWLL, eADVLFES, HÆRIWOLÆFA, HARIWULFS, HÆÐUWOLÆFA, HYÐUWULÆFA, ROAUL, SKWLFS. TÆNULU. — WULFIA, nom. s. f.   See HYERUWULÆFIA. — WÜLIF, *Franks Casket.*   Nom. s. f. (WYLF), she-wolf. — WULFHERE, *Bewcastle.*   Mansname. nom. WULÐU. — OWLÐU-ÐEWÆA, *Thorsbjerg Sword.*   Mansname, dat.

giwUNDAD, *Ruthwell.*   P. p. WOUNDED.

Y. see I.

MARKER.

**NOTE:- none of the above have been reprinted by
Llanerch; they are probably only available through
reference libraries.**

Also published by Llanerch:

A HANDY BOOK OF RULES AND TABLES FOR
VERIFYING DATES WITH THE CHRISTIAN ERA. J. F.
Bond. Calendars; Western, Orthodox, Assyrian, Coptic,
Indian, Chinese, etc. Facsimile of 1859 edition. ISBN
0947992804.

NORTHUMBRIAN CROSSES OF THE PRE-NORMAN AGE.
W. G. Collingwood. Facsimile. ISBN 0947992359.

THE INDUSTRIAL ARTS OF THE ANGLO-SAXONS. Baron
de Baye. Facsimile of one of the first texts on the
subject. ISBN 0947992502.

SYMBOLISM OF THE CELTIC CROSS. Derek Bryce, with
drawings by J. Romilly Allen, and others. ISBN
0947992332.

OGHAM MONUMENTS IN WALES. John Sharkey, ISBN
094799288X.

From booksellers. For a complete list; write to
LLANERCH PUBLISHERS, Felinfach, Lampeter, Dyfed,
SA48 8PJ.